9

D1145812

370.1

Becoming Critical

Education, Knowledge and Action Research

Wilfred Carr
School of Education
University College of North Wales

Stephen Kemmis
School of Education
Deakin University

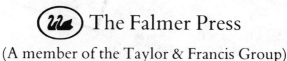 The Falmer Press
(A member of the Taylor & Francis Group)
London and Philadelphia

UK   The Falmer Press, Falmer House, Barcombe, Lewes, East Sussex, BN8 5DL

USA   The Falmer Press, Taylor & Francis Inc., 242 Cherry Street, Philadelphia, PA 19106–1906

First published by Deakin University Press 1986.
Reprinted 1988, 1989, 1990, 1991, 1993, 1994

Library of Congress Cataloging in Publication Data

Carr, Wilfred.

  Becoming critical.

  Includes bibliographies.

  1. Education—Philosophy. 2. Education—Research.
3. Action research in education. I. Kemmis, Stephen.
II. Title.
LB1025.2.C275 1986 370'.1 85-29403
ISBN 1-85000-089-1
ISBN 1-85000-090-5 (pbk.)

370·1

Typeset in 11/13 Bembo by
Imago Publishing Ltd, Thame, Oxon.

*Printed in Great Britain by Burgess Science Press, Basingstoke
on paper which has a specified pH value on final paper
manufacture of not less than 7.5 and is therefore 'acid free'.*

Contents

Contents

Preface

Joint authorship is a risky business which can only succeed if it is founded on personal and intellectual cooperation, a sense of common purpose and some shared commitments and concerns. This book was no exception: it emerged from an extended dialogue between us both which was often conducted from opposite ends of the world, which was sometimes difficult and protracted, but which was always anchored by our shared convictions and beliefs. One of these was a dissatisfaction with the way in which educational research was increasingly becoming divorced from its philosophical and historical roots; another was our conviction that current conceptions of the relationship between educational theory and practice could no longer be vindicated; yet another was our commitment to the development of forms of enquiry in which educational research and the professional development of teachers could be more readily integrated. The book represents our collaborative effort to give some expression to these beliefs and to show how they are related to one another.

To those who are familiar with the literature of curriculum theory, educational philosophy and educational research, our larger intellectual debts will be easily recognized. We would like here to record the assistance of Susan Dawkins, Dilys Parry and Pat Rankin in preparing and typing the manuscript and our gratitude to Marisse Evans and Sheila Kemmis for their encouragement and support during the period in which the book was written.

Our final acknowledgement recognizes a debt of a quite different character. Without the work and ideas of the late Lawrence Stenhouse this book could not have been written; without his personal encouragement and support, progress towards its completion would have been a much more arduous task. It is to his memory that the book is dedicated.

Wilfred Carr and
Stephen Kemmis
June 1985

Introduction

There is now a growing movement to extend the professionalism of teachers by providing them with greater opportunities to engage in curriculum theorizing and educational research. This is evidenced in a variety of ways: school-based curriculum development, research-based in-service education and professional self-evaluation projects are just some of the signs that the 'teacher as researcher' movement is well under way.

The reasons why teachers have become researchers vary. Some teachers have become researchers because they are the products of a period of intense intellectual and social ferment: they are committed to a view of themselves that is bound to reflect upon their educational practice; to justify it and transcend its limitations. Others have been drawn into research and evaluation roles as they have been required to debate and justify innovative practices for which they have been responsible. Still others have more or less spontaneously arrived at the general idea of the teacher-researcher simply as a reasonable aspiration for a professional. And some have been enthused by a time of major change in education in which teachers and schools have been offered greater autonomy and responsibility in curriculum matters.

The 'teacher as researcher' movement, then, is a response to a variety of social conditions, political pressures and professional aspirations and for this reason its development has, to a large extent, been pragmatic, uncoordinated and opportunistic. Moreover, because the pace of change has allowed little opportunity for careful reflection on the significance of these developments, the movement lacks the sort of theoretical rationale which can clarify its meaning, arm it against criticism and promote its future progress.

The purpose of this book is to offer such a rationale by outlining a

1

philosophical justification for the view that teachers have a special role as researchers and that the most plausible way to construe educational research is as a form of critical social science. By exposing and critically assessing some of the key philosophical positions in the field of educational research, the book aims to give teachers, teacher educators and educational researchers access to the language and arguments with which they may resist the claim that educational research should be the sole preserve of the academic 'experts' and defend the claim that the professional development of teachers requires that they adopt a research stance towards their educational practice.

Of course, in many ways, teachers today are better prepared for their profession than ever before. They have better qualifications, more opportunities for continuing professional education, better communication opportunities, better-developed and more differentiated professional organizations and associations, and (although there are signs that their increasing professional responsibility is under threat) more freedom from the domination of the central authorities which control educational provision in large government education systems. They are more conscious of themselves as professionals, not only in the sense that they are expert in subject-matters to be taught and learned, but also in the sense that they are professional *educators*.

Yet the profession remains conformist in many ways. Unlike previous eras, conformity is not now assured through domination by imposed curricula or rigid systems of inspection and control. It is now a far more insidious and subtle matter, achieved through offering predesigned packages, through creating a profession with limited views of its professionalism, and through the consumerist activity of some school communities which demand that schools and teachers live up to 'standards' shaped in a culture and society whose own predilections for conformity are the product of a time when great consensus could be assumed about social and educational values. One of the purposes of this book is to question this conformist view of education by questioning some of the beliefs on which it rests.

Among the most powerful and enduring of these beliefs are those surrounding the concepts of 'theory' and 'practice'. To most researchers and teachers, these concepts have more or less settled meanings. 'Practice' is particular and urgent; it is what teachers do in meeting the tasks and demands confronting them in their everyday work. 'Theory', in sharp contrast, is timeless and universal; it is something produced by researchers through the careful process of enquiry. This tendency to regard educational theory as something different from educational practice is, of course, just a particular manifestation of the widespread disposition to draw a sharp distinction between 'theoretical' matters concerning what is the case and 'practical' matters concerning what ought to be done. Moreover, the disposition to think and act in terms of this dichotomy did not develop in an historical vacuum. Rather, it developed within the context of a particular intellectual tradition which shaped both the questions about educational theory and practice that were posed, and the criteria in terms of which answers to these questions were given. For this reason, it would be a mistake to believe that a correct understanding of theory and practice can be elucidated in a way that assumes that the history of these concepts is only of secondary or incidental importance. Understanding the meaning of these concepts is, in part, understanding the intellectual traditions in which they have been, and still are, embodied. For present preconceptions to be broken down, therefore, some historical understanding of the way in which these concepts acquired their present meaning is of the first importance.

So much for general considerations. In seeking to substantiate its central claims, the book aims to accomplish four general tasks. The first is to provide an overview of some of the dominant views of educational theory and research and their relationship to educational practice. The second is to offer a critical examination of these views. The third task is to outline the different images of the teaching profession which these different views of theory and practice suggest. The fourth task is to try and develop a philosophical position within which a more adequate account of theory, research and practice can emerge and a view of the teaching profession as a critical community can be justified.

The first task — that of outlining some different ideas about educational theory, research and practice — is tackled in Chapter 1 by trying to reveal something of the diversity in the field of curriculum research. The purpose of this chapter is to show that there are different images about what curriculum research is, what it is for and who is best placed to do it. Particular emphasis is given to the way in which these different images of curriculum research convey different ideas about the professional role of teachers and the kind of knowledge that they require.

The way in which curriculum research should relate to the professional role of the teacher is, of course, a particular instance of the more general issue of how educational theory should relate to educational practice. The range of possibilities presented in Chapter 1, therefore, helps to relate the specific problem of curriculum research and teacher professionalism within a broader context of educational theory and practice. Chapters 2 and 3 focus on this broader context by outlining two major intellectual traditions — positivism and the interpretive approach — and examining how they have affected the conduct of educational enquiry and research. Chapter 2 traces the emergence of the positivist approach by retrieving some of the principal arguments that have been used to establish educational research as an essentially scientific enterprise. In particular, attention is focused on the way in which positivist principles entail a definite conception of how theory is to relate to practice.

Chapter 2 also offers some arguments critical of positivist views of educational research. These make use of recent developments in the history and philosophy of science and also draw on some familiar themes in the philosophy of education. These arguments provide a point of departure for the critical consideration, in Chapter 3, of the idea of an 'interpretive' approach to educational research. The third task, concerning teacher professionalism and research, is dealt with by exploring how teachers' professional knowledge relates to the theoretical knowledge generated by positivist and interpretive educational research.

The somewhat negative conclusions derived from the critical examinations of positivism and the 'interpretive' approach provide the starting point for tackling, in Chapter 4, the fourth aim of trying to develop a more coherent account of the nature of educational theory and practice. This takes the form of an attempt to elucidate some of the formal criteria that any coherent account of an *educational* science would need to incorporate. The purpose of Chapter 5 is to identify critical theory as the form of enquiry that seems to incorporate these criteria and to describe the kind of educational research methodology that this theoretical perspective entails.

Chapter 6 takes up the challenge of Chapter 5: it outlines a form of educational research which is compatible with the aspirations of a critical social science. It does so, first, by presenting an argument for a form of educational research which is grounded in the concerns and commitments of practitioners, and which engages them as researcher-participants in the critical development of education. This view of educational research fulfils the general aspirations of a critical educational science to 'name those for whom it is directed', and to assist them in the critical analysis and development of education as they experience it. It therefore views educational research not as research *about* education but as research *for* education. Second, Chapter 6 describes a concrete and practical process by which this aspiration may be realized: the process of collaborative action research. In Chapter 7, the claim of collaborative action research to be a way of enacting a critical educational science is examined in detail; the chapter shows how collaborative action research meets the formal criteria for an adequate and coherent educational science developed in Chapter 4.

In Chapter 7, the argument of the book is concluded. It examines the different views of educational reform implicit in different views of educational research and defends the idea that the teacher is a member of a critical community made up of teachers, students, parents and others concerned for the development and reform of education. The professional responsibility of the teacher is to offer an approach to this task: to create conditions under which the critical community can be galvanized into action in support of educational values, to model the review and improvement process, and to organize it so that colleagues, students, parents and others can become actively involved in the development of education. The participatory democratic approach of collaborative action research gives form and substance to the idea of a self-reflective critical community committed to the development of education.

Chapter 1

Teachers, Researchers and Curriculum

1   Curriculum Research and Teacher Professionalism

The aim of this chapter is to introduce some of the recent history of educational research. Many of the themes and arguments touched on in this chapter will recur in greater detail in the chapters that follow, but a general introduction should provide a useful perspective within which the issues to be raised later can be located. The method employed to convey this kind of historical and contextual understanding of research in education is by focusing on recent developments in 'curriculum' as a field of study and research.

One reason for concentrating on the field of curriculum research is that it tends to be more uncertain and problematic than other more established forms of educational enquiry. These uncertainties and problems arise in many ways. Sometimes they emerge as academic disputes about the nature of curriculum research; at others as problems about the role of the teacher in curriculum development and change. Now although these two areas of concern are normally treated separately, an attempt to exemplify the complexities of curriculum research which treats them as closely related has some important advantages. In particular, it makes it possible to examine how different conceptions of curriculum research convey different images of teaching as a distinctively *professional* activity. In consequence, it allows for a discussion of curriculum research which perceives methodological considerations and questions about teachers' professionalism as intrinsically related.

Most discussions about teaching as a profession focus on the extent to which teaching conforms to the criteria normally employed in distinguishing professional from non-professional occupations. Briefly, these are, first, that the methods and procedures employed by members of a profession are based on a body of theoretical knowledge and research. Part of the reason why medicine, law and engineering are regarded as professional occupations is because they involve techniques and skills supported by a body of systematically produced knowledge. A second distinguishing feature of professions is that the overriding commitment of their members is to the well-being of their clients. Both the medical and legal professions are governed by ethical codes which serve to ensure that the interest of clients is always the predominant concern. Thirdly, to ensure that they can always act in the interest of their clients, members of a profession reserve the right to make autonomous judgments free from external non-professional controls and constraints. This professional autonomy usually operates at both the individual and the collective levels. Individually, professionals make independent decisions about which particular course of action to adopt in any particular situation. Collectively, professionals have the right to determine the sort of policies, organization and procedures that should govern their profession as a whole. The medical and legal professions, for example, select their own membership and determine their own disciplinary and accountability procedures.

Even this very brief description of the characteristics of a profession is sufficient to convey some idea of the limited extent to which teaching, as we know it today, can legitimately be regarded as a professional activity.[1] It is clear, for example, that theory and research play a much less significant part in teaching than they do in other professions. Indeed, what little evidence there is suggests that most teachers regard research as an esoteric activity having little to do with their everyday practical concerns.[2] Likewise, the relationship of teachers to their clients is much less straightforward than in other professions. To doctors and lawyers, the client is either 'a patient' or 'a case' and professional concern is limited to effecting a cure or winning a case. A teacher's professional concern for his pupils, however, cannot be limited in this sort of way. In the case of the doctor or lawyer, a specific condition, such as an illness or a real or alleged grievance, exists before the professional is called in. This is not so for the teacher. A lack of education is a diffuse and open condition, too general to be regarded as specific 'ignorance', except in some special cases of a very basic kind (total illiteracy, for example). The business of educating is diffuse and prolonged, and teaching requires a much more diverse range of skills than those required by either doctors or lawyers. A further complication arises because it is not at all self-evident that the pupils are the teachers' only clients. Parents, the local community, government and employers all make claims to be considered as legitimate clients and their interests may not coincide with what teachers believe to be in the educational interest of their pupils.

It is, however, in the area of autonomy that the professionalism of teachers is most seriously limited. For although teachers can, and do, make autonomous judgments about their everyday classroom practices, the broad organizational context within which these practices occur is something over which they have little control. Teachers operate within hierarchically arranged institutions and the part they play in making decisions about such things as overall educational policy, the selection and training of new members, accountability procedures, and the general structures of the organizations in which they work is negligible. In short, teachers, unlike other professionals, have little professional autonomy at the collective level.

What all this suggests is that if teaching is to become a more genuinely professional activity, three sorts of development will be necessary. First, the attitudes and practices of teachers must become more firmly grounded in educational theory and research. Secondly, the professional autonomy of teachers must be extended to include the opportunity to participate in the decisions that are made about the broader educational context within which they operate; that is, professional autonomy must be regarded as a collective, as well as an individual matter. Thirdly, the professional responsibilities of the teacher must be extended so as to include a professional obligation to interested parties in the community at large.

Now these three requirements are closely related. For example, any extension of the professional autonomy of teachers will have important implications both for the kind of knowledge required from research and the kind of relationship that exists between researchers and teachers. Thus, the sort of knowledge required from research would not be limited to that which affects classroom practices and teaching skills. Rather, it would include the sort of knowledge that would facilitate collaborative discussion within the teaching profession as a whole about the broad social, political and cultural context within which it operates. Moreover, if professional autonomy was extended in this way, research findings could not be regarded as something that teachers accepted from researchers and slavishly implemented. Instead, researchers would be required to devise ways of helping the teaching profession to organize its beliefs and ideas (both individually and collectively) so as to facilitate the making of informed judgments about professional activities and to fulfil its responsibility to defend these judgments to other interested parties.

It is clear, then, that the professional development of teachers not only involves extending the range of their autonomous judgments and the range of clients to whom they have responsibilities and obligations. It also involves a more generous view about the kinds of knowledge that research should provide. It is also clear that the diverse range of views about the aims, methods and products of curriculum research will reflect an equally diverse range of attitudes about the desirability of this kind of professional development. The next section aims to show something of the wide spectrum that exists in the field of curriculum research by describing several different traditions of educational study and various dimensions of curriculum research. Against the background of this kind of review it will then be possible to identify the potential of different approaches to curriculum research for either impeding or assisting the development of the autonomy and responsibilities of the teaching profession.

2 Eight General Traditions in the Study of Education

a *Philosophical Studies of Education*

So far as our western intellectual traditions are concerned, the earliest 'researchers' into education were philosophers. The study of education was a *philosophical* study linked to the study of knowledge, ethics and political life. Plato, for example, had a good deal to say about education; the Greek philosophers in general had much to say about knowledge that is directly relevant to education even today. The aim of their enquiries was as much to discover the nature of knowledge and its role in political life as it was to understand education.

b *Grand Theorizing*

In much more recent times, *grand theorizing* about education became more common. For example, in 1762 the French philosopher Jean Jacques Rousseau published his *Emile*, arguing that nature provided the motive force for child development and that the teacher should not interfere too much in this unfolding but rather remove blockages to development. Froebel (1782–1852) developed this theory further and opened a school for which he coined the term 'kindergarten' — a garden in which children, like plants, could grow.

Grand theorizing is also evident in the work of John Dewey (1859–1952) who was a philosopher, founder of an experimental school and author of a number of books in which his theory of education was expounded.[3] Perhaps Dewey was the last of the 'grand theorists' in the English-speaking world. What makes this kind of work 'grand theory' is that it has a consciousness of the need to place education as a process of 'coming to know' in the context of a general theory of society on the one hand and a theory of the child on the other. The schemes of the grand theorists were, relatively speaking, whole accounts of the nature and role of education. More recent thinkers have tended to eschew this grand theorizing tradition, focusing on narrower problems.

c   The Foundations Approach

After the 'grand theory' tradition, the study of education began to become more specialized. Psychology quickly became a focus for research, pursuing questions about the nature of the child and of learning. Philosophy and sociology, too, became arenas for relevant specialist study. Knowledge *about* education began to become fragmented into specialisms, and by the mid-twentieth century curriculum as a field had emerged to hold the fragments together by maintaining a 'practical' focus on the organization of teaching and learning in schools.

Out of this fragmentation, the *foundations* approach to the study of education emerged.[4] The rapidly developing specialisms needed to be focused on the life of education, but each specialist domain was growing too fast for unification to be feasible. Teacher education institutions began to teach sociology, psychology, philosophy and history as they were relevant to education. From these domains, philosophy of education, sociology of education and psychology of education emerged as distinct specialisms, and began to become inward looking and somewhat separated from their 'parent' disciplines. By this time the knowledge industry was driving the development of the study of education: the development of knowledge about education and 'educational phenomena' began to have a dynamism of its own which could sustain momentum almost independently of the development of practice. The specialist fields were sufficiently advanced to pose their own intellectual problems and capable of keeping a growing army of researchers occupied. This is not to say that researchers were indifferent to the work of schools. On the contrary, two distinct kinds of research began to emerge: research on particular *educational* 'phenomena' (like learning, motivation or social groupings in schools) or 'issues' (like authority, discipline or knowledge), and *service research*, a research service to school systems and to schools which could collect and collate information for decision making.

d Educational Theory

In Britain in the 1960s, the academic study of education began to achieve a new, though extremely frail, unity with the development of a new version of *educational theory*. Like the 'foundations' approach, the separate disciplines were all given their place, but an attempt was made to give them a common focus on the nature (rather than the practice) of the educational process. Paul Hirst (1966)[5] outlined the characteristics of this view of educational theory:

> (i)   It is the theory in which principles, stating what ought to be done in a range of practical activities, are formulated and justified.
>
> (ii) The theory is not itself an autonomous 'form' of knowledge or an autonomous discipline. It involves no conceptual structure unique in its logical features and no unique tests for validity. Many of its central questions are, in fact, moral questions of a particular level of generality; questions focused on educational practice.
>
> (iii) Educational theory is not a purely theoretical field of knowledge because of the formulation of principles for practice in which it issues. It is, however, composite in character in a way similar to such fields.
>
> (iv) Educational principles are justified entirely by direct appeal to knowledge from a variety of forms, scientific, philosophical, historical, etc. Beyond these forms of knowledge it requires no theoretical synthesis. (p. 55)

It is striking in this characterization of educational theory that knowledge from other disciplines provides the justification for educational practice and that the development of educational theory is contingent upon developments in those disciplines: it cannot develop of its own accord. The view expressed here echoes some of the views of

D.J. O'Connor[6], a scientifically minded philosopher who had intended to go even further, claiming that educational theory had no overriding practical purpose and confining it to the production of empirically established findings.[7]

This step from the 'foundations' approach to the 'educational theory' perspective of Hirst and O'Connor is remarkable in completing a development in the study of education from the concerns of the Greeks about knowledge and action, rich in practical interests about education and the conduct of political life, through a fragmentation by increasing specialism, to the state where knowledge about education could be valued almost for its own sake, though it reserved the right to issue pronouncements in the form of principles for practice. One might say that educational practice had become instrumental — a technical activity — under the aspect of an increasingly 'pure' or academic educational theory.[8]

e The Applied Science or Technical Perspective and the New Practicality

In America in the late 1950s and early 1960s the scene was changing also, but it was changing differently. The pragmatism of C.S. Pierce and John Dewey was a more 'practical' philosophy. But the essentially practical perspective in America, too, had been increasingly directed towards technical concerns: towards education as a technology for upbringing. American studies in education, too, began to take a technical turn towards an applied science or technical perspective. But in 1957 (the same year that O'Connor published his *Introduction to the Philosophy of Education*) *Sputnik* was launched and, in its wake, the American curriculum development movement began. Academic subject-matter specialists took over the specification of content of the new curricula and academic educationists were pressed into service in curriculum design. Curriculum became very much a technical matter.

Before pursuing this line, it may be worth pausing to reflect on the American scene before the launching of *Sputnik*. Dewey and the progressives had made a major impact on the educational world for the first quarter of the century. In the 'grand theory' tradition, they had always kept educational and social and political theory in contact with one another and with philosophy. Their concern was very much with the cultivation of the 'whole man'. The 'reconstructionists' (like Harold Rugg, who developed the first social studies curriculum in the early twenties) had given education a distinctly political role and character, which flourished with the New Deal politics of Roosevelt in the thirties. In this, they also kept faith with the classical view of education as the cultivation of the morally sensitive, civilized person.

By the end of the Second World War, however, the enemy had changed from fascism on the extreme right to communism on the extreme left. Where the vision of New Deal politics had been one of men and women working together to achieve social justice and developing a new consensus from common striving towards a better society, with social ideas and ideals being tested for their capacity to contribute to the development of society, the vision of post-war American politics was different. It was conservative: its social vision was that the mechanisms for the good society were already present in American political structures; individuals rather than ideas differed in the strivings for development. New Deal politics now seemed dangerously left-wing, and some of the reconstructionist curricula which had previously prospered were unceremoniously dumped (for example, Harold Rugg's books were burned for their leftist tendencies). Behaviourist psychology and educational measurements began to exert a stronger influence on the practice of education.

In 1949, Tyler's classical curriculum text *Basic Principles of Curriculum and Instruction*[9] appeared and soon had a major influence on curriculum through teachers' colleges. Tyler's work made it clear that curriculum was a means to given ends. Discussion about educational aims was to take place, followed by specification of objectives which, once agreed, allowed curriculum development to proceed. After instruction had taken place, educational measurement could be used to test whether the objectives had been attained; if they were, the instruction was successful; if not, it should be modified.

Tyler's approach was rapidly appropriated by behaviourist psychology and became a foundation stone for instructional psychology.[10] What was significant here was that discussions about goals were now to be decided before curriculum development could proceed, that the aim of developing the cultivated person was now discarded in favour of developing conformity to an agreed image of the educated person (implied by the goals), and that teaching and curriculum became instrumental — the means for achieving these given ends.

By the time *Sputnik* was launched and America was mobilizing education to ensure the production of scientists able to compete successfully with the Russians, educationists were already prepared for the challenge. Studies in education were already studies of the 'phenomena' of education; educational phenomena could be construed as phenomena about the behaviour of systems; educational problems could be construed as technical problems to be solved by educational technology, not only in the physical form of teaching machines, but also in the form of programmed instruction and packaged curricula (sometimes described as 'teacher proof'). The curriculum had become a 'delivery system'.

The 'educational theory' approach to studies in education evident in Britain did not really make a major impact on the American scene. But the technical implications of educational theory were now explicitly evident in the Tylerian (objectives-based) technical view of curriculum. (Tyler focused on the technology of curriculum while the British educational theorists focused on the theory from which its guiding principles could issue.)

The distinction between theory and practice upon which technical rationality depended was there in the technical view of curriculum; and the 'pure' vs 'applied' science debate was under way, with the high-status 'pure' science being developed as a means of legitimizing the development of curriculum as technology. A technical view of educational research now reigned supreme.

American curriculum theorizing had always been a kind of 'mongrel' discipline. It had elements left over from the 'grand theory' tradition (for example, liberal ideas about the cultivation of the person), from the 'foundations' approach (for example, in the discussion of the social context of education or the nature of child development), and from the technical perspective (for example, in a means-ends approach and educational measurement). The distinctiveness of curriculum as a field was its concern with practice and the preparation of teachers for practice. It became increasingly concerned with specific subject-matter content (thus swinging away towards pedagogy in its focus on 'principles of education' or, later, towards teaching 'method' in particular subject areas). The special role of 'curriculum' was to give substance to the form or method of a particular subject domain. For this reason, curriculum, too, began to fragment as a field but (unlike educational theory which specialized in the direction of academic or scientific theory) its fragmentation and differentiation was towards the special demands of teaching school subjects. Mathematics curriculum, social studies curriculum, language curriculum, science curriculum and the like, provided domains in which specification of content could usefully take place. In this rush towards content (filling the school-day with content and instructional activities), the overarching character of the field was submerged. The 'grand theory' and 'foundations' approaches, which had posed educational questions capable of reshaping the nature of education, were increasingly neglected, and the technological perspective began to be *assumed* as the ordering image. Fundamental questions could thus be neglected, since more 'practical' questions (in fact, pseudo-practical, 'technical' questions) pressed their demands: the demands to provide material for schools and teachers. Curricula were thought of as visible products, appearing in the forms of schemes of activities, teaching ideas, subject-matter content and textbooks. The *new practicality*, that is, a pseudo-practicality oriented by a technical view of education, was the basis for an industry of education: providing texts for students and scripts for teachers in the form of curriculum packages.

In this shift of emphasis, teachers became actors on the stage of education or, to use an unkinder image, operatives in its factories. The profound questions of education became the preserve of the academic designers of curricula, not teachers themselves. To the extent that teachers were to be concerned with these questions (during their teacher education, for example), it would be so that they could appreciate the educational designs worked out by the curriculum specialists.[11] Teachers would not generate educational ideas in their teaching or school curricula, they would use the curricula developed by others. When they were to be educational actors in their own right, it would be as a form of mimickry of what professional curriculum developers did, not as an autonomous educational activity.

Curriculum as a field was thus transformed from one concerned with *doing* to one concerned with *making*. Curriculum as 'making' thus took a view of the work of education as being like the work of the craftsman, instrumentalizing educational situations to the technical means and given ends (that is, only comprehending the situation in terms of the means and ends decided before an educational encounter took place and neglecting the essential openness of the situation and the transitivity of the human relationship between teacher and student). At this point, with the launching of *Sputnik* and the curriculum development movement, this view of curriculum achieved a sudden and almost complete dominance.

And then, in American education at least, a peculiar thing happened.

f   The Practical

The peculiar thing that happened was that the flurry of technological making of curricula needed a guiding framework. Curriculum as a specialism needed an explicit theory to guide its technology. The development of the new self-consciousness meant that the technological *assumptions* needed to be examined and recovered from the realm of the taken-for-granted, examined and explicitly ordered. To some extent, Tyler's technical approach provided a compatible theory. But the emphasis on the *practical*, which had been suppressed with the decline of the 'grand theory' and 'foundations' approaches, was now recovered (it had remained present in theoretical courses in teacher education but had become increasingly irrelevant under the technological aspect of the 'new practicability') as a source for educational thought. The more genuine practicality identified by the Greeks as *praxis* (guided by an image of the wise man aiming to act appropriately, truly and justly in a social-political situation) had always allowed ends as well as means to be problematic, and to be a matter of choice — choice about right action in a given situation, not guided by singular ends. With the new self-consciousness about curriculum as a field, the technical and the practical approaches to the study of education were once again in contention.

The practical erupted into the curriculum theory of the 1960s with the publication of Joseph J. Schwab's paper, 'The practical: a language for the curriculum'.[12] In the paper, Schwab distinguished the 'theoretic' approach (what we have described as the foundations approach, though Schwab's critique is equally telling against Hirst's view of 'educational theory') from the practical. He argues that the theoretic approach fragments curriculum as a field and as practice, that it leads to confusion and contradiction, and that it does not help the practitioner in the real work of making wise choices about what to do next. Schwab's guiding image is of the curriculum committee in a school deciding about the school's curriculum, taking into account practical constraints and the concerns of the school community. It is an image remarkably close to Aristotle's view of the wise man choosing the right course of action in the political context of the Greek state.

But Schwab's concerns also found a new place for the idea of the cultivated person which had so much preoccupied the progressives. (Indeed, they sprang from the same intellectual roots.) Cultivation of the reasoning person, rather than cultivation of conformity, was once again placed in its social and political context. Schwab's *tour de force*, written exemplifying the method of the practical, *College Curricula and Student Protest*[13], demonstrates both the Aristotelian method and an Aristotelian message. It set curriculum debate in a political context and argued that students found their curricula 'irrelevant' to their own development as reasoning persons and to contemporary concerns for the political development of society.

With Schwab's paper, the practical approach to contemporary curriculum theorizing and practice became as explicit as the technical approach had done in the work of the educational theorists and the Tylerian curriculum technologists. Picking up adherents quickly from the ranks of those disaffected by the increasingly technical perspective of the applied science and educational theory paradigms, Schwab's views became significantly influential. The tide of the 1950s — the Korean War, McCarthyism and the technical approach to social problems — had turned. The Vietnam War was unpopular (enthusiasm for the fight against communism was waning) and there was increasing protest against technological domination of political and social systems.[14] The concerns of the curriculum were seen once again as essential concerns for teachers.

The publication of 'the practical' had a major effect on academic work in curriculum. It focused some of the unease about technical approaches to curriculum design which were prospering among educational technologists. It recognized that the life of schools as the domain in which curriculum thinking must take place is from the perspective of the academic theorists or the educational systems designer, and it reinstated practical judgment as an essential art in the doing of curriculum.

g   Teachers as Researchers

It would be too simplistic to assert that Schwab's view of the practical prepared the ground for the notion of *teachers as researchers*. Nevertheless, it is true to say that both Schwab and Stenhouse were spokesmen for the practical: both recognized the need for teachers to be central to the curriculum exercise as doers, making judgments based on their knowledge and experience and the demands of practical situations. The teachers-as-researchers 'movement' to which Stenhouse (1975) contributed so great an impetus is perhaps more accurately seen as a response to political conditions.

Certainly Stenhouse's work had a major impact on the British

scene. It followed the Humanities Curriculum Project[15] which cele-
brated the 'extended professionalism' of the teacher; in Britain, the
notion of teacher-as-researcher appealed to the profession as an
element of its professionalism. It could be accepted because it affirmed
and justified a well-developed sense of professional autonomy and
responsibility.

Also, the teacher-as-researcher movement 'arrived' at a time of
breathtaking change in educational structures and systems. It seemed
a time of professional liberation. But it is also apparent that elements of
the *teacher*-as-researcher movement were at odds with the *school*-based
curriculum development movement. They had different foci: the
individual teacher and the school. The rationale for the teacher-as-
researcher approach was individualistic; the rationale for school-based
curriculum development collectivist.[16] At the time, the distinction
could go unheeded: both points of view were devolutionary, and under
some circumstances the two could be reconciled. The changes were
underway in the profession; the ideas found ready acceptance. The
Stenhouse approach to the field of curriculum provided a justification
(or a rationalization) for the reforms which preceded it.

h Emerging Critical Tradition

'Teachers-as-researchers' was a singularly acceptable slogan for the
period in curriculum theory and practice. Its theoretical roots, however, were elusive. Schwab's view of the practical could have provided
further justification, but to enact Schwab's approach required a profound change in thinking about curriculum issues. There does not seem
to be much evidence that this profound change took place, unless one is
prepared to dignify references made by teachers to the mysterious
'professional judgment' as evidence of the change. In fact, teachers and
curriculum developers turned to the somewhat wooden and almost
technical 'model' of curriculum development proposed by Skilbeck and
Reynolds (the situational analysis-goals definition — curriculum
development-evaluation model) as a guide to their activities. At least
privately, Skilbeck acknowledges that the model may simplify complex issues to a misleading degree. Where it attempted to provide a
framework for practical judgment, it was often used as a framework for
legitimation of curriculum ideas — as a formula rather than a sequence
of problematic issues to be resolved in practice. It became increasingly
clear that the political changes in education had not been matched by

intellectual changes in curriculum and the profession. New participatory and consultative organizational structures in schools and systems would be necessary to create a climate in which the intellectual framework for curriculum could be developed. At the school level, participatory decision-making structures and whole-school curriculum planning provided forums for practical curriculum debate.

These consultative and participatory structures had to be understood as essential elements in curriculum: curriculum theory has to embody a social theory. It is in this context that a *critical tradition* in curriculum is beginning to be established, incorporating not only theories about educational events and organizations, but also a theory about how participants in these events and organizations can learn about them and collaborate in changing them in the light of their learning.

3 Five 'Dimensions' of Curriculum Research

There is some contention about exactly how 'curriculum' should be defined. There are also ambiguities about the precise focus for the researchers. To what extent is the curriculum to be found in a specific act of teaching or learning? To what extent does it refer to a programme of work across a whole year? To what extent is it to be understood in relation to historical circumstances and general educational policies? To what extent is it to be found in materials, and to what extent in educational practices? To what extent does curriculum refer to general systems, and to what extent to human encounters?

Some argue that all these different foci are appropriate for curriculum research and that they can be systematically related to one another. Kallos and Lundgren[17] take this view in their report of research on the 1962 comprehensivization of the Swedish school system. There is much to be said for this view — but it is no mean achievement to devise the theoretical framework within which they can be related.

Not all curriculum research is of this kind, however. Individual studies often fail to make their general theoretical frameworks clear, and the student of curriculum is left with the uneasy feeling that the different foci of different studies simply fail to relate either to a consistent framework in the researcher's mind or to more general theoretical frameworks.[18] So it is problematic whether the different studies can be related consistently to one another. Joseph Schwab[19] used the notion of the commonplaces of education (teachers, students, subject-matter and the teacher-learning milieu) as a set of ordinary-language categories which we use in describing educational activities. We can agree that these terms do find a place in our discussions of educational affairs, but they do not define a clear focus for curriculum research.

Individual curriculum researchers focus their research efforts on different grounds: as a matter of personal interest; in the light of other contemporary research; because the practical or policy implications are of contemporary concern; because they hope to contribute to the progress of a research literature or the debate in a community of researchers; or even because they have particular research techniques to try out or improve. And because the range of potential foci for curriculum study is so vast (does it include everything which can be described using the four commonplaces in conjunction?), there is a certain 'messiness' about the field.

In an attempt to draw attention to some of the features of curriculum research which are of theoretical and methodological interest for the field as a field of enquiry, we turn to a brief discussion of five dimensions along which different kinds of curriculum research studies may be distinguished:

1   Different *levels* of educational study (from macro- to micro-perspectives).
2   Different perspectives on the *character* of educational situations (as 'systems', 'programmes', 'human encounters', or 'historical moments').
3   Different *views of educational events as objects of study.*
4   Different degrees of emphasis on education as a *distinctively human* and *social process.*
5   Different degrees of emphasis on *intervention* by the researcher in the situation being studied.

a   Different Levels: Macro- to Micro-Perspectives

For many years, curriculum theorists have studied the relationship between *curriculum* and *culture*. Dewey and the progressives were interested in this relationship the social reconstructionists (including Harold Rugg, and, much more recently, Malcolm Skilbeck) take the

21

view that education has a role in reshaping society. For some time curriculum theorists and researchers have been interested in the role of education in the development of 'the cultured person' and, more recently, in the role of education in anticipating different social and cultural forms (the reconstructionists); however, contemporary concern focused on the interaction between *education and the structure of society*.[20] In fact, these contemporary theorists have done much to show how schooling may reproduce the social structure, rather than change it.

Still at the macro-level, there are also relevant studies of curriculum as it is related to the concerns of whole education systems. Mention has already been made of the work of Kallos and Lundgren in Sweden. The work of Jencks and his associates[21] was concerned with the effects of family and schooling in relation to inequality in America. And curriculum and educational researchers have studied the effects of many educational policies at the systems level.[22]

Then there are studies at the *school* level. For example, sociologists David Hargreaves[23] and Colin Lacey[24] carried out case studies of individual schools. *Classrooms*, too, have been the subject of intense curriculum research efforts. An excellent review of the classroom research of the 1970s has been made by Ian Westbury.[25]

Finally, there has been great attention to the *specifics of interaction between teachers and students*. Micro-analyses of these interactions have proved to be extremely revealing, not only about learning outcomes, but also about the consequences of different kinds of learning opportunities and learning processes.[26]

To a greater or lesser degree, all of these 'levels' of research have curriculum implications, at least on Stenhouse's definition. In any real curriculum situation, factors related to the different levels affect the initiation or implementation of an educational proposal. Lundgren has attempted to put some order into the conceptualization of the relationships between the levels by using the notion of 'frames' or 'frame factors': frameworks of constraints and opportunities which shape what can happen in the classroom, progress through a syllabus, school decision-making and student-teacher interactions.[27]

Different curriculum researchers focus on different levels; from the point of view of curriculum as a field, the problem is one of relating the different levels to one another. Are they different levels in a purely organizational or administrative sense (corporate management to the factory floor)? Are they different in an ecological sense (the difference between macro- and micro-environments)? Are they different kinds of components in a technical system (drive shaft to motorcar)? Or are they different 'layers' in an historical process (national history to local history)?

It turns out that different researchers make different assumptions about these relationships. The assumptions they make lead them to focus on different kinds of educational happenings, and to make recommendations for action by different groups: policy-makers, teachers, curriculum designers, other researchers, or the community at large. Some of these differences in perspective will become clearer as we consider other dimensions along which curriculum research studies may be differentiated.

b   Different Perspectives on the Character of Educational Situations

It is difficult from our perspective in the late twentieth century to think about formal educational processes, especially in relation to schooling, without thinking of educational *systems*. Education as a responsibility of the state, and the rapid expansion of educational opportunities (or obligations) for all, especially in western industrial societies, are relatively recent phenomena. The preoccupations of governments and government advisers have often been with the construction and reconstruction of educational systems. In our century, administrative concerns have led thinkers about education to focus on the organization of educational provision to an expanding number of potential 'clients'. From this perspective, it is natural to think of education as a *commodity* (or an investment) and to think of educational organizations as *delivery systems* which make the commodity available to the 'clients'.

At the macro-level, the administration of education consequently appears as the management of the system. At the micro-level, curriculum issues appear to be issues in organizing the transmission of content and skill from knowledgeable teachers to relatively ignorant students.

In a technological society, especially one in which knowledge is viewed as a commodity (where credentials can 'buy' opportunities, power and status) the systems view is extremely attractive. Under this view it seems that opportunities can be fairly provided to all, and the most deserving (the most able) will emerge from the selection processes of the schooling system with access to positions of the greatest opportunity, influence and reward in society.

At the micro-level, individual teachers, students and parents are also encouraged to accept this view, and to see the process of education as the accumulation of 'knowledge' (and qualifications). Opportunities are regarded as available to all; a competition takes place to decide who accumulates most 'knowledge' (with access to later opportunities being contingent upon success in earlier competitions), and the 'winners' are rewarded with access to privileged places in the social structure. The task of the teacher is to create systems for the transmission of content which are 'fair' in the bureaucratic sense; that is, which provide open access and treat individuals without regard to personal interests or idiosyncrasies, differentiating their subsequent treatment only on the basis of performance.

The 'systems' view of education, with its notions of knowledge as transmissable content, the organization of educational provision as bureaucratically 'fair', and education as a social commodity, is assumed by a very great proportion of contemporary educational researchers. It is evident in much research on educational administration, instructional psychology and curriculum development. It is also evident in certain schools of educational sociology.

Under the 'systems' view, it is compelling to think of curricula as 'programmes' which are designed to make certain knowledge (information, skills) available and to create, maintain, monitor and assess student progress.

Alternative views of the educational situation are also available, however. A *humanistic* perspective emphasizes that education is a human encounter whose aim is the development of the unique potential of each individual. Progressive education has this perspective. It is also compatible with the liberal philosophy of individualism, and with egalitarian elements of the social-democratic approach.

Educationists taking a humanistic approach are often concerned with a different set of issues. Assuming the intrinsic worth of each individual, they study issues related to such topics as self-esteem and self-concept, intrinsic motivation in learning, and the personal structuring of knowledge by each learner. At another level, they may also be interested in cultural issues in education and social reconstruction through education. They may take an existentialist or phenomenological approach in their studies, reflecting their philosophical commitments in the methodologies they choose.

A third perspective on education takes still another view. It sees educational issues in a social-political context and attempts to identify the *political-economic* structures which shape educational provision and practices. It sees education in an historical and social dimension. Topics of interest to such educationists include the issue of cultural reproduction (the reproduction of the social structure of society by education and other social processes), the political economy of education (the study of the production and distribution of knowledge in society), and even the social and political structures of educational research itself.

These different perspectives take different positions on the character of social processes, the role of education, and the nature of the person. And each addresses the curriculum differently. The 'systems' approach may address curriculum problems as problems of the technology of delivery systems; the humanistic approach addresses them as problems of the development of persons, society and culture; and the political–economic approach addresses them as problems of ideology and the control of society.

c   Different Perspectives on Educational Events as Objects of Study

Partly as a consequence of the different philosophical outlooks just discussed, different curriculum researchers address different aspects of educational events, to the point where the objects of their studies seem to be quite different kinds of things. For example, some describe educational phenomena in terms of *abstract, universal categories* like motivation, ability, social class or achievement, attempting to discover causal relationships between different variables in the framework of relevant categories. In some versions, they attempt to identify patterns in the interactions between these variables so that they can control educational arrangements more effectively, to maximize the achievement of all learners. They see educational processes as *complex*, but nevertheless open to analysis; the complexity is regarded as penetrable and consequently susceptible of technological control.

Others see all educational events as unique, so *diverse* and *manifold* in character that it would simply be unreasonable to hope for any precise analysis of their character or for a technology capable of controlling educational processes in any effective or feasible way. They are more inclined to focus on 'practicalities' (rather than technologies) and perspectives of participants (rather than theoretical perspectives) as productive points of reference for educational research and curriculum enquiry.

Still others regard educational events as *social-historical entities* which will not yield to analysis, except in developmental or historical terms, and as *reflexive* (changing as the knowledge of participants changes; as both products and producers of historical and social states of affairs and interactions). More than those who take the 'manifold' view, they are likely to focus on participants and participants' perspectives, but use the tools of language and strategic action to change educational situations and enlighten participants about the nature and consequences of different practices.

Again, different approaches to the task of curriculum research are required, depending on which of these different perspectives one adopts, and different issues will merit attention. The abstract/universal approach will focus on manipulable variables in educational settings; the diverse/multiplex approach will focus on changing perspectives and identifying wise practices appropriate for different contexts; and the social-historical/reflexive approach will focus on the language and strategic action of those involved in particular educational processes.

d Different Degrees of Emphasis on Education as Distinctively Human and Social

Some educationists use the model of the *physical sciences and technology* in their research on educational phenomena. They argue that education can be understood reliably only to the extent that its phenomena are amenable to this kind of scientific analysis. They see evidence of educational phenomena in the behaviour of those involved, and study patterns of behaviour in relation to external determinants of behaviour. In short, they regard educational processes as caused and determined and therefore as likely to be controllable.

Others do not accept the analogy of the physical sciences so easily. They see the extent to which human activity is guided by intentions and reject the exclusive claims of the determinist view. They see education as distinctively human and social in the sense that it is a product of our language and interactions with others and a part of its social and cultural framework. Moreover, they argue, our educational actions are consequences of our moral choices and commitments and can only be understood in the context of our values, aspirations and intentions. To these people, education can only be understood in terms of its *meaning* to those involved in educational processes.

This difference reflects a more general difference in perspectives on the nature of social science. The debate has gone on in social science since the late nineteenth century, especially among German sociologists. The British empiricists regarded social science as similar in principle to physical science. Indeed, John Stuart Mill (1816–1883) argued strongly in favour of this view, asserting that the social sciences (like the contemporary study of the tides, or 'tidology') were simply 'inexact' while other phenomena could be studied using 'exact' methods.[28] But some German sociologists rejected Mill's arguments in relation to the study of social life. The *Geisteswissenschaften*, or 'human sciences', they argued, were not merely different from physical sciences in their exactitude, but also in their character. Human and social events were to be understood differently, and different methods would be appropriate in studying them.[29]

In curriculum research, there are advocates of both views.[30] The alternative points of view have often been caricatured (for example, as between 'quantitative' and 'qualitative' methods, or 'objectivity' and 'subjectivity') by advocates of one or the other perspective, and the debate between them has often been doctrinaire. Yet the history of social science shows that both approaches have substantial critical literatures.[31] Moreover, the relationship between these points of view has, in recent times, been more clearly understood and there are signs that a new framework may be constructed within which the opposition between the points of view can be comprehended.[32] Curriculum researchers and theorists have moved quickly to explore the potential of this new framework, *critical social science*, in relation to the problems of curriculum, and have demonstrated its promise.[33]

In short, it is clear that curriculum is human and social in character, and that there are differences among curriculum researchers, as among social scientists in general, about the degree to which its questions and issues can be examined through the physical sciences approach. To the extent that the methods of the physical sciences are inappropriate for the study of social life, it is argued, curriculum researchers must reject the methods of the physical sciences and instead use methods which are more appropriate to the study of social life.

    e   Different Degrees of Intervention by the Researcher in the Situation Being Studied

Few physical or social scientists today believe that their observations are 'non-reactive'; that is, that the act of observation does not in some way change the object being observed, or at least the context in which it is understood. Observations often have an impact on the observed, and the framework within which observations take place is not neutral or indifferent about the theoretical or practical consequences of the observation. In short, observation is nowadays generally regarded as theory- and value-laden.[34] But there is disagreement about the degree to which intervention by the researcher in the situation being studied is necessary to understand it.

For example, some curriculum researchers and evaluators have attempted to develop methods which are as non-interventive as possible. The 'responsive' or 'illuminative' evaluator does not regard his or her work as non-reactive, but attempts to represent as faithfully as possible the perspectives of those already in a situation.[35] As far as possible these approaches attempt to leave the power for change in a situation with participants rather than with the observer.

'Participant-observer' and 'observer-participant' studies also abound. In the first, the observer attempts to participate in the situation but to exercise caution about the degree to which his or her presence will influence it. Some participant-observers prefer to err on the side of having an influence, others on the side of avoiding influence, but both tend to regard understanding, rather than change, as the immediate and direct aim of participant-observation.[36]

The experimental approach in curriculum study, however, does require intervention into a situation. By observing the effects of the intervention, the observer hopes to learn something about cause-effect relations within it. This kind of intervention is regarded as strictly for the purposes of the study; the experimenter, however, will take the view that subsequent changes in the situation will be rationally justifiable on the basis of evidence and the theoretical fruits of his or her enquiries. But the intervention the experimentalist hopes will follow from the theoretical developments is understood as a matter of applied science or technology; the initial interventions are for purposes of explanation, not application.

Finally, action researchers also aim at intervention, but expect advances in theory or understanding to be consequences of their real-world interventions. In other words, they are inclined to see the development of theory or understanding as a by-product of the improvement of real situations, rather than application as a by-product of advances in 'pure' theory.[37]

In short, different approaches to the study of educational events imply different views on the nature of the intervention they make into the situations they study. Interventions may be made for the development of theories or interpretations, with the view that the language in which situations are understood can be systematically developed and decisions made subsequently about whether and how permanent changes might be made. Some interpretive researchers and some experimentalists share this view that their interventions can be made more or less independently of the day-to-day life of the situation being studied. Other researchers aim for intervention in order to change the situation, expecting advances in theory or understanding to follow. Action researchers, in particular, have this view.

There are corresponding differences between researchers in their view of their own relationship to those in the situations being studied. Participants may be regarded as objects of study (or part of the phenomenon: 'experimental subjects') or as cooperators with the researcher in the quest for knowledge; or the researcher may be regarded by participants as a collaborator in the quest for improved practice. These distinctions have important consequences in terms of the kind of knowledge and action 'produced' by the research.

4   Curriculum Research and Professional Competence

From the overview of traditions in, and dimensions of, curriculum research, it is clear that there are different ways of characterizing teacher professionalism and hence of what the professional development of teachers entails. For underlying the diversities and complexities characterizing the study of the curriculum there is a discernible range of assumptions about the kind of professional knowledge that teachers require and about the role of the researcher in making this knowledge available. In order to draw attention to these features of curriculum research it is possible to set out five different views of what the professional competence of teachers involves.

a   The Commonsense View

This refers to all those approaches which seek to ground research knowledge in practical commonsense experience rather than theory and which are, therefore, confined to codifying knowledge of existing educational ideas and practices. On this view, the task of the researcher is to facilitate the successful conformity of teachers to traditional patterns of conduct. Professional development simply requires an increasingly skillful use of an existing stock of pedagogical knowledge.

b   The Philosophical View

This refers to all those approaches which stress the need for teachers to adopt a reflective stance towards the fundamental assumptions and ideals on which their 'philosophy of education' depends. The purpose of research, therefore, is to provide teachers with the sort of concepts and insights that are required to formulate a coherent understanding of the nature and purpose of the educator's role. Teaching is a professional occupation, on this view, because it is guided by a self-conscious understanding of basic educational principles, rather than by any narrow concern with instrumental or utilitarian goals and motives. Professional competence is, therefore, a matter of making judgments in accordance with fully articulated principles, values and ideas.

c   The Applied Science View

Those who regard research as an applied science take the view that the task of the researcher is to produce scientifically verified knowledge that can be used to ensure that pre-established educational goals are achieved by the most effective means. According to the 'applied science' view, the professional expertise of teachers does not derive from any overriding concern with educational values and goals. Rather, it stems from the possession of the technical skills required to apply scientific theories and principles to educational situations. The professional development of teachers, on this view, requires teachers to adopt a technical approach to their work, seeking to optimize the efficacy of learning by utilizing scientific knowledge. Professional competence, therefore, is judged not by reference to the way in which teachers formulate their aims, but by the effectiveness of their practices in achieving whatever aims are being pursued.

d   The Practical Approach

This view, like the 'philosophical' view, sees curriculum research as a form of enquiry which is reflective and deliberative and which results, not in the production of theoretical knowledge, but in morally defensible decisions about practice. The role of the researcher is not that of an external investigator providing solutions to educational problems, but that of a consultant whose task is to assist teachers to arrive at sound practical judgments. The distinctive professionalism of the teacher, therefore, does not stem from skillful mastery of existing practical knowledge or an ability to apply scientifically accredited technical rules. Rather, it emerges out of the fact that teachers, like members of other professions, profess an ethic. As with the 'philosophical view', it is recognized that teaching is a professional activity because it involves the pursuit of essentially moral purposes and goals. However, while the 'philosophical' view tends to view questions about these moral purposes as somehow separate from questions about their realization, the 'practical' view emphasizes how they are realized not *by* teaching but *in* and *through* teaching. Professional competence is, therefore, to be judged not by the ability to articulate and defend moral principles, nor as a matter of traditional conformity or technical accountability. Rather, it is assessed in terms of moral and prudential answerability for practical judgments actually made within the context of existing educational institutions. It is a matter of wise and prudent deliberation, not conformity to general traditions or narrowly specified prescriptions for practice.

e The Critical View

Those who subscribe to this view accept much of the thinking that informs the 'practical' view. Both, for example, accept that individual practitioners must be committed to self-critical reflection on their educational aims and values. Where they differ is in the additional claim of the 'critical' view that the formulation of these additional aims may be distorted by ideological forces and constraints and their realization may be impeded by institutional structures. In the critical view, educational problems and issues may arise not only as *individual* matters, but as *social* matters requiring collective or common action if they are to be satisfactorily resolved. The outcome of critical research, therefore, is not just the formulation of informed practical judgment, but theoretical accounts which provide a basis for analyzing systematically distorted decisions and practices, and suggesting the kinds of social and educational action by which these distortions may be removed. Furthermore, while these theories may be made available by the researcher, they are not offered as 'externally given' and 'scientifically verified' propositions. Rather, they are offered as interpretations which can only be validated in and by the *self-understandings* of practitioners under conditions of *free and open dialogue*. Hence, professional development, on this view, is a matter of teachers becoming more enlightened about the ways in which their own self-understandings may prevent them being properly aware of the social and political mechanisms which operate to distort or limit the proper conduct of education in society. Professional competence, therefore, requires a capacity for continuous deliberation and critical discussion by the teaching profession as a whole of the way in which political and social structures relate to and influence educational aims and practices. This professional discussion must also relate to a wider social debate about the role of education in society.

In many ways, this divergent range of research stances, each incorporating different attitudes towards the purpose that research serves and its value to the teaching profession, is no more than a contemporary confirmation of the classical Greek view that the appropriateness of any particular form of knowledge will depend on the *telos*, or purpose, it serves. The most influential attempt to articulate this view and to differentiate forms of enquiry in terms of their different purposes, was Aristotle's three-fold classification of disciplines as 'theoretical', 'productive' or 'practical'.

Briefly, the purpose of a theoretical discipline is the pursuit of truth through contemplation; its *telos* is the attainment of knowledge for its own sake. The purpose of the productive sciences is to make something; their *telos* is the production of some artifact. The practical disciplines are those sciences that deal with ethical and political life; their *telos* is practical wisdom and knowledge.

Now while the form of thinking appropriate to *theoretical* activities was essentially contemplative, the kind of knowledge and enquiry appropriate to the *productive* disciplines was what Aristotle called *poietike*, which roughly translates as 'making action' and which is evident in craft or skill knowledge. The Greeks described the disposition of the craftsman as *techne*, a disposition to act in a true and reasoned way according to the rules of the craft. A guiding image or idea, *eidos*, guided the act of production, providing a perfect model of the performance or the product, and the product would more or less adequately demonstrate the idea which guided its production. The situation in which the production took place was only significant to the extent that it furnished materials for the act of production. Today we could say that a local situation is only significant to the extent that it can be instrumentalized to the production process. We would call the form of reasoning involved in *poietike* 'means-end' or instrumental reasoning. In this kind of thinking, the guiding image is so powerful that it dominates the action and directs it towards the given end.

The form of reasoning appropriate to the 'practical sciences' was called *praxis*. *Praxis* is distinguished from *poietike* because it is informed action which, by reflection on its character and consequences, reflexively changes the 'knowledge-base' which informs it. Where *poietike* is 'making-action', *praxis* is 'doing-action'. *Techne* is a disposition which guides and directs action, but is not necessarily changed by it; its goals and general character remain unchanged even though the craftsman becomes more skilled and has greater understanding of the craft. Craft or technical knowledge is not reflexive; it does not change the framework of tradition and expectation within which it operates. Nor does it take the view that, through the exercise of the craft, the fundamental character of the social setting will be reconstructed. *Praxis*, however, does have this character — it remakes the conditions of informed action and constantly reviews action and the knowledge which informs it. *Praxis* is always guided by a moral disposition to act truly and justly, called by the Greeks *phronesis*.

This way of thinking is *dialectical*. The dialectic is often described as the opposition of a 'thesis' against its 'antithesis', with a new 'synthesis' being arrived at when the thesis and antithesis are reconciled. For example, one might pose the view that individualization of instruction allows each student to reach his or her full potential as a human being; then oppose it with the antithesis that individualized instruction promotes the interests of the already advantaged and selects out the disadvantaged quickly, consigning them to a life of limited potential. This contradiction might be resolved by describing a system which had this effect as oppressive (the synthesis), and planning a programme of positive discrimination in favour of the disadvantaged.

Dialectical thinking involves searching out these contradictions (like the contradiction of the inadvertent oppression of less able students by a system which aspires to help all students to attain their 'full potential'), but it is not really as wooden or mechanical as the formula of thesis-antithesis-synthesis suggests. On the contrary, it is an open and questioning form of thinking which demands reflection back and forth between elements like *part* and *whole, knowledge* and *action, process* and *product, subject* and *object, being* and *becoming, rhetoric* and *reality*, or *structure* and *function*. In the process, *contradictions* may be discovered (as, for example, in a political *structure* which aspires to give decision-making power to all, but actually *functions* to deprive some access to the information with which they could influence crucial decisions about their lives). As contradictions are revealed, new constructive thinking and new constructive action are required to transcend the contradictory state of affairs. The complementarity of the elements is dynamic: it is a kind of tension, not a static confrontation between the two poles. In the dialectical approach, the elements are regarded as mutually constitutive, not separate and distinct. Contradiction can thus be distinguished from paradox: to speak of a contradiction is to imply that a new resolution can be achieved, while to speak of a paradox is to suggest that two incompatible ideas remain inertly opposed to one another.

In *praxis*, thought and action (or theory and practice), are dialectically related. They are to be understood as *mutually constitutive*, as in a process of interaction which is a continual reconstruction of thought and action in the living historical process which evidences itself in every real social situation. Neither thought nor action is pre-eminent. In *poietike*, by contrast, thought (a guiding idea or *eidos*) is pre-eminent, guiding and directing action; theory directs practice. In *praxis*, the ideas which guide action are just as subject to change as action is; the only fixed element is *phronesis*, the disposition to act truly and rightly.

Considered against the background of these Aristotelian distinctions, many of the contemporary disputes about curriculum research can be viewed as arguments about whether curriculum research should be a *theoretical, productive* or *practical* science. While, to those advocating the 'philosophical' view, curriculum research is a species of *theoria*, the advocates of an 'applied science' approach clearly presume that it is a form of *poietike*. Those advancing both the 'practical' and 'critical' views, however, explicitly believe curriculum research to be one of Aristotle's 'practical arts': a matter of *praxis*.

Also, but perhaps less obviously, the Greek distinction between the basic dispositions of *techne* and *phronesis* helps to locate and characterize the underlying motives and attitudes that inform the two major styles of thought pervading contemporary understanding of education, curriculum and teaching. The most dominant of these two forms of consciousness is one in which education is seen as essentially technical and, hence, echoes the attitude of *techne*. The second outlook sees education as practical, echoing the attitude of praxis. There is, however, an alternative outlook now emerging which is explicitly informed and guided by *phronesis* and that involves a view of education which is essentially *strategic*. The purpose of the next section is to explore and examine these three modes of consciousness.

5 Technical, Practical and Strategic Views

a The Technical View

Among teachers, a technical view of education is altogether more prevalent in our society, which is so thoroughly a technological one. A technical view of teaching and curriculum treats educational provision as a set of means to given ends. It is assumed there are alternative means available to given ends, and that the role of research is to evaluate their effectiveness and efficiency. Teachers' knowledge is assumed to be about the means available and their relative effectiveness under different circumstances.

Given this view of knowledge about teaching and curriculum, the role of research is to inform the craftsman about technical matters, just as research on the colloidal properties of different clays or on the temperature ranges which could be achieved in a certain kiln might be of help to the potter. The potter is still an individual, still a craftsman, but the dimensions of the craft are set by traditions about the work, by expectations about the products, and the physical environment in which the work is done.

A teacher may be regarded by some as bound to a craft in just this way. There are traditions about education, expectations about the 'products' of schooling, and physical constraints on what can be achieved. These physical constraints serve also as a model for understanding other kinds of psychological, social and economic constraints on teaching. Like clay which is insufficiently elastic, some children are thought to be insufficiently intelligent or motivated by school work; like a kiln which is not properly sealed, some families are thought not to create an intense enough climate of support for students; like tools which are inadequate, some classrooms are regarded as inadequate resource bases for teaching and learning.

The idea that teaching and curriculum are craftlike is a reassuring one. To regard them so is to sustain our beliefs about the continuity of the traditions of education, our expectations of teachers and schools, and our materialist views that education can be improved by providing better tools, resources and environments (that is, by believing that more money, more resources and better environments could solve our problems for us). It is also reassuring because we can easily think of educational problems as blockages in a 'delivery system' which can be overcome through the improvement of the technology. In short, we need not ask about the purposes of education, the side-effects of unjust traditions or inadequate systems, or the unsettling changes in society which require different kinds of skills, knowledge and critical capacities in the young.

b The Practical View

By contrast with the technical view, education, curriculum and teaching may be considered as practical. Considered from this perspective, education is essentially a process or an activity. It takes place in social situations of great complexity, calling for many decisions from those involved if it is to be regulated at all. While the technical view of education sees teaching and learning behaviours as elements in a system which can, in principle at least, be controlled as means to given ends, the practical view asserts that the social world is simply too fluid and reflexive to allow such systemization. It regards social life as in principle fluid and open. Such control as is possible in the social process of education will only enter through the wise decision-making of practitioners — through their deliberation on practice. Wise and experienced practitioners will make highly complex judgments and act on the basis of these judgments to intervene in the life of the classroom or school to influence events in one way or another. But the events of school and classroom life will always have an open, undetermined character. The action of those in the situation will never completely control or determine the unfolding of classroom or school life. In short, under the practical view, educational processes cannot be viewed as means-ends systems, with clear and definite ends and alternative means (techniques) to achieve them. Those taking the practical view believe that influence can only by exerted by practical deliberation and wise and prudent intervention into the life of the classroom. Practice cannot be reduced to technical control.

This description of educational processes accords with experience, at least for many practitioners. They do not feel such a singlemindedness about the pursuit of objectives — on the contrary, they feel that they pursue many different aims and objectives more or less simultaneously (for example, pursuing specific knowledge outcomes in a classroom activity, while at the same time pursuing general learning about wider views of knowledge, wider learnings about society, learnings about right conduct in the classroom and beyond, and even maintaining a readiness to change direction away from the specific topic under consideration to pursue an incidental topic which can engage the students and promote learnings which were unanticipated at the outset). Equally, practitioners tend not to experience their expertise as a set of techniques or as a 'tool kit' for producing learning. They can identify some 'tricks of the trade' and techniques, certainly, but these are employed in complex patterns, in overlapping sets, in combinations dictated as much by the mood or climate of the class, the particular set of aims being pursued, the kinds of subject matter being considered, the particular image which governs the teaching/learning exercise at hand as a kind of dramatic performance for the 'players' involved, and by all sorts of other factors which shape the situation moment by moment (like the time of day, the force of the wind outside, the dramatic opportunities of the classroom talk of the moment, and so on). Expertise under this view does not consist of designing a set of sequenced means or techniques which 'drive' learners towards expected learning outcomes. It consists of spontaneous and flexible direction and redirection of the learning enterprise, guided by a sensitive reading of the subtle changes and responses of other participants in the enterprise.

To exert a consistent influence in this spontaneously changing and evolving drama, the practitioner finds guidance not in the pursuit of fixed goals or the certainties of particular known techniques (although these things may provide some direction). Instead, he or she uses professional judgment responsively, guided by criteria for the process itself: criteria based on experience and learning which distinguish educational processes from non-educational processes and which separate good from indifferent or bad practice.

This view of education does not see the process as a craft: the moulding of classroom life like clay into definite shapes. It treats it as a practice which is guided by complex, sometimes competing intentions, which are themselves modified in the light of circumstances. The underlying disposition is that of *phronesis*, the disposition to act truly and rightly, which expresses itself differently in different situations. In fact, this is a time-honoured view of the role of the teacher, with roots reaching back to the ancient Greeks. Perhaps it is only the institutionalization of schooling, the relative uniformity of the organization of classrooms, the systematization of curricula and the bureaucratization of the profession which have allowed the technological image of education to emerge. Once given the image, it becomes possible to believe that the work of classrooms is comprehensively described by the language of technology. Yet, as we have sought to demonstrate here, another language for describing education processes (the language of the practical) identifies and names aspects of education which are not captured in the technical view. And they are aspects of education which many practitioners would want to defend as the hallmarks of their professional life.

In education today, these two images of education as a profession rest uneasily alongside one another. On the one hand, professional teachers want to point to the complex aims for contemporary education apparently imposed by a society which requires sophisticated skills in its youth and which has given schools complex tasks in social education in addition to their tasks of inculcating 'cognitive' knowledge and skills. Moreover, teachers want to point to the complex technical knowledge about teaching methods now available, supported by theories of child development, learning and social structure. These provide evidence of technical sophistication appropriate to a profession. But, on the other hand, teachers want to point to their autonomy and responsibility as professionals guided by a disposition to act truly and rightly in the interests of their clients; to their capacity to judge their own conduct and the conduct of their students wisely; and to interpret society reflectively so that they can give their students access to the social world through their understanding. This aspect of their professionalism requires practical deliberation which expresses itself as much in personal and social conduct as in institutional rituals and forms. These competing technical and practical views of education are not much distinguished in talk about education. It is easy to slip into one language or the other and believe that one is speaking about the whole of the process. Recent developments in curriculum theory, however, have distinguished these languages and have made it clear what is lost when one language is regarded as sufficient for the whole purpose of examining education. In particular, it has become clear what is lost when technical language dominates, for when it does, the 'moral' dimension of education is inadvertently suppressed, and education becomes a purely technical matter — or, some would say, a matter only of training or indoctrination.

It has been the task of some educational theorists to untangle these two views and to attempt to see them in relation to one another. To do so, they have had to create a new language for describing education which recognizes both technical and practical aspects: which recognizes the systemic, institutional and instrumental (means–end) elements of education, and which also recognizes its practical and moral character. We will begin the discussion of this perspective in relation to the strategic view.

c   The Strategic View

A consciousness of teaching and curriculum as strategic is a consciousness, first, that educational activities are *historically located*. They take place against a social-historical background and project a view of the kind of future we hope to build. Second, it is a consciousness that education is a *social activity* with social consequences, not just a matter of the development of the individual. Third, it is a consciousness that education is intrinsically *political*, affecting the life chances of those involved in the process by affecting their access to an interesting life and material well-being. Moreover, it is a consciousness that those who can influence the nature of education can influence the character and expectations of future citizens. And finally, it is a consciousness that educational acts — every act of teaching and every learning opportunity embodied in a curriculum — are *problematic* in a deeper sense than the craft or technical view can admit. Under the strategic view, all aspects of an educational act may be regarded as problematic: its purpose, the social situation it models or suggests, the way it creates or constrains relationships between participants, the kind of medium in which it works (question and answer, recitation, simulation, game, rote-learning exercise), and the kind of knowledge to which it gives form (knowledge of content, appreciation, skills, constructive or reconstructive power, tacit understanding). In the hurly-burly of life in schools, teachers must use their practical judgment in decisions about these matters. But each can be reflected upon and reconsidered (made problematic) to inform future practical judgments, and each can be seen in social and historical context as facilitating or debilitating progress towards a more rational and just society.

Each educational act is determinate and embodies ideas about each of these aspects of educational acts. The teacher who regards them as problematic is conscious that he or she gives life to one among many possible educational acts; one among many possible forms of social life. Not every act can be thought about this way (it would be too morally and intellectually demanding), but every educational act *could* be. And so a constant debate is necessary in education to continue the process of examining its frameworks of tradition, expectation and action, and to understand the consequences of different kinds of provision and performance. Only through open and informed debate about these matters can education improve the chances of achieving a just and rational society.

The teacher who regards teaching and curriculum as strategic therefore submits some part of his or her work (and, in principle, all of it) to *systematic examination*. To the extent that it is possible to do so, he or she *plans thoughtfully, acts deliberately, observes the consequences of action systematically, and reflects critically on the situational constraints and practical potential of the strategic action being considered*. He or she will also construct opportunities to carry this private discourse into discussion and debate with others — teachers, students, administrators and the school community. In so doing, he or she helps to establish *critical communities of enquirers* into teaching, the curriculum and school organization, and administration with groups within the school, the whole school or between schools. This *critical self-reflection*, undertaken in a self-critical community, uses *communication* as a means to develop a sense of comparative experience, to discover local or immediate constraints on action by understanding the contexts within which others work, and, by converting experience into discourse, uses language as an aid to analysis and the development of a critical vocabulary which provides the terms for reconstructing practice.

Treating teaching and curriculum in a strategic way thus leaves great scope for research. And it is readily apparent that the kind of research it suggests requires that teachers become critical figures in the research enterprise. At times, the 'research' will be only a restless, enquiring attitude about teaching and curriculum; at other times, a particular domain of strategic action will be selected for more sustained, systematic enquiry. In the latter case, we may speak of a 'research project'. In such a case, the teacher will adopt a 'project perspective', from which the particular domain selected (for example, the organization of remedial reading provision in the school) may be regarded as problematic. In this area, *actions* taken will be regarded as 'tentative' or 'experimental' (though they will be deliberately thought through), the *language* in which actions are described and understood will be critically examined, *social consequences* will be scrutinized and reflected upon, and the *situation* in which action takes place will be examined to see how it creates and constrains the potential of the chosen strategy. When teachers adopt a project perspective, they will also create opportunities to learn from their experience and to plan their own learning. Very probably, they will arrange to discuss their unfolding experience with others. In short, such teachers 'become critical' — not in the sense that they become negativistic or complaining, but in the sense that they gather their intellectual and strategic capacities, focus them on a particular issue and engage them in critical examination of practice through the 'project'.

It should now be clear that part of the intention of this book is to argue for the sort of theoretical framework within which teachers can become critical in just this way. It should also be obvious that the development of such a critical theory of education must be related intrinsically to the professional development of teachers. More extensive professional autonomy and responsibility require that teachers themselves build educational theory through critical reflection on their own practical knowledge.

But not all the knowledge that teachers have provides an equally profitable starting point for the enterprise of critical reflection. The next section sets out some of the kinds of knowledge that teachers have and employs in their work and examines the part that teachers' knowledge plays in developing a more critical approach to curriculum research.

6 Teachers' Knowledge

Some of the knowledge teachers have, like the notion that classrooms are the appropriate place for education to go on in, has its roots in habit, ritual, precedent, custom, opinion or mere impressions. Its rationale must first be recovered from assumption before critical work can begin. Other knowledge, like a theory of individual differences in ability, is essentially abstract, and its concrete implications must be worked out to reclaim it for critical analysis (or else the critical enterprise will dissolve into mere word games or polemics). Strategic action, which has some framework of thought or rationale informing it, and a practice which gives it material significance, is more suited for critical reflection. An example of strategic action would be the use of cooperative teaching by a regular classroom teacher and a reading specialist in an attempt to improve remedial reading teaching. Its rationale is based on the idea of collaborative effort among teachers and students, and its practical significance is that it is a workable arrangement which will benefit students and teachers in their common enterprise. But both theory and practice are regarded as tentative and subject to change in the light of experience.

To emphasize the point that some kinds of knowledge provide a more effective foundation for critical reflection than others, it may be helpful to simply list some of the kinds of knowledge teachers have and use in their work. First, there is the *commonsense* knowledge about practice that is simply assumption or opinion; for example, the view that students need discipline, or that not knowing the answer to a student's question is a sign of lack of authority in a teacher. Then there is the *folk wisdom* of teachers: like the ideas that students get restless on windy days, or that they can't easily learn on the day that the doctor visits to give injections, or that Friday afternoons are difficult times in the classroom. After that, there is an array of *skill-knowledge* which teachers use: how to get students to line up, or how to prevent students speaking while instructions about a task are being given. Next, there is a body of *contextual knowledge*: knowledge about *this* class, *this* community, or *this* student, providing background against which the achievability of aspirations or the 'relevance' of tasks can be evaluated. Fifth, there is a body of *professional knowledge* about teaching strategies and curriculum: their potential, their forms, their substance and their effects. Sixth, there are ideas about *educational theory*: ideas about the development of individuals or about the role of education in society, for example. And finally, there are ideas about *social and moral theories and general philosophical outlooks*: about how people can and should interact, the development and reproduction of social classes, the uses of knowledge in society, or about truth and justice.

Some of these kinds of knowledge have the roots of their rationality well hidden 'underground' in the life of practice. Others have their heads in clouds of talk. The former must be reclaimed from the taken-for-granted to be analyzed; the latter must be made real and concrete before their implications can be understood. Put at its simplest, critical analysis is only possible when both theory (organized knowledge) and practice (organized action) can be treated in a unified way as problematic — as open to dialectical reconstruction through reflection and revision.

Certain habits of mind prevent us from treating theory and practice as problematic (and especially from thinking of them as jointly problematic). It is easy to think of theory as something more than an organized body of knowledge — too often is it regarded as something close to 'The Truth' — as certain or complete. And it is easy to think of practice as habitual, self-evident or inevitable (just 'as it is'). To break these habits of mind, we must restore the problematic element of both. We must reawaken the moral disposition of *phronesis*; the disposition to act rightly, truly, prudently and responsively to circumstances.

Few competent social researchers fall into the trap of treating their theories as 'truths'. They treat them as problematic, as open to recon-struction. But they do not always make it clear that their theories have this problematic character. Unfortunately, many who read their work do regard their theories as 'truths' (or relative certainties) and their social life as the unfolding of fixed patterns (which researchers can identify and describe in their theories, thus creating new 'truths'). There are serious consequences in treating these theories as 'truths' or certainties (as unproblematic). Once they are regarded as already sufficiently justified and then applied uncritically, observation of their consequences is forgotten about. Only when significant problems occur will those involved cast doubt on the theories (and the problems may have to be massive — like a nuclear spillage, to borrow an analogy from natural science and technology).

In short, taking theories too much for granted leaves us at the mercy of yesterday's good ideas. While to some extent we do this, just because practices which have been justified and have 'worked' seem validated by our experience, we should remember that the phenomena of social life are different from those of physics and chemistry. While there are *some* general tendencies and well-attested social 'facts', real practical situations are idiosyncratic, social conditions often change unpredictably, and different points of view lead us to judge similar situations differently.

Social life is reflexive; that is, it has the capacity to change as our knowledge and thinking changes, thus creating new forms of social life which can, in their turn, be reconstructed. Social and educational theories must cope with this reflexivity: the 'truths' they tell must be seen as located in particular historical circumstances and social contexts, and as answers to particular questions asked in the intellectual context of a particular time.

'Knowledge' is sometimes defined as 'justified true belief'. Not all the kinds of knowledge we described in relation to teachers is 'knowledge' in this sense. It may not be true, it may not be justified, or it may not be believed sincerely by anyone. Paradoxical though it may seem, belief reaches the special status of 'knowledge' only when it survives examination: when it can be and has been treated as problematic. For someone to claim that they know, they must convince us that their ideas survive critical examination: that they can be justified, that they can survive attempts to show them to be false, and that they are not incredible.

This is a severe test for teachers' knowledge. Apart from the difficulty of getting ideas 'out in the open' so that they can be analyzed critically, there is the difficulty that social and historical cricumstances of teaching and curriculum may differ widely from school to school and classroom to classroom. Knowledge about education turns out to be bound to particular action-contexts. This, in turn, suggests that we should expect few certainties in education (unlike physical scientists, we cannot assume that the phenomena of interest in education are uniform over place and time). The best we can expect in social science is knowledge which is tried (in analysis and in action in an historical and social context) and not found wanting.

How then should we regard the different kinds of 'knowledge' teachers have and use? We should regard it as problematic. To do this, it may be helpful to think of *policies* which embody the knowledge we claim to have, to use it in *planning action*, and to test it in *strategic action*. For example, we might think of a policy of equalizing opportunity in education, use it in planning a programme of positive discrimination in favour of children arriving at school without having mastered pre-reading skills, and implement our plan reflectively, gathering data about how the different groups get on in learning to read. In this way, we can readily submit our ideas to critical examination and begin to build, not only a critical theory of education, but also a critically informed practice. Some of our 'knowledge' will crumble as soon as we begin to think about it seriously as a guide to action; some will be modified, deepened and improved through analysis and active testing.

Teachers' knowledge provides a starting point for critical reflection. It cannot simply be taken for granted and systematized into theory, nor can it be taken as definitive in prescribing for practice. This is not because teachers' knowledge is any less compelling than the knowledge others have; it is because educational acts are social acts, which are reflexive, historically located, and embedded in particular intellectual and social contexts. So knowledge about education must change according to historical circumstances, local contexts and different participants' understandings of what is happening in the educational encounter. And it is clear that the knowledge we have will, to a very great extent, be rooted in local historical and social contexts.

We have discussed teachers' knowledge because it is one essential aspect of education as *praxis*: the aspect which 'resides in' the knowledgeable actor or knowing subject. A critical theory of education requires a disposition to think critically and a critical community of professionals committed to an examination of the teaching profession and the circumstances within which it carries out its task.

7 Conclusion

This chapter has revealed something of the diversity of curriculum research. But historically and in terms of the foci, methods and roles of researchers and teachers it is clear that the field is open: it has not converged neatly upon a unified view of its problems, substance, methods, or community of enquirers. In this diversity, it is difficult to discern stable patterns. It has responded to a variety of interests and policy and practical concerns in a variety of social, political and cultural contexts.

Yet there are themes which embrace some of this diversity. Perhaps these are most easily understood in relation to views of the relationship between theory and practice. One view regards theory as a source of principles that can be applied in practice; another regards practice as a matter of professional judgment which can be developed as the wisdom of practitioners and policy makers is developed; and a third regards theory and practice as dialectically related, with theory being developed and tested by application in and reflection on practice, and practice as a risky enterprise which can never be completely justified by theoretical principles. Different approaches to the study of education and curriculum reflect these alternative views of theory and practice.

Moreover, each of these alternative views reflects a different general position concerning the nature and purpose of social scientific enquiry. These positions, the 'positivist', the 'interpretive' and the 'critical' are described and examined in the chapters that follow, but it is hoped that what will be learned is not just the intellectual history of these traditions. Rather, the aim of the book is to make their assumptions and character more accessible and so increase the capacity for entering into critical discussion and debate about the nature of educational and curriculum research. Also, and more positively, the intention is to justify a critical approach to educational theory, and action research as its concrete methodological expression. Indeed, the principal contention of this book is that action research as an expression of a critical approach can, in its turn, inform and develop a critical theory of education.

Further Reading

This chapter has covered much ground and raised numerous issues and problems. The 'classical' texts that have largely determined and shaped most of the issues are Tyler's *Basic Principles of Curriculum and Instruction*; Stenhouse's *Introduction to Curriculum Research and Development*; and Schwab's paper, 'The practical: A language for curriculum'.

For an interesting philosophical analysis of the nature of teaching as a profession see Glen Langford's *Teaching as a Profession*. A sociological analysis of teaching as a profession is given by Eric Hoyle, in 'Educational innovation and the role of the teacher'. Aristotle's discussion of the technical, productive and practical arts is to be found in *The Nicomachean Ethics*.

Notes

1 For an extended analysis of the professional character of the teachers' role, see HOYLE, E. (1974), 'Professionality, professionalism and control in teaching', *London Educational Review*, vol. 3, no. 2, pp. 15–17.
2 See, for example, CANE, B., and SCHRODER, C. (1970), *The Teacher and Research*, Slough, NFER.
3 See, for example, (1916) *Democracy and Education*, Macmillan, and (1938) *Experience and Education*, Collier-Macmillan.
4 For classical expositions of the 'foundations approach', see STANLEY, W.O., SMITH, B.O., BENNE, K.D. and ANDERSON, A.W. (1956), *Social Foundations of Education*, New York, Dryden; SMITH, B.O., STANLEY, W.O. and SHORES, J.H. (1950), *Fundamentals of Curriculum Development*, New York, World Book; CONNELL, W.F. *et al.*, (1962), *The Foundations of Education*, Sydney, Novak; and CONNELL, W.F., DEBUS, R.L. and NIBLETT, W.R. (Eds) (1966), *Readings in the Foundations of Education*, Sydney, Novak.
5 HIRST, P.H. (1966), 'Educational theory', chapter 2 in TIBBLE, J.W. (Ed.) *The Study of Education*, London, Routledge and Kegan Paul.
6 O'CONNOR, D.J. (1957), *An Introduction to the Philosophy of Education*, London, Routledge and Kegan Paul.
7 See, for a critique of this view, CARR, W. (1980), 'The gap between theory and practice', *Journal of Further and Higher Education*, vol. 4, no. 1, pp. 60–9.
8 It is tempting to draw the parallel here to the distinction between owners, managers and workers in nineteenth-century industry: the owning class could develop 'pure' science, the managers 'applied' science, and the workers became instruments or operatives who did the practical work. Hirst and O'Connor seem to be struggling to create a 'pure' science of education, even though it is 'composite', which can transcend the apparently technical concerns and constraints of education as an 'applied' study.
9 TYLER, R.W. (1949), *Basic Principles of Curriculum and Instruction*, Chicago, University of Chicago Press.
10 Tyler's views were stripped to their most technical (almost to the point of caricature) by MAGER, R.F. (1962), in his influential book, *Preparing Instructional Objectives*, Palo Alto, CA. Fearon.
11 Questions about general goals of education and the cultivation of the person were increasingly regarded as irrelevant — endured by student-teachers as a necessary part of their education, but hardly as compelling for them. After all, they were to fit into large and complex education systems

and needed to know (they thought) how to *implement* education (curricula) rather than how to *create* it. The goals were decided, the systems were there: they needed to know how to play their roles when they entered the classroom alone, aided only by their knowledge, skills and (especially) the resources (materials) provided by others for their use.

12 In *School Review*, 1969, vol. 78, pp. 1–24.

13 (1969), Chicago, University of Chicago Press.

14 See, for example, REICH, C. (1970), *The Greening of America*, New York, Random House; and MARCUSE, H. (1964), *One-dimensional Man*, Boston, Beacon Press.

15 He had directed the Humanities Curriculum Project. See STENHOUSE, L. (1968), 'The humanities curriculum project', *Journal of Curriculum Studies*, vol. 1, no. 1, pp. 26–33.

16 For example, REYNOLDS, J., and SKILBECK, M. (1976), *Culture and the Classroom*, London, Open Books.

17 KALLOS, D., and LUNDGREN, U.P. (1979) 'Lessons from a comprehensive school system for curriculum theory and research', *Journal of Curriculum Studies*, reprinted in TAYLOR, P.M. (Ed.), (1979) *New Directions in Curriculum Studies*, Lewes, Falmer Press.

18 Indeed, there is disagreement about the kinds of theoretical frameworks which might be employed. See, for example, EISNER, E.W. and VALLANCE, E. (Eds) (1974), *Conflicting Conceptions of Curriculum*, Berkeley, CA. McCutchan.

19 In SCHWAB, J.J. (1969), *College Curricula and Student Protest*, Chicago, University of Chicago Press.

20 There is space here only to list a few relevant authors: APPLE, M. (1979), *Ideology and Curriculum*, London, Routledge and Kegan Paul; BOWLES, S., and GINTIS, H. (1976), *Schooling in Capitalist America*, London, Routledge and Kegan Paul; GINTIS, H. (1972), 'Towards a political economy of education', *Harvard Educational Review*, vol. 42, pp. 70–96; MUSGROVE, F. (1979), 'Curriculum, culture and ideology', *Journal of Curriculum Studies*, reprinted in TAYLOR, P.H. (Ed.) (1979), *New Directions in Curriculum Studies*, Lewes, Falmer Press; SHARP, R., and GREEN, A. (1976), *Education and Social Control: A Study in Progressive Primary Education*, London, Routledge and Kegan Paul.

21 JENCKS, C. et al. (1975), *Inequality: A Reassessment of the Effect of Family and Schooling in America*, Harmondsworth, Penguin.

22 For example, Bennett's influential (and hotly disputed) study of formal and informal teaching: BENNETT, N. (1976), *Teaching Styles and Pupil Progress*, London, Open Books.

23 HARGREAVES, D. (1967), *Social Relations in a Secondary School*, London, Routledge and Kegan Paul.

24 LACEY, C. (1970), *Hightown Grammar*, Manchester, Manchester University Press.

25 WESTBURY, I. (1979), 'Research into classroom processes: A review of ten years' work', *Journal of Curriculum Studies*, reprinted in TAYLOR, P.H. (Ed.) (1979), *New Directions in Curriculum Studies*, Lewes, Falmer Press.

26 For a few examples, see BERNSTEIN, B. (1975), 'Class and pedagogies:

Visible and invisible', *Educational Studies*, vol. 1, no. 1, pp. 23–41; KEDDIE, N. 'Classroom knowledge' in YOUNG M.F.D. (Ed.) (1971), *Knowledge and Control*, London, Collier Macmillan; LUNDGREN, U.P. (1977), 'Model analysis of pedagogical processes', *Studies in Curriculum Theory and Cultural Reproduction*, vol. 2, Lund, CWK Gleerup.

27 LUNDGREN, U.P. (1972), *Frame Factors and the Teaching Process*, Stockholm, Almqvist and Wiksell.

28 The distinction between 'exact and inexact' sciences and its implications for social science are set out in the final section of Mill's, *A System of Logic* (see volumes 7 and 8 of MILL, J.S. (1963 onwards) *Collected Words*, Toronto, University of Toronto Press, originally written in 1843). David Hamilton has written a most perceptive essay on Mill's impact on educational research entitled 'Educational research and the shadow of John Stuart Mill', in SMITH, J.V. and HAMILTON, D. (Eds) (1980), *The Meritocratic Intellect: Studies in the History of Educational Research*, Aberdeen, Aberdeen University Press.

29 The work of Windelband, Dilthey, Rickert and Simmel is relevant here. These authors attempted to test the degree of distinctiveness of social life from physical events, and to devise distinctive forms of explanation or understanding appropriate for the study of social life. The history of the debate has been presented in OUTHWAITE, W. (1975), *Understanding Social Life: The Method Called Verstehen*, London, George Allen and Unwin.

30 The methodology of the physical sciences/causal/explanatory approach was classically expounded in a number of contributions to the influential first *Handbook of Research on Teaching*, GAGE, N.L. (1963), Chicago, Rand McNally, especially the chapters by BRODBECK, M.'Logic and scientific method in research on teaching', GAGE, N.L. 'Paradigms for research on teaching', TATSUOKA, M. and TIEDEMANN, D., 'Statistics as an aspect of scientific method in research on teaching', and CAMPBELL, D.T. and STANLEY, J.C. 'Experimental and quasi-experimental designs for research on teaching'. The non-physical sciences/interpretive/understanding approach is well presented in the various chapters of TAYLOR, P.H. (Ed.) (1979), *New Directions in Curriculum Studies*, Lewes, Falmer Press.

31 For example, by von WRIGHT, G.H. (1971), in his book *Explanation and Understanding*, London, Routledge and Kegan Paul.

32 See, for example, HABERMAS, J. (1972), *Knowledge and Human Interests*, tr. SHAPIRO, J.J., London, Heinemann.

33 See, for example, the work of APPLE, M. (1979) (notes 20) and LUNDGREN, U.P. (1972) (notes 17 and 27) quoted earlier.

34 Quantum physicists, too, have recognized this phenomenon (see, for example, David Bohm's analysis of the famous Heinsenberg experiments in his paper 'Science as perception-communication' in SUPPE, F. (Ed.) (1974), *The Structure of Scientific Theories*, Urbana, Ill, University of Illinois Press).

35 See, for example, STAKE, R.E. (Ed.) (1975), *Evaluating the Arts in Education: A Responsive Approach*, Colombus, Ohio, Charles E. Merrill; and PARLETT, M., and HAMILTON, D. (1976), 'Evaluation as illumination: A new approach to the study of innovatory programs' in TAWNEY, D.A. (Ed.)

Curriculum Evaluation Today: Trends and Implications, London, Macmillan Education.

36 See BECKER, H.S. (1958), 'Problems of inference and proof in participant observation', *American Sociological Review*, vol. 23.

37 LEWIN, K. (1946), 'Action research and minority problems', *Journal of Social Issues*, vol. 2, pp. 34–46.

Chapter 2

The Natural Scientific View of Educational Theory and Practice

1 Introduction

Most contemporary textbooks assume that questions about the aims and methods of educational research can be answered by reference to the aims and methods of the established sciences. Lovell and Lawson, for example, in their book on understanding educational research maintain that 'the aims of research in education are the same as those of research in science generally'[1], while Travers' well-known text is based on the assertion that educational research is 'an activity directed towards the development of an organized body of scientific knowledge'.[2] 'When the scientific method is applied to educational problems,' says Ary, 'educational research is the result.'[3]

In similar fashion, most philosophical accounts of the nature of 'educational theory' proceed by adumbrating the logical merits of scientific theories and assessing the extent to which educational theories can conform to them. For example, in his influential discussion of the subject, D.J. O'Connor argues that the scientific notion of 'theory' provides the logical standards 'by which we can assess ... any claimant to the title "theory"' and 'which enables us to judge the value of the various theories that are put forward by writers on education'.[4] Numerous other examples could be cited but this is hardly necessary. Few would dispute that there is now a widespread belief that science provides the methods of enquiry that educational research should seek to emulate and that scientific theories provide the logical criteria to which educational theories should aspire to conform.

The attractions of placing educational theory and research on scientific foundations are obvious enough. Over the last few centuries science has provided a corpus of knowledge about the natural world which has enabled the environment to be controlled with ever-greater sophistication and has allowed for a range of practical problems that were once considered insurmountable to be successfully resolved. If the methods of science are enlisted by educational research, then the seemingly intransigent problems of education can be overcome and practical progress achieved. Just as science allows us to control the natural world, so it will allow us to control education and make it more congruent with the needs of society and its members.

The aims of this chapter are to trace the historical emergence of this view of educational research, to describe some of its principal features and to critically assess its claims. The emergence of this view is described, first, by retrieving the main arguments used to substantiate the claim that science, rather than philosophy, should be the legitimate source of educational theory and, secondly, by setting these arguments within their general philosophical context. The chapter concludes with a critical discussion of these arguments which indicates the weakness of the natural-scientific view of educational theory and how it relates to practice.

2 The Foundations of Educational Theory: From Philosophy to Science

Around the turn of the century, when education began to emerge as an academic discipline, it was commonly assumed that educational theory was essentially philosophical in character. What people meant by this varied, but common to them all was the view that the task of educational theory was to encourage teachers to develop a comprehensive understanding of their role as educators, by engaging in a process of philosophical reflection. Teachers required this kind of educational theory because, as educators, they needed a substantive 'philosophy' which would justify and support the educational aims and ideals they pursued. L.A. Reid put the case like this:

> If we are to educate sensibly ... we must above all things do it
> with a sense of direction and proportion, and to have this is to
> have a philosophy. Philosophy is love of wisdom; the philo-
> sopher is the lover of wisdom and it is wisdom that we need.[5]

From the outset, then, the concern of educational theory was with 'wisdom' and, hence, with the need for teachers to abandon their unreflectively held attitudes towards established educational creeds. In consequence, the relationship of theory to practice was not such that theory was to provide knowledge which could be converted into rules of action for teachers to apply. Rather, the value of theory stemmed from the way in which philosophical self-reflection helped to transform the manner in which teachers' existing values and beliefs were held. The practical purpose of this kind of educational theory was to transform unconsidered and unexamined modes of thought and practice into thoughtful and reflective ones. Educational theory did not so much 'imply practice' as transform the outlook of the practitioner.

Now although this justification for a philosophical approach was frequently enunciated in the early textbooks on educational theory, what actually occurred was somewhat different. Sir John Adams, writing in 1928, described the situation in this way:

> When education as such began to be recognized . . . as a separate study and afterwards as a subject in university curricula, it was only natural that lecturers in education should look out through world literature for great names wherewith to adorn their list of prescribed readings. Quite naturally, Socrates, Plato and Aristotle were seized on at the very start and a good deal of ingenuity was shown in bringing out educational principles from their work. . . . Even at the present day the best way for a young lecturer on education to establish his claims as an educationalist is to select some well known writer and publish a book under the title 'so and so as educator'.[6]

As these comments make clear, most of the early books on educational theory, as well as the courses for which they were produced, conformed to a recognizable pattern in which the general ideas of some major philosopher would be described and the 'educational implications' of those views abstracted. Originally, the most popular philosophers were Plato and Rousseau, but they were soon joined by other 'great names' and a large ancillary literature offering potted accounts of the educational implications of their central philosophical doctrines.[7]

From the outset, then, there were serious discrepancies between the rationale for a philosophical approach to educational theory and the particular way in which it was put into practice. In practice, educational theory was never concerned with developing reflective and philosophical thinking in teachers, but only with presenting the summarized results of the philosophical thinking of others. Educational theorizing emerged, not as a distinctive way of thinking in which teachers actively engaged, but as the passive digestion of chronologically arranged factual accounts of philosophical doctrines. The original promise of an approach to educational theory that took a philosophical, and hence questioning, stance towards fundamental educational ideas, never actually got off the ground.

Needless to say, the most common complaints levelled by teachers against this kind of theory pointed to the wide gulf between the abstract nature of the 'educational implications' that teachers were being offered and the concrete educational realities to which they were supposed to be applied. Consequently, educational theory was invariably perceived as a self-contained academic pursuit different from, and unrelated to, the educational practices it was supposed to illuminate and inform. It is not surprising, therefore, that this whole approach to educational theory was eventually discarded. What is surprising, is that it was not discarded because of its practical failure to generate more reflective and self-critical attitudes in teachers. Rather, it was rejected on the theoretical grounds that it operated with a confused and outdated understanding of the nature and scope of philosophy. For, according to the emerging view, philosophy was not, as educational theory assumed, a method for arriving at ideals from which practical educational principles could be derived. It was simply a method for analyzing language and concepts. To think that philosophy could provide valid knowledge about educational aims and values was misguided.

Some of the methodological arguments responsible for this reduction in the scope of philosophy were adumbrated in A.J. Ayer's famous book called *Language, Truth and Logic.*[8] According to Ayer, the question of whether sentences or propositions are meaningful and intelligible, or meaningless and nonsensical is decided by whether or not rational procedures exist for confirming or denying their truth. Since however, the only rational procedures for testing the validity of empirical propositions are those of the natural sciences, it follows that empirical propositions that cannot be tested by an appeal to experimental evidence are meaningless or, at best, linguistically confused.

The implications of this modern view of philosophy were far reaching. No longer conceived as an activity of reflection concerned with substantive questions, philosophy became limited to tackling non-substantive analytic questions about the meaning of concepts.[9] Furthermore, since value statements were a prime example of the sort of substantive claims that philosophy could no longer verify, philosophy could not be prescriptive. Stripped of its traditional concern with substantive moral problems, it emerged as a value-neutral analytical activity concerned with clarifying the meaning of concepts. As one distinguished educational philosopher, P.H. Hirst, puts it:

> Philosophy . . . is above all concerned with the clarification of the concepts and propositions through which our experiences and activities are made intelligible. It is interested in answering questions about the meaning of terms and expressions. . . . As I regard it, philosophy . . . is not the pursuit of moral knowledge. . . . It is rather . . . primarily an analytical pursuit. . . . Philosophy as I see it is a second-order area of knowledge. Philosophical questions are not about some particular facts or moral judgments but what we mean by facts, what we mean by moral judgments. [10]

Given this view of philosophy, the implications for the conventional appoach to educational theory were more or less obvious. Since this approach had proceeded on the assumptions that philosophy offered a method for answering substantive moral questions about the nature and purpose of education, and since it was precisely *this* assumption that had been repudiated, it followed that the role of philosophy in educational theory should be severely restricted. Furthermore, since there were no adequate criteria in terms of which answers to questions about the nature and purpose of education could be answered, it followed that they were pseudo-questions and that educational theory should surrender all interest in them. Indeed, the fact that the only educational questions that could be rationally answered were those that were amenable to empirical methods of testing, suggested that scientific knowledge should replace philosophical beliefs as the proper source of educational theory. Knowledge and understanding should be based on scientific experimentation rather than philosophical reflection. The concern of educational theory with reflective teaching and enlightened practice should be replaced by a concern for the scientific ideals of explanation, prediction and control.

3 Education as an Applied Science

The idea that educational theory should be established on a scientific basis was hardly new. During the nineteenth and early twentieth centuries a number of educationists had argued that education would be improved if the thought and beliefs of teachers became subject to the critical attitudes characteristic of scientific enquiry. The educational psychologist E.L. Thorndike, for example, had argued that:

> The profession of teaching will improve in proportion as its members direct their daily work by the scientific method.[11]

In a similar vein, John Dewey had argued for a science of education that would . . .

> enter into the heart, head and hands of educators and which, by entering in, render the performance of the educational function more enlightened.[12]

What is interesting about these early versions of the scientific view of educational theory is that they retain some of the important assumptions of the philosophical approach. For example, in both cases, the value of theory lies in its capacity to 'enlighten' the teachers' thinking. In both cases, theory relates to practice by providing for the critical examination of practical educational experiences. The only major point of disagreement concerned the relative claims of philosophy and science to offer a mode of thought conducive to this task. In this sense, root assumptions about the purpose of educational theory and its relationship to practice remained more or less undisturbed.

It was just these root assumptions, however, which were challenged by the 'scientific approach' that actually emerged to govern the conduct and organization of educational theory and research. For with this approach, educational theory sought to improve practice not by improving the thinking of practitioners, but by providing a body of scientific knowledge in terms of which existing educational practices could be assessed and new, more effective practices devised. Educational theory, on this view, was something to be applied to practice. In short, educational theory was to become an 'applied science'.

Although, at one time, this concept of 'application' was taken to mean that educational research should apply the methods and techniques of the natural sciences to educational events, this interpretation was quickly replaced by the view that what was to be applied were the concepts, theories and methodologies of the social sciences. However, views about the particular ways in which these applications should be made varied. Some, for example, saw educational research as being an applied science in the same sense as engineering; others saw medicine as a more appropriate model.

To those advocating the engineering view, the task of educational research was to develop an educational technology in which appropriate psychological knowledge is applied to the practical tasks of teaching and classroom organization. The most ardent and influential advocate of this approach was B.F. Skinner who, along with other behaviourist psychologists, maintained that

> ... a special branch of psychology, the so-called experimental analysis of behaviour, has produced a technology of teaching from which one can ... deduce programs and schemes and methods of instruction.[13]

The basis of this 'technology of teaching' was a recognition of how behaviourist principles of operant conditioning provided a scientific knowledge of learning that was rich in educational implications. Thus, in Skinner's opinion:

> ... the advances which have recently been made in our control of the learning process suggest a thorough revision of classroom practices and, fortunately, they tell us how the revision can be brought about.[14]

What, specifically, this revision entailed was that teachers should adopt the role of a learning technician applying the principles of operant conditioning so as to ensure effective learning. Just as the engineer may apply the theories and principles of aerodynamics to the practical task of designing and building an aeroplane, so

> the application of operant conditioning to education is simple and direct. Teaching is the arrangement of contingencies of reinforcement under which students learn ... teachers arrange special contingencies which expedite learning, hastening the appearance of behaviour which would otherwise be acquired slowly....[15]

The view of educational theory and research as the application of the principles and theories of behaviourist psychology has been highly influential. As well as leading directly to the development of a technology of teaching, behaviourist principles have also been applied to educational problems concerned with discipline, classroom control, motivation and assessment. They have also been employed to provide a scientific basis for the construction of models for curriculum planning and design, for curriculum evaluation and for educational administration.

To those who pursued the image of education as an applied science in the same sense as medicine, the emphasis was not on applying psychological theories to educational situations, but on identifying the body of scientific laws governing these situations and defining the parameters within which teachers can operate. Just as the medical practitioner must take account of the laws of biology, chemistry and physiology, so, it was argued, must the educational practitioner take account of the appropriate framework of psychological and sociological laws operative in educational situations. Like the doctor who diagnoses and treats some illness by using his knowledge of the scientific laws governing the functioning of the human body, the educational theorist should also be able to recognize, diagnose and treat educational problems by using knowledge of the scientific laws governing human and social development.

The task of educational theory and research that relies on the medical analogy, then, is twofold. The first is to discover the relevant scientific laws operative in educational situations so that knowledge of the limits of what it is possible to achieve will be available. It is only on the basis of this kind of knowledge that realistic choices about which educational purposes and goals to pursue can be made. The second task follows from the fact that the extent to which any scientific laws effectively operate in any educational situation will depend on the extent to which certain conditions are satisfied. Just as the laws governing physical growth can operate more successfully when an organism is given certain kinds of food and a certain kind of natural environment, so will the laws governing intellectual growth similarly be encouraged or impeded. So, by manipulating the conditions and circumstances in which laws operate, desired effects can be either encouraged or minimized and, to this extent, controlled. The purpose of educational research, therefore, is to identify the sort of practical arrangements which would ensure that scientific laws conducive to desirable educational goals are able to operate effectively, and that the impact of any laws impeding their achievement would be minimal.

An approach to educational theory and research that incorporates much of this view is the functionalist approach to educational sociology.[16] Basic to this perspective is the conviction that sociology explains human actions by showing how the regular patterns displayed in human action are caused by social laws operating to ensure the order and cohesion necessary for the preservation of society. Society is, therefore, regarded as an independent entity maintained through impersonal law-like processes that operate without the intervention of human purpose. Particular institutions, such as education, are presumed to be 'functional', in the sense that they are taken to exist in order to serve some of the functions that must be fulfilled for society to survive. Individuals operating within educational institutions, such as teachers and students, are, therefore, perceived as incumbents to socially defined 'positions' whose actions are regulated by the 'norms of behaviour' imposed by institutions in order to ensure that they accomplish their allocated social tasks. In effect then, the action of individuals is always regarded as something governed by invariant functional laws that operate beyond the individual actors' personal control.

Given this view of sociology, a primary task for the sociology of education is to identify those laws to which educational institutions must respond by identifying the particular social functions that they are required to undertake. The particular 'laws' affecting educational institutions are, of course, those that operate to ensure the transmission of values across generations and those that ensure that individuals are allocated to the social, economic and occupational positions that society makes available. The principal functional requirements of education are, therefore, first, to socialize the young into prevailing norms and attitudes so as to preserve social stability, and secondly, to stratify individuals in accordance with the complex network of roles that sustain the existing social order.

In practice, the sociology of education examined these twin functions of socialization and stratification by focusing on the relationship between social class and educational achievement. This in turn led to detailed investigations into how the various selective mechanisms employed in education, such as IQ tests and public examinations, operate to match social class with educational opportunity. When 'applied' to education, therefore, the results of these investigations were used to suggest how the existing procedures for socializing and stratifying pupils could be changed so as to ensure that these functions were fulfilled more effectively. In this sense, the functionalist sociology of education provides knowledge of how the social mechanisms already operating in educational institutions could be modified so that the equilibrium of society could be maintained.

Although functionalist sociology and behaviourist psychology employ quite different methods and techniques, they clearly share some common features. Both, for example, adhere to the view that educational theories must conform to scientific standards and criteria. Both assume that the purpose of educational research is, as in the natural sciences, to discover knowledge of law-like regularities which can be applied to educational practice in order to improve its efficiency.

Finally, both see educational theory as being, in comparison with physics and chemistry, an immature science standing in need of development and sophistication.

Now it needs to be noted that, in adopting these beliefs, educational theorists and researchers were simply following a path that had already been travelled by political theory, psychology, sociology, economics and anthropology. These, and other social scientific disciplines, had all passed through a period in which the role of philosophy had declined and a new optimism had emerged about what could be achieved once firm scientific foundations had been provided for the investigation of human and social phenomena. Moreover, this rejection of philosophy and subsequent allegiance to science did not occur just because of philosophical arguments favourable to this stance. On the contrary, the growth of a diverse range of methodologies consistent with the requirements of science, and the appearance of philosophical theories to justify them, were both symptoms of a deep-seated and all-pervading intellectual mood that had dominated western thought since the first half of the nineteenth century. In this sense, the popularity of philosophical theories supporting the extension of scientific methods to the study of social phenomena was itself due to the power of the dominant intellectual climate within which they emerged. Rudolph Carnap, one of the principal architects of this supportive philosophy, described, in the preface to his famous *Aufbau*, how his philosophical theories and the prevalent intellectual outlook were mutually reinforcing:

> We feel that there is an inner kinship between the attitude on which our philosophical work is founded and the intellectual attitude which presently manifests itself in entirely different walks of life; we feel this orientation ... in movements which strive for meaningful forms of personal and collective life, of education and of external organization in general. We feel all around us the same basic orientation, the same style of thinking and doing ... our work is carried by the faith that this attitude will win the future.[17]

The 'philosophical work' to which Carnap refers was a series of epistemological doctrines produced by a group of thinkers who became known as the Vienna Circle. The title usually attached to their work, Logical Positivism, reflected its close affinity to the basic 'attitude' which Carnap and others believed would 'win the future'. This attitude, this 'style of thinking', is now known simply as Positivism.

The purpose of next section is to clarify and examine positivism as a 'style of thinking' about educational theory and research.

4   The Positivist Approach to the Problem of Theory and Practice

'Positivism' is not a systematically elaborated doctrine. Rather, as Carnap suggested, it is the name usually associated with the general philosophical outlook which emerged as the most powerful intellectual force in western thought in the second half of the nineteenth century. Its ancestry can be traced back at least as far as Francis Bacon and the British Empiricists of the eighteenth and nineteenth centuries. But it was the French writer, Auguste Comte, who introduced the term 'positivist philosophy' and whose own work clearly exemplifies the positivist attitude. Comte's choice of the word 'positive' was intended to convey an opposition to any metaphysical or theological claims that some kind of non-sensorily apprehended experience could form the basis of valid knowledge. It was this desire to liberate thought from dogmatic certainties, coupled with an optimistic belief in the power of 'positive' knowledge to solve major practical problems, that gave positivism its original appeal. However, as the promise of intellectual freedom and practical improvement has remained unfulfilled, so the appeal of positivism has faded. Ironically, the attractions of positivism have now declined to such an extent that the word has become a derogatory epithet stripped of its original association with the ideas of progress and liberation. It comes as no surprise, therefore, to find that one contemporary writer has to recognize that:

> The term (positivism) has become one of opprobrium, and has been used so broadly and vaguely as a weapon of critical attack ... that it has lost any claim to an accepted and standard meaning.[18]

Although there are wide variations in the way the term is used, 'positivism' is usually taken to refer to a style of thought that is informed by certain assumptions about the nature of knowledge. The most important of these assumptions is what Kolakowski calls 'the rule of phenomenalism'[19]; the claim *that valid knowledge can only be established by reference to that which is manifested in experience.* It is, then, a claim to the effect that the label 'knowledge' can only be ascribed to that which is founded in 'reality' as apprehended by the senses. One of the major implications to follow from the rule of phenomenalism is the belief that value judgments, since they cannot be founded on empirical knowledge, cannot be given the status of valid knowledge.

The ways in which positivist principles have been expressed and the inferences that have been derived from them have been many and varied. They were, as the previous reference to the work of Ayer suggests, at the heart of positivists' attempts to produce a more restricted conception of the nature and scope of philosophy. Positivist thinking has also been influential in the study of history, theology and ethics. When applied to the social sciences, however, positivism is usually taken to imply two closely related contentions. The first is the belief that the *aims, concepts and methods* of the natural sciences are also applicable in social scientific enquiries. The second is the belief that the model of *explanation* employed in the natural sciences provides the logical standards by which the explanations of the social sciences can be assessed. Most positivist accounts of educational theory and research, therefore, advocate research strategies that are based on the logic and methodology of the natural sciences. Indeed, in one of the most influential of these accounts, the author concludes that:

> The construction of educational theories, in so far as it is a rational activity, is subject to the same standards as the paradigm instances of theorizing that we meet in science. (And, in so far as it is not a rational activity, it is a pretentious and contemptible waste of time.)[20]

But why must educational theory be subject to these same standards? And why must educational research be based on the methodology of the natural sciences? The argument offered for adopting scientific methods is relatively straightforward. Traditional philosophical methods of educational theorizing confused empirical assertions with a range of non-empirical and subjective elements, such as metaphysical speculations, ideological views and value judgments. In consequence, they provided no public or objective standards in terms of which their theories could be rationally assessed. In order to put educational theory on a more rational basis, therefore, it must be purged of its metaphysical, ideological and normative elements and adopt a more objective and neutral stance. This requires discarding traditional philosophical methods in favour of the methods of science. Science, and only science, offers a neutral stance because it alone employs methods which guarantee knowledge which is not infected by subjective preferences and personal bias. Since these methods are uniformly applicable to both natural and human phenomena, their application to education would lead to a body of educational theory which would reveal what is actually happening in educational situations, rather than stipulate what somebody thinks ought to be happening.

The account of the methods that create these theories and which, within most accounts of educational research, now enjoys a position of near orthodoxy, is the *hypothetico-deductive* account suggested by the modern empiricist philosophy of science and defended by philosophers as different as J.S. Mill, Nagel and Hempel.[21] The name given to this view summarizes its main contentions, namely, that scientific enquiries proceed by proposing *hypotheses*, preferably in the form of universal laws which can be assessed by comparing their *deductive* consequences with the results of observations and experiments. Usually the hypothetico-deductive method is represented as consisting of three steps which can be represented schematically as follows:

1 Proposal of hypothesis	All As are B	for example, all metal expands when heated.
2 Deduction from hypothesis	If all As are B then C	for example, if all metals expand when heated then iron will expand when heated.
3 Assessing deduction by observation on experiment.	C or not C	for example, experiment to find whether iron does or does not expand when heated.

Certain features of this method are worth noting. First, the hypothesis must be such that it will have observable consequences. Secondly, for the hypothesis to be true, these consequences must actually occur. Thirdly, the fact that a prediction deduced from a hypothesis does occur, does not establish that the hypothesis is true; it merely strengthens its plausibility. If the deductive implications of the hypothesis do not occur, however, (if, that is, iron did *not* expand when heated) then the hypothesis is conclusively refuted.

The insistence, conveyed by the hypothetico-deductive method, that knowledge claims must stand or fall by the results of observation and experiment, serves as a demarcation criterion for distinguishing scientific knowledge from metaphysical, prescriptive and ideological claims. For whereas these claims may reflect the personal motives and prejudices of those who make them, such matters have nothing to do with assessing the truth of hypotheses in a scientific way. Science is not concerned with how hypotheses originate or with the motives of those who propose them, it is only concerned with how they are validated. All that this requires is that empirical predictions can be deduced from a proposed hypothesis and then set against the neutral facts. Metaphysical, ideological and normative assertions have no deductive implications, are not objectively testable and can, therefore, reflect subjective and personal opinions. In contrast, science represents an impersonal method for assessing claims to knowledge by bringing them into confrontation with what actually happens. It is above all the use of this method that distinguishes science from non-science, pseudo-science and ideology.

The second major contention of the positivist view is that educational theories must conform to the logical requirements of scientific explanations. Although Nagel[22] identifies four major patterns of scientific explanation, the most comprehensive type, and the one which positivist educational theorists regard as the ideal to emulate, is what Nagel calls the Deductive Nomological model. These are those explanations which attempt to explain why some event occurs, why some situation persists, or why some object has certain features, by showing how — given some general laws and some other state of affairs — the event, situation or object to be explained could not have been otherwise. In their well-known paper on 'The logic of explanation', Hempel and Oppenheim[23] clarify the logical features of this kind of explanation and identify the formal conditions that have to be satisfied for it to be acceptable. The most important of these features and conditions can be brought out by resorting to the example used to demonstrate the hypothetico-deductive method of science. This will also reveal how the scientific method and scientific explanations are closely related.

Explanans { General Law (L)   All metals expand when heated
           { Initial conditions (C)   This metal is heated
Explanandum event (E)   This metal expands

A scientific explanation may be divided into two parts — an *explanandum*, which refers to the event to be explained, and an *explanans*, which contains the information explaining its occurrence. A deductive nomological explanation is so called because its explanans must contain at least one General Law (L) which, together with some particular information of 'Initial conditions' (C) deductively entail the explanandum event. The importance of the general law, then, stems from the fact that the deduction of the explanandum event is only possible because of the presence of a scientifically verified, or at least well-confirmed, hypothesis which states that for every case in which particular initial conditions of type C occurs an event of type E will also occur. In short, to explain something is to show that it can be subsumed under a scientific law. For this reason the deductive nomological model is frequently called the 'covering law' model.

Obviously, for a deductive-nomological explanation to be acceptable, it must contain at least one general law and its explanandum has to follow deductively from its explanans. Among the further conditions stipulated by Hempel and Oppenheim is the requirement that the explanans must have *empirical content*; that is, it must be capable of testing by experiment and observation. Another formal condition is that the premises constituting the explanans must be *true*. Furthermore, the scientific laws in a valid explanation must not only be true, but must also express *a uniform and invariant connection between different empirical phenomena*. Scientific laws, therefore, express an unrestricted universality in that they claim to be true for any place at any time. They express, in short, some sort of 'nomic necessity'.

In most, but not all, deductive explanations, the kind of necessity that is asserted is *causal*. In such cases, the law employed in the explanation asserts a general and unexceptional connection between specific types of events, so that the circumstances described in the initial conditions may be said to have 'caused' the explanandum. Hence, to assert a 'cause' is to assert that there is a causal law which shows that the occurrence of one event is sufficient for the occurrence of some other. The previous example can be described as a causal explanation in the following way:

Explanans	{	Causal Law (L)	Heat causes metal to expand
	{	Initial conditions (C)	This metal is heated
Explanandum event (E)			This metal expands

Thus, the Explanandum event E is explained by showing how the regularities expressed by Causal law L entail that whenever conditions of type C occur an event of type E will follow. Finally, adequate causal explanations must fulfil certain conditions in addition to those required for an adequate deductive nomological explanation. For example, the relationship between cause and effect asserted in the causal law must be *invariable and uniform*. The cause, in other words, must be *both necessary and sufficient* for the occurrence of the effect. Another condition is that *the cause must temporally precede the effect*.

Acceptance of the Hempel-Oppenheim characterization of deductive nomological explanations, together with a recognition of the fact that these are frequently causal explanations, leads to some important conclusions about the relationship between explanations and predictions. For, reverting to the example, if the Causal law L and state of affairs described in the initial condition C are true, and the Explanandum event E is *not* known to have occurred, then its occurrence *could* have been predicted by deduction from the explanans. If the Explanandum event E has already occurred, however, it is explained by providing the General law L and the Initial conditions C from which it can adduced.

In this sense, the knowledge provided in any adequate explanation of an event that *has* occurred, could, in principle, also have served to predict that event before it actually happened. For this reason, argue Hempel and Oppenheim, *the explanation and prediction of an event are symmetrical.* To claim to have adequately explained some event is to claim to have been able to predict it. They write:

> ... the same formal analysis applies to scientific prediction as well as to explanation. The difference between them is of pragmatic character ... an explanation is not fully adequate unless its explanans, if taken account of in time could have served as a basis for predicting the phenomena under consideration.[24]

Although the discussion of scientific method and explanation advanced in the positivist view of educational theory has been rather brief, what has been said about the structural identity of explanation and prediction should be enough to indicate their relevance to the question of educational theory and practice. Because a scientific explanation of an educational process provides the knowledge required to predict its occurrence, it also provides the means for its practical *control.* Just as scientific predictions can be used to control events in the natural world, so educational theory can use causal laws to predict, and hence control, the outcomes of different courses of practical action. Travers' textbook on educational research reveals this stance very clearly. Educational research, he says

> in an activity directed towards the development of an organized body of scientific knowledge ... which reveals laws of behaviour that can be used to make predictions and control events within educational situations.[25]

So, it is the predictive value of scientific theories that give them their practical value for, by laying the foundations for the manipulation of educational situations, they provide the opportunity for bringing about desirable educational goals. Thus, educational theory guides practice by making predictions about what would happen if some aspects of an educational situation were modified. On the basis of these predictions it becomes possible, by manipulating a particular set of variables, to control events so that desirable goals are achieved and undesirable consequences eliminated. In effect, by pursuing the standard scientific ideals of explanation and prediction, educational theory — when conceived as an applied science — provides the foundations on which rational educational decisions can be made.

Clearly, if educational decision-making was to be based on an application of scientific knowledge, the whole character of educational arguments and disagreements would change. For these would be no longer regarded as expressions of incompatible values, but as 'technical' problems which could be resolved objectively through the rational assessment of evidence. Just as the disagreements that arise in medicine and engineering are not treated as if they express conflicting ideological or subjective stances, so it would be recognized that in education the correct way of resolving issues and making decisions was to employ the rational procedures of science.

It may be useful at this point to translate this view into practical educational terms. It is usually assumed that disputes about teaching methods arise out of differences in teachers' 'educational values and ideologies'. It is further assumed that these disputes cannot be finally settled because they reflect different moral, social and political attitudes which, in the last resort, are the product of incompatible and irreconcilable value stances. If, however, education were to become an applied science, these disputes could be resolved in the same neutral way as are similar questions that occur in medicine and engineering. If scientific methods were brought to bear in this way, objective answers to questions about teaching methods could be established, evidence would replace opinion and the influence of arbitrary personal values would be eliminated. The belief that an applied science of education could answer questions that, at present, are regarded as contentious is clearly evident in O'Connor's claim that:

> The techniques of teaching and the theories that explain and justify them are matters that can be determined only by the methods of the positive sciences.... The questions of what techniques are most effective for teaching ... are questions of

fact to be determined by observation refined by experiment and aided by statistical devices for weighing the evidence obtained. There is no other way of settling such questions.... The theories of the educational psychologists about such matters as the nature of learning, motivation, the nature and distribution of intelligence, child development and so on are (or ought to be) the theoretical basis on which particular educational techniques ... are recommended or explained.[26]

It is, of course, recognized by O'Connor that not all educational questions can be made amenable to scientific solution. There are, he acknowledges, also questions about educational purposes and goals which involve 'non-scientific components ... value judgments ... religious concepts, political and social ideals which cannot be explained or justified by the application of scientific knowledge'.[27] It is, therefore, necessary to separate these questions of educational purposes and goals from questions about the best means to achieve them and to relate this division to a parallel distinction between values and facts. For once this distinction is made it becomes immediately apparent that since questions of educational goals involve values, they must be removed from the realm of scientific enquiry. However, because questions of means are questions about the best way to accomplish desired goals, they are empirical questions that can be rationally answered on the basis of scientific knowledge. Being questions about how to maximize the achievement of whatever values are chosen, 'means' questions can only be rationally decided if the outcomes of available courses of action are known. Science can provide this knowledge because the causal laws it produces can, when employed in scientific explanations, predict what these outcomes will be. Just as doctors and engineers decide on the basis of scientific knowledge what medicines or building materials are best suited to their purposes, so the educational theorist can provide knowledge of the most efficient means to the achievement of whatever educational ends are deemed desirable. To quote O'Connor again:

Education, like medicine and engineering, is a set of practical activities and we understand better how to carry them out if we understand the natural laws that apply to the material with which we have to work....[28]

Moreover, although these natural laws do not themselves reveal any particular educational goals, they still have important implications for how such goals are to be chosen. For by establishing the parameters within which any realizable educational goals can be chosen, they set limits to the range of goals that can be realistically pursued. If, for example, science can, as O'Connor suggests, provide 'objective knowledge of human inequalities'[29] then clearly educational aims based on some ideal of equality may have to be discarded or, at least, reinterpreted so as to take this scientific knowledge into account.

The impact of science on the choice of educational aims and values then, should not be minimized. Indeed, it is partly because of the spread of scientific knowledge that there is now a more realistic vision of the limited range of ends that it is feasible for education to pursue. Moreover, it is precisely because discussions about educational goals are now tempered by scientific knowledge of what it is possible to achieve that these matters are no longer as contentious as when they were decided on the basis of intuition and experience. For this reason, the sort of educational questions now dominating educational discussion are no longer about educational ends, but about the most appropriate means of achieving those educational ends accepted as appropriate in contemporary society. And it is just these questions that an applied science of education can tackle and resolve. To quote O'Connor once more:

> Educational policy ... is usually a matter of establishing the most efficient use to be made of scarce resources — time, building, intelligence, teaching skills and so on. The important point to remember in all such cases is that where something proposed as an educational advance or reform is recommended, as it usually is, on the ground that it is a means to some socially accepted end, the proposal is an empirical matter which stands or falls by the evidence that can be adduced in its favour.[30]

The major implications of adopting an 'applied science' view of educational theory are not hard to identify. For the educational researcher, the most important implication is the recognition that there are objective solutions to educational problems and that these can be established by using the methods of science. Furthermore, these methods can be employed in two different ways. First, they can be utilized for 'pure' research which provides well-confirmed theories that explain educational phenomena by showing how they can be derived from nomological statements. Secondly, however, there is also a need for 'applied research' in which these theories are employed as the basis for formulating educational policies designed to increase the efficiency of educational practice. As an applied scientist, the educational researcher operates as a 'social engineer' who recommends institutional and practical changes on the basis of established scientific theories.

In pursuing these different tasks, 'pure' educational researchers are, like natural scientists, pursuing objective knowledge through scientific enquiry. They therefore remain aloof from decisions about how their findings can or should affect educational practice. But the 'applied' educational researcher, even though the possibility of his or her activity depends on a specification of educational goals, also remains disinterested in educational values. The task of the applied researcher is to provide answers to scientific questions that arise within a given framework of educational ends. In doing this, the applied researcher may propose policies for improving the ways in which educational institutions try to accomplish their goals, or may scientifically evaluate the consequences of existing policies in terms of their avowed purposes. But in neither of these cases does the applied researcher decide which educational goals are desirable. Just as engineers do not determine whether a building should be erected but only how it should be built, so the role of the applied educational researcher is confined to determining the best way to accomplish the educational goals that have already been agreed. In this sense the 'social engineering' of the applied educational researcher remains, like 'pure' research, a value-free activity.

What are the implications of this scientific view of educational theory for the teacher? First, the fact that both pure and applied educational research demands considerable scientific expertise, implies that the only people competent to make decisions about educational policies and practices would be those who had acquired this expertise. Teachers, although they can be expected to adopt and implement educational decisions made on the basis of scientific knowledge, would not themselves participate in the decision-making process. Just as it would be inconceivable for doctors to allow their patients, or even nurses, to decide how medical problems should be cured, so is it unnecessary for educational theorists to collaborate with teachers in order to decide how educational problems should be resolved. In short, the role of the teacher is one of passive conformity to the practical recommendations of educational theorists and researchers. Teachers are not themselves regarded as professionally responsible for making educational decisions and judgments, but only for the efficiency with which they implement the decisions about how educational practice can be improved that are made by educational theorists on the basis of their scientific knowledge.

5   Criticisms of Positivism

Even the most cursory glance at the relevant theoretical literature immediately reveals how, in recent times, positivism has been subject to severe critical scrutiny and debate.[31] Although it would be impossible to consider the numerous objections to positivism, some are particularly pertinent to the natural scientific view of educational theory and, for this reason, worth mentioning. For convenience, these objections can be divided into two groups. First, there are those which have their origins in the very general field of the philosophy of science. Secondly, there are some specific objections to the positivist view of the relationship of theory to practice.

The Positivist View of Science

Some of the most influential challenges to positivism have emerged out of a set of arguments that derive from an historical analysis of the nature of progress in science. According to these arguments, the positivist notions of knowledge, objectivity and truth lay down ideals for the conduct of research that are incompatible with the history of science and, to this extent, are unrealistic and irrelevant. A close examination of how science has developed reveals that subjective and social factors play a crucial role in the production of knowledge. Indeed, the significance of these factors is such that 'knowledge' can be more accurately understood in psychological and sociological terms than in purely logical or epistemological terms. Moreover, once understood in this way, it becomes apparent that the positivist conception of objective knowledge is nothing more than a myth. The most influential version of this thesis is to be found in Thomas Kuhn's (1970) book, *The Structure of Scientific Revolutions*. Kuhn's basic argument can be summarized in the following way.

Within the positivist tradition it is assumed that scientific knowledge is in a continuous state of accumulation and growth. As more areas are explored, old areas examined in more detail, more accurate observations made and more sophisticated experiments conducted, so new concepts and theories are formulated, new law-like regularities are discovered and the stock of true, valid, knowledge grows. For Kuhn, this view is incoherent. A more realistic way of interpreting the development of scientific knowledge, he argues, is by seeing it as a succession of 'revolutions' in which dominant 'paradigms' are overthrown and replaced.

Typically, argues Kuhn, this process begins with attempts to resolve a particular range of problems or develop a body of theoretical knowledge about a specific aspect of the world. At this stage, interpretations of the problems under enquiry are disorganized and diverse. Initial research studies are not structured by any coherent methodology. This 'pre-scientific' period comes to an end when those engaged in this activity form a social community and adhere to a single 'paradigm'. A 'paradigm' embodies the particular conceptual framework through which the community of researchers operates and in terms of which a particular interpretation of 'reality' is generated. It also incorporates models of research, standards, rules of enquiry and a set of techniques and methods, all of which ensure that any theoretical knowledge that is produced will be consistent with the view of reality that the paradigm supports. The production of theories from *within* a paradigm is what Kuhn calls 'normal science' and it usually takes the form of 'puzzle solving' — the puzzles always being defined by and soluble in terms of the dominant paradigm. In attempting to discover solutions to puzzles, researchers will eventually run into difficulties. Puzzles which persistently resist solution, within the terms of the paradigm, become 'anomalies'. When sufficient anomalies emerge a state of 'crisis' develops. The research community begins to turn away from 'normal science' and to express discontent with the existing paradigm. Researchers begin to lose their 'faith' and debates over fundamental issues are initiated. After some 'recourse to philosophy', alternative paradigms emerge. The 'crisis' is finally resolved when the existing paradigm is overthrown and abandoned and a new paradigm attracting the allegiance and support of the research community takes its place. This 'paradigm shift' is not based on any systematic, logical or rational assessment of the rival alternatives. It is not based on 'proof', or any appeal to reason. Rather, it is a 'scientific revolution' brought about by the 'conversion' of the research community. Needless to say, when such a revolution takes place, it entails changes in the conduct of research that are so fundamental that the nature and scope of the whole enterprise are perceived in an entirely different way. Not only does 'normal science' and its 'puzzles' change; so also does the way in which the research community interprets 'reality' and defines such notions as 'knowledge', 'theory' and 'truth'.

The implications of Kuhn's arguments are many and complex but, for present purposes, four of them are worth mentioning. Firstly, since paradigms structure observations in particular ways, observations are always made in the light of the concepts and theories impregnated in the paradigm which they presuppose. In short, observations are dependent on the theory in terms of which they are made. Now although at first sight it may appear that arguments about the theory dependence of observations are purely 'theoretical', their practical effects are not unimportant. For example, if the positivists' separation of theory and observation is untenable, if observations are indeed impregnated with theory, then theoretical advances are not constrained by 'neutral' observations. Rather, the development of radical, creative and imaginative theories offers the possibility of making radical, creative and imaginative observations. This sort of theory development does not depend on rejecting observations of one event in favour of some observations of some alternative event. Instead, radical theoretical innovations may be seen as attempts to transform the conventional observations of the *same* event by challenging the adequacy of the theoretical categories in terms of which existing observations are made. Positivism, by accepting 'neutral observation' as the secure basis from which 'objective' knowledge can be derived, thereby commits itself to a confinement within whatever pre-existent theoretical framework these observations presuppose. And, as a result, the knowledge that is discovered by positivist research effectively reinforces the theoretical perspectives operating in any given situation. It serves, in other words, the conservative task of insulating the theoretical 'status quo' from criticism and rejection.

Secondly, if, as Kuhn suggests, a change from one paradigm to another is a matter of 'conversion', then, more than anything else, it reflects a commitment to new values and beliefs. In consequence, there is no impartial way of demonstrating the superiority of one paradigm over any other. Knowledge and experience, far from providing a rational basis for a commitment to a particular way of interpreting 'reality', are themselves a projection of just these sorts of commitments. It is precisely because there are no neutral criteria for deciding whether any paradigm offers a better way than any other for producing valid knowledge, that they are, to use Kuhn's term, 'incommensurable'. 'The choice between paradigms,' he says, 'is a choice between incompatible modes of community life. . . . There is no standard higher than the ascent of the relevant community'. And if there is any truth in this then knowledge is not, as positivism suggests, the objective, universal and value-neutral product of the 'disinterested' researcher. Rather, it is subjective, context bound, normative and, in an important sense, always political.

A third effect of Kuhn's arguments is that they draw attention to the fact that research is an activity performed within social communities and that the ways in which these communities are organized is of crucial significance in the production of knowledge. Two features of this social aspect of research are worth stressing. First, the 'paradigm' within which any research is pursued provides the ways of thinking and acting regarded as appropriate for the institutional setting in which the research is conducted. To talk of scientific researchers, therefore, is to talk of a group of individuals whose actions are governed largely by the expectations that a research community has of its members; expectations which are justified by reference to the attitudes, beliefs and values that the governing paradigm sustains. Secondly, although the theoretical frameworks incorporated in any paradigm may be acquired through a systematic introduction to its concepts, methodology and techniques of research, this does not alter the fact that paradigms are prescribed and settled ways of thinking that are transmitted across generations of researchers by a process of initiation. In this sense, a paradigm is an inherited mode of thinking that is acquired in a largely non-reflective way.

Finally, paradigms are informed by a whole complex of beliefs, values and assumptions. These are never made explicit in the theories produced by research, but they nevertheless structure the perceptions of researchers and shape their subsequent theorizing. They enter into decisions about such things as what constitutes a research problem, what kind of knowledge is considered appropriate to its solution, and how this knowledge is to be acquired. In this sense, theories are always 'infected' by the beliefs and values of the research community and are, therefore, always social products.

Although the effects of these challenges to the orthodox positivist philosophy of science are still to be fully worked out, their overall impact on the idea of an applied science of education are already clear. In the first place, they seriously undermine the minimal claim of the scientific view of education that there is, or can be, some description of facts that is neutral between competing theories. The facts to which the scientific educational theorist appeals are not some unmistakable and immediately recognized 'given', but are dependent on the theories within which they operate. 'Facts' are always facts as interpreted by prior assumptions and beliefs. Furthermore, if theories are underdetermined by facts (that is, they presuppose empirical content greater than the body of observations so far coordinated under the theory), then the activities of scientists cannot be understood by reference to the image of science that positivism suggests. In the alternative Kuhnian picture, science only has the appearance of being an impersonal, objective activity because most ideological and normative conflicts are suppressed by researchers in their allegiance to a dominant paradigm; an allegiance which is necessary to get the scientific enterprise going at all. But of course a paradigm is not itself impersonal or objective. Rather, it stipulates a particular 'view of the world' which incorporates ideological preferences and normative assumptions. As such, it yields that particular conception of reality which will be amenable to the empirical tests and causal theories used by scientists to explore and explain it.

Now if the assumptions and beliefs incorporated in a dominant paradigm are, as Kuhn suggests, imposed on the scientific community, then science itself begins to resemble something like an ideology and the original arguments supporting the scientific approach to educational theory begin to crumble. For it becomes immediately apparent that the main attraction of the positivistic approach — namely, its claim to rescue educational theory from value conflicts and ideological bias — is only achieved by indoctrinating educational researchers into the values and ideology that the dominant scientific paradigm prescribes. But now 'science' appears to have some close resemblance to the sort of value-laden philosophy of education that it claimed to replace. Science, no less than traditional philosophy, stipulates the kind of total conceptual framework considered appropriate for understanding and guiding a practical pursuit. In short, educational philosophy and a scientific paradigm are attempts to stipulate the kind of perspectives for determining what is allowed to count as an educational or a scientific practice at all.

The difference between the traditional philosophical approach to educational theory and the scientific approach, then, is not that science escapes the normative and ideological conflicts that infect philosophy. Rather, it is that while the philosophical approach was explicitly concerned with critically discussing the plausibility of different 'views of the world', the scientific approach ensures that such considerations remain covert, invisible and unquestioned. But in doing so, a scientific approach to education does not eliminate normative and philosophical issues. It simply avoids them by making an uncritical adherence to the philosophical preconceptions entrenched in its own 'view of the world', a precondition of membership to the scientific community.

The Positivist View of Theory and Practice

The positivist approach to the problem of theory and practice rests on the conviction that it is possible to produce scientific explanations of educational situations which can be employed to make objective decisions about possible courses of action. Of course, although it is recognized that decisions about the ends for which such action is to be taken involve values, and therefore cannot be decided scientifically, it is still the case that questions about the most effective means to whatever ends are chosen are empirical questions, amenable to scientific solution. Thus, although the scientific educational researcher may not be competent to choose educational goals, he is competent to recommend educational policies that are instrumental to the achievement of whatever educational goals are to be pursued.

Unfortunately, the idea that educational decisions can be neatly divided into instrumental questions concerned with means, and value questions concerned with ends is incoherent. Moreover, as far as education is concerned, any attempt to relate theory and practice to a simple division between facts and values always makes some appeal to the sort of value-laden considerations that it was designed to eliminate. Various arguments have been put forward to support this conclusion.[32] Some of these are designed to show how questions of 'educational means' are always value laden. Others argue that implicit in the positivist view of theory and practice, there is a commitment to the values that underlie existing educational arrangements and a latent antagonism towards any radical attempt to revise established educational goals.

One of the obvious reasons why decisions about educational 'means' are always value laden is that they always incorporate attitudes towards other people and, therefore, they cannot be assessed in terms of instrumental value alone. For example, the instrumental criterion of 'efficiency' will, when applied in an educational context, always presuppose a background of moral constraints. For this reason, what is allowed to count as an 'efficient' means must take account of some notion of what is permissible. For example, educational theories demonstrating that the most efficient way to teach something is by using some form of brainwashing would be rejected, not on the grounds of their inefficiency, but because of the unacceptable moral standards inherent in the criterion of efficiency being employed. That this may appear to be an 'extreme' example does not alter the general point. For example, in response to the instrumental question of deciding the most effective way of grouping children, the educational scientist might recommend a system of selection based on intelligence tests. But this may be rejected because it infringed egalitarian values. The scientist may then propose that pupils should not be grouped or segregated at all. But this could also be opposed on the moral grounds that it curtails the freedom of parents to decide their children's education. Hence, no matter how 'neutral' some educational decisions may seem, they always incorporate some moral notion of what it is permissible to do to other people and what is not. Any estimation of the worth of alternative 'educational means' is, therefore, always open to question on moral, as well as instrumental, grounds.

Apart from problems stemming from the fact that the moral values enter into all educational decisions, there are other objections to the positivist conception of theory and practice that arise from a consideration of the peculiar nature of educational aims. For a point constantly stressed by educational philosophers is that educational aims are not descriptions of some desirable end state that can serve as criteria for assessing some extrinsically related 'means'. Rather, they are attempts to specify the sort of values to which any distinctively educational means must (if they are to be *educational* means) conform. R.S. Peters' argument to this effect is worth quoting at length:

> Talk about 'the aims of education' depends to a large extent on a misunderstanding about the sort of concept that 'education' is ... Education is not a concept that marks out any particular process ... rather it suggests criteria to which processes ... must conform. One of these is that something of value should be passed on.... However, this cannot be construed as meaning that education itself should lead on to or produce something of value. This is like saying that reform must lead to a man being better.... The point is that making a man better is not an aim extrinsic to reform; it is a criterion which anything must satisfy which is to be called reform. In the same way a necessary feature of education is often extracted as an extrinsic end. People thus think that education must be for the sake of something extrinsic that is worthwhile, whereas being worthwhile is part of what is meant by calling it 'education'. The instrumental model of education provides a caricature of this necessary feature of desirability by conceiving of what is worthwhile as an end brought about by the process....[33]

Educational aims, then, are not the end product to which educational processes are the instrumental means. They are expressions of the values in terms of which some distinctive educational character is bestowed on, or withheld from, whatever 'means' are being employed. So, to talk of 'creative' thinking, 'critical awareness', or 'rational autonomy' as educational ends is not to describe some valued end state to which teaching and learning are the instrumental means. Rather, it is to talk of the sort of values, or what Peters calls 'principles of procedure', to which appeals are made in justifying the educative value of whatever 'means' are being employed. In this sense, educational 'ends' are constitutive of means as *educational* means. To say, for example, that 'critical thinking' is a desirable educational end is to express a 'procedural principle' governing the kind of 'educational means' that are permissible. It is, in other words, to imply that rote-learning memorization, passive instruction or any other teaching methods that impede critical thinking are inadequate as 'educational means'. This is not the same as saying they are ineffective. More accurately, it is to say that they are unacceptable because they do not accord with the values implicit in this end. Indeed, if any proposed 'means' do not conform to the evaluative criteria suggested by any avowed educational end, then questions about their effectiveness do not even arise. For when this happens the proposed 'means' will serve no distinctively educational purpose at all.

What this suggests is that the sort of relationship between 'means' and 'ends' which the positivist view of theory and practice assumes fails to recognize how, in education, aims, policies and methods are all intrinsically related. In particular, by regarding value questions as only concerned with ends, it ignores the peculiar relationship between educational aims and the means employed to achieve them, 'What is the educational aim?' and 'How can this aim be achieved most effectively?' are not separate questions parallel to a fact-value distinction. Because the end largely determines what is to count as an *educational* method, the range of empirical hypotheses that it is possible to generate about the most effective educational means is severely limited. To go beyond this limit is not simply to operate with an unsophisticated conception of education. It is also to ignore the way in which decisions about 'means' in education always reflect educational values. Any attempt to remove these values in order to make questions of means purely instrumental would, in the last analysis, result in them not being educational means at all.

Another area of criticism focuses on the positivist claim to offer ways of guiding educational practices that are not supportive of any particular value orientation towards the educational situations it studies. These criticisms stem from the fact that, insofar as it studies educational situations in the same way as natural scientists study natural phenomena, scientific research inevitably assumes that these situations operate according to a set of 'general laws' that regulate the behaviour of individuals. Furthermore, because these laws are assumed to be independent of the purposes of the individuals whose actions they determine, it follows that the only way to affect practice[34] is by discovering what these 'laws' are and manipulating educational situations accordingly. This implies that educational research can only function by presuming that those aspects of educational situations that are governed by these 'laws' are beyond control and, consequently, that any research recommendations the research supports will have to accept that certain basic features of education are unalterable. But by so treating these basic features as 'natural entities', this kind of research will always be biased towards prevailing educational arrangements and its theories will be structured in favour of the 'status quo'.

Of course the actual achievements of the positivist search for these laws are not very impressive and theories that could be used to predict and control educational situations are almost non-existent. In accounting for this state of affairs, some researchers have pointed to the practical difficulties caused by the immense complexity of the variables involved in educational situations; others have pointed to the fact that the social sciences are still in their infancy and make a plea for patience. In recent times, however, some educational theorists and researchers have argued that the failures of this sort of research are the inevitable outcome of its positivist epistemology and a confused belief in the applicability of the methods of the natural sciences to human and social phenomena. They argue, in particular, that for educational researchers to be able to understand education at all, they must refrain from mimicking the surface features of the natural sciences and recognize how the natural and social sciences operate with different purposes and employ different methods. What is distinctive of educational research is that it employs a methodology which enables it to describe how individuals interpret their actions and the situations in which they act. This alternative view of the social sciences as descriptive and interpretive rather than explanatory and predictive, provides the topic for discussion in the next chapter.

Further Reading

B.F. Skinner's *Technology of Teaching* remains one of the major attempts to establish educational theory as an applied natural science. Chapters 1–3 of D.J. O'Connor's, *An Introduction to the Philosophy of*

Education, offers a positivistic account of philosophy, while chapters 4 and 5 of the same book, together with his article, 'The nature and scope of educational theory', constitute the most influential philosophical rationale for a scientific view of educational theory.

Probably the best critical overview of positivism in its many forms is Kolakowski's, *Positivist Philosophy*. Good critical examinations of a positivist approach to the social sciences are to be found in chapters 1 and 2 of Brian Fay's, *Social Theory and Political Practice*; and part 2 of R.J. Bernstein's, *The Restructuring of Social and Political Theory*.

The most influential criticisms of the positivist view of science are Popper's *Conjectures and Refutations*; Feyerabend's *Against Method: Outlines of an Anarchist Theory of Knowledge*; and Kuhn's *The Structure of Scientific Revolutions*. For a good summary of the ideas of all these writers see Max Charlesworth's *Science, Non-Science and Pseudo-Science*.

Detailed philosophical arguments designed to show how means-end and fact-value distinctions are inappropriate in educational theory are to be found in R.S. Peters', 'Must an educator have an aim?' and Hugh Sockett's, 'Curriculum planning: taking a means to an end', both of which are published in R.S. Peters (Ed.) *The Philosophy of Education*.

Notes

1 Lovell, K., and Lawson, K.S. (1970), *Understanding Research in Education*, London, University of London Press, p. 24.
2 Travers, R.M.W. (1969), *An Introduction to Educational Research*, London, Macmillan, p. 16.
3 Ary, D. *et al.* (1972), *Introduction to Research in Education*, Holt, Rinehart and Winston, p. 21.
4 O'Connor, D.J. (1957), *An Introduction to the Philosophy of Education*, London, Routledge and Kegan Paul, p. 76.
5 Reid, L.A. (1962), *Philosophy and Education*, London, Heinemann, p. 4.
6 Adams, J. (1928), *Educational Theories*, London, Ernest Benn, p. 32.
7 For an example of one of the most widely used textbooks of this type see Rusk, R.R. (1979), *Doctrines of the Great Educators*, New York, St. Martin's Press.
8 Ayer, A.J. (1946), *Language, Truth and Logic*, New York, Dover Publications.
9 *Ibid.*, p. 78.
10 Hirst, P.H. (1974), *Knowledge and the Curriculum*, London, Routledge and Kegan Paul, pp. 1–2.
11 Jonicich, G.M. (Ed.) (1962), *Psychology and the Science of Education: Selected Writings of Edward L. Thorndike*, New York, Teachers College Columbia University Press, p. 63.
12 Quoted in Cronbach, L.J., and Suppes, P. (1969), *Research for Tomorrow's*

Schools, London, Macmillan.
13 SKINNER, B.F. (1968), *The Technology of Teaching*, Prentice Hall, New York, p. 59.
14 *Ibid.*, p. 19.
15 *Ibid.*, pp. 65–6.
16 See, for example, BANKS, O. (1976), *The Sociology of Education*, New York, Schoken Books.
17 CARNAP, R. (1967), *The Logical Stucture of the World*, tr. GEORGE, R.A. University of California Press, p. ix.
18 GIDDENS, A. (1974), *Positivism and Sociology*, London, Heinemann, p. i.
19 KOLAKOWSKI, L. (1972), *Positivist Philosophy*, Harmondsworth, Middlesex, Penguin, pp. 11–12.
20 O'CONNOR, D.J. (1973), 'The nature and scope of educational theory' in LANGFORD, G. and O'CONNOR, D.J. (Eds) *New Essays in the Philosophy of Education*, London, Routledge and Kegan Paul, p. 64.
21 See MILL, J.S. (1963), *Collected Works*, Toronto, University of Toronto Press; NAGEL, E. (1961), *The Structure of Science*, London, Harcourt Brace Jovanovich; HEMPEL, C.G. (1966), *Philosophy of Natural Science*, Englewood Cliffs, NJ, Prentice Hall.
22 NAGEL, E. (1961), *The Structure of Science*, London, Harcourt Brace Jovanovich.
23 HEMPEL, C.G. and OPPENHEIM, P. (1948), 'The logic of explanation', *Philosophy of Science*, vol. 15, no. 2, April, pp. 135–74.
24 *Ibid.*
25 TRAVERS, R.M.W. (1969), *An Introduction to Educational Research*, London, Macmillan, p. 16.
26 O'CONNOR, D.J. (1957), *op. cit.*, p. 5.
27 O'CONNOR, D.J. (1973), *op. cit.*, p. 48.
28 O'CONNOR, D.J. (1957), *op. cit.*, p. 48.
29 O'CONNOR, D.J. (1973), *op. cit.*, p. 63
30 O'CONNOR, D.J. (1957), *op. cit.*, p. 54.
31 See POPPER, K.R. (1963), *Conjectures and Refutations*, London, Routledge and Kegan Paul; FEYERABEND, P.K. (1975), *Against Method*, London, New Left Books; HANSON, N.R. (1958), *Patterns of Discovery*, Cambridge, Cambridge University Press.
32 See, in particular, SOCKETT, H., (1973), 'Curriculum planning: taking a means to an end', in PETERS, R.S. (Ed.) *The Philosophy of Education*, London, Oxford University Press, p. 150–60.
33 PETERS, R.S. (1965), 'Education as initiation' in ARCHAMBAULT, R.D. *Philosophical Analysis and Education*, London, Routledge and Kegan Paul, p. 92.
34 Note the use of the term 'educational practice' in this kind of formulation. From the perception of such researchers, 'practice' is something pervasive, widely occurring and general — a kind of 'phenomenon' like 'air pressure'. This abstract and decontextualized view of practice makes it amenable to study by 'scientific' methods. Such a use of the term 'practice' robs it completely of the Aristotelian connotations and connections which identify practice as *praxis*: informed action which flows from certain particular commitments in the light of certain particular circumstances and issues.

Chapter 3

The Interpretive View of Educational Theory and Practice

1 Introduction

The case for a positivist approach to educational theory and research rests on the twin assumptions that only a scientific approach to education can ensure a rational solution to educational questions, and that only instrumental questions about educational means are amenable to scientific solution. Because of the barrage of criticisms that have been levelled at both of these assumptions, there is now a growing realization that educational research based on positivist principles does not really conform to the image of a non-ideological activity that was once supposed. As a result, positivist approaches to educational research have been challenged and new epistemologies have been sought. In recent times, educational psychology, curriculum theory and educational administration have all explored the possibilities offered by alternative research methodologies for structuring their activities in more appropriate ways.

By far the most popular area of exploration has been those methodologies which derive from the 'interpretive' tradition of social enquiry, and which seek to replace the scientific notions of explanation, prediction and control, with the interpretive notions of understanding, meaning and action. The first task of this chapter is to describe the way in which an 'interpretive' approach based on social phenomenology emerged in the sociology of education. The second is to set this development against the background of a general discussion of the interpretive approach to social science. The third aim is to examine the interpretive view of the relationship between educational theory and educational practice. The chapter concludes with a critical assessment of the strengths and weaknesses of this approach to educational theory, and a brief discussion of the view of teaching which it sustains.

2 The Sociology of Education from Functionalism to Phenomenology

Until the end of the 1960s it was generally agreed that 'functionalism' provided the most appropriate framework for the sociological study of education. As noted in the previous chapter the positivist characteristics of this kind of educational theory are clearly visible in its view of social reality as a self-regulating mechanism and in its concern to provide value-neutral explanations. A positivist orientation is also clearly evident in the functionalist image of human behaviour as something that is determined by impersonal laws that operate beyond the individual's control.

Partly because of this in-built positivism, the consensus about the value of functionalism broke down and the sociology of education took a 'new direction' that adopted a radically different stance. The main expression of this new approach was *Knowledge and Control* edited by Michael F.D. Young and published in 1971.[1] What united most of the papers in this book was a recognition of the persistent failure of functionalism to question the positivist assumptions on which much of the sociological research in education was based. In order to overcome this deficiency, the 'new direction' in the sociology of education endorsed a preference for an 'interpretive' approach derived largely from the social phenomenology of Alfred Schutz[2] and the sociology of knowledge developed by Berger and Luckman.[3] This 'New Sociology' argued that society is not an 'independent system' maintained through the relationship of factors external to its members. Rather, the crucial character of social reality is that it possesses an *intrinsic meaning structure* that is constituted and sustained through the routine interpretive activities of its individual members. The 'objective' character of society, then, is not some independent reality to which individuals are somehow subject. Rather, society comes to possess a degree of objectivity because social actors, in the process of interpreting their social world, externalize and objectify it. Society is only 'real' and 'objective' in so far as its members define it as such and orient themselves towards the reality so defined.

It follows from this that to regard social order as a given feature of society not only suggests an illegitimate 'reification' (treating perceived patterns as objective realities) but also fails to explain how such order is produced and continually reaffirmed through the everyday interpretations of social actors. Sociological research must therefore be more concerned with how social order is produced by revealing the network of meanings out of which this order is constituted and reconstituted by its members. Within the field of education, therefore, enquiry should focus on understanding the social processes through which a given educational reality is produced and becomes 'taken for granted'. In particular, there should be a move towards treating 'what counts as knowledge' as 'problematic', so as to facilitate research into the ways in which knowledge is socially organized, transmitted and assessed in schools.

What has become a 'classical' example of this kind of 'interpretive' research in education is Keddie's study of the ways in which 'classroom knowledge' is defined and organized in schools.[4] The aim of Keddie's research was to examine what teachers 'know' about their pupils and how this 'knowledge' is related to the organization of curriculum knowledge in the classroom. In effect, by regarding 'knowledge' and 'ability' as socially constructed organizing concepts, Keddie sought to show how they are employed both in the interpretation of pupils' behaviour and in the organization of the knowledge made available to them.

Another example of an 'interpretive' approach to the study of education is the pioneer investigation of Cicourel and Kitsuse into the organizational practices of schools.[5] In more traditional educational research 'school organization' is usually seen as a formal structure with rules regulating the activities of members and goals towards which these activities are directed. Cicourel and Kitsuse, however, do not regard an organization as a 'real thing' and instead pose the question of why organizations are so experienced. Once a belief in the 'objective reality' of formal organizations is abandoned, they argue, the organizational rules operative in schools can be seen to be the result of their continual affirmation through the everyday decision-making practices of teachers and administrators.

What the work of Keddie and Cicourel and Kitsuse have in common is a refusal to accept the orderly character of the use of educational institutions as given, and a research perspective which explore how this order is produced and maintained. Neither study uses methodologies which merely impose order or regards the interpretations of teachers as illustrating a given reality to which research enquiry can naively be addressed. Both are concerned to show how teachers' accounts of what they are doing creates a 'reality' which has the appearance of 'objectivity', but which can be investigated by exploring the social activities through which it is produced. As such, both operate with a conception of social reality which takes the 'interpretive' stance that social reality can only be understood by understanding the subjective meanings of individuals. It is with the general features of this approach that the next section is concerned.

3   The Interpretive Approach to Social Science

One of the most important controversies in the history of social thought has concerned the relationship between the understandings people have of their own actions and the purpose of the social sciences.[6] Those who have argued that the social sciences should adopt the aims and methods of the natural sciences have maintained that this kind of everyday understanding merely constitutes a starting point in the search for testable hypotheses and general laws. Others, however, have argued that since social life is the product of these everyday under-standings, the social sciences should aim at 'interpretation' rather than scientific explanation.

This 'interpretive' view of the nature of the social sciences has a long history. It was first elaborated by seventeenth-century Protestant theologians who wanted to develop a method that would show how the meaning of the Bible could be directly understood from a reading of the text — without the intervention of any ecclesiastical explanations. The technical method developed for this method of interpreting meanings was called 'hermeneutics'. In the eighteenth century it was used not only for interpreting biblical texts but also for interpreting literature, works of art and music. Jurisprudence and philology also took up the 'hermeneutic' method and in the nineteenth century, 'interpretive understanding' became the central concept in a major methological discussion between German-speaking historians, about the nature of history. It was not, however, until the late nineteenth century and early twentieth century (the period when in Britain and elsewhere a positivist approach to the social sciences held sway) that a succession of German social theorists like Dilthey, Rickert, Simmel and Weber sought to extend and elaborate the idea of hermeneutic interpretation into an alternative epistemological basis for the social sciences.

Until recently, theoretical and methodological reflection on the role of 'interpretive understanding' in the social sciences was largely confined to Germany. However, because of the growing criticisms levelled at positivist conceptions of knowledge in the English-speaking world, the 'interpretive' alternative has begun to attract widespread support. As noted in the previous chapter, functionalism, as a model for sociological research, was heavily criticized in the 1960s and 1970s and replaced by models which draw on the 'interpretive tradition'.[7] Similarly, behaviourist models of curriculum research and evaluation have given way to 'illuminative' perspectives in which the task of interpretation is given in a central place.[8] Furthermore, recent developments in neo-Wittgensteinian analytical philosophy have generated accounts of action, language and social life which not only undermine the positivist account, but also provide logical support for the interpretive view of how social phenomena are to be explained and understood.[9]

The notion of 'interpretive social science' is a generic term that includes a variety of positions. It can also be explicated from a variety of different sources, ranging from German hermeneutics to British analytical philosophy. Perhaps the clearest expression of the interpretive standpoint is Max Weber's famous definition of sociology:

> Sociology ... is a science which attempts the interpretive understanding of social action.... In 'action' is included all human behaviour when and in so far as the acting individual attaches a subjective meaning to it. Action in this sense may be either overt or purely inward or subjective; it may consist of positive intervention in a situation, or of deliberately refraining from such intervention or passively acquiescing in the situation. Action is social in so far as, by virtue of the subjective meaning attached to it by the acting individual (or individuals), it takes account of the behaviour of others and is thereby oriented in its course.[10]

The key elements in Weber's definition are easily identified. Social science, he claims, is concerned with the 'interpretive understanding' of social action and the most significant feature about action is its 'subjective meaning'. But what does it mean to talk of 'subjective meanings' and why is 'interpretive understanding' so important in the social sciences?

The notion of 'subjective meaning' is closely related to the distinction between human action and human behaviour, where the latter refers to overt physical movement. The importance of this distinction becomes immediately apparent once it is realized that the behaviour of physical objects can only be made intelligible if some interpretive categories are imposed on it. To say, for example, that 'metal expands when heated' reflects the way in which the behaviour of heated metal is endowed with meaning by the causal explanations of the scientist. It is not to say anything about the way in which metals interpret their own behaviour.

The behaviour of human beings, however, consists, in the main, of their actions, and a distinctive feature of actions is that they are meaningful to those who perform them and become intelligible to others only by reference to the meaning that the individual actor attaches to them.[11] Observing a person's actions, therefore, does not simply involve taking note of the actor's overt physical movements. It also requires an interpretation by the observer of the meaning which the actor gives to his behaviour. It is for this reason that one type of observable behaviour may constitute a whole range of actions. A.J. Ayer demonstrates this point by describing how the raising and drinking of a glass of wine could be interpreted as:

> ... an act of self-indulgence, an expression of politeness, a manifestation of loyalty, a gesture of despair, an attempt at suicide, a religious communication....[12]

Hence actions cannot be observed in the same way as natural objects. They can only be interpreted by reference to the actor's motives, intentions or purposes in performing the action. To identify these motives and intentions correctly is to grasp the 'subjective meaning' the action has to the actor.

Another way of putting the point is to say all descriptions of actions must contain an interpretive element. To describe somebody as teaching, for example, is not simply to describe their observable behaviour. What is observed may be somebody baking a cake, standing on his head, reading a book, playing the piano or talking to a child. What allows any of these behaviours to be interpreted as teaching is an identification of the particular 'subjective meanings', according to which those performing these actions understand what they are doing. Actions, unlike the behaviour of most objects, always embody the interpretations of the actor, and for this reason can only be understood by grasping the meanings that the actor assigns to them. A task of 'interpretive' social science is to discover these meanings and so make action intelligible.

The claim that human actions are meaningful involves more than a reference to the conscious intentions of individuals. It also involves understanding the social context within which such intentions make sense. Actions cannot be private; the very identification of an action as an action of a certain kind involves employing rules of identity in terms of which any two actions are deemed to be the same. Such rules are necessarily public; if they were not then it would be impossible to distinguish a correct identification of an action from a mistaken one. And this 'public' characteristic of the rules of interpretation entails that an action can only be correctly identified when it falls under some description which is publicly recognizable as correct. Hence, to describe somebody as 'teaching' is to implicitly appeal to a background of rules operative in a particular society which specify what is to count as teaching. Indeed they constitute the very possibility of teaching at all.

This social character of actions implies that actions arise from the networks of meanings that are given to individuals by their past history and present social order and which structure their interpretation of 'reality' in a certain way. To this extent, the meanings in terms of which individuals act are predetermined by the 'forms of life' into which they are initiated. For this reason, another task of an 'interpretive' social science is to uncover the set of social rules which give point to a certain kind of social activity and so reveal the structure of intelligibility which explains why any actions being observed make sense.

If human actions are considered in this way then clearly any attempt to explain them in the same way as the natural sciences explain the behaviour of natural objects deprives them of their intended meanings and substitutes in their place the sort of causal interpretations that the positivist conception of explanation requires. When this happens, meaningful actions are reduced to patterns of behaviour which, like the expanding metal, are assumed to be determined by some external forces so that they can be made amenable to conventional scientific explanations. Action is denuded of its meaning and finds a place in a calculus of movements which have meaning only illicitly, through the meanings and values which the positivist scientist tries vainly to extirpate from his or her theories. If this is to be avoided, if attempts to understand human and social phenomena are to be taken seriously, it must be recognized that the social sciences deal with entirely different kinds of subject matter from the natural sciences and that the methods and the form of explanation used in the two types of science are fundamentally different.

Historially, the kind of methods and explanations concerned to offer theoretical interpretations of the subjective meanings of social action are the methods and explanations of Verstehen.[13] In seeking to uncover the meanings of action, Verstehen explanations do not regard intentions, purposes and motives as some 'inner' mental event that somehow causes overt physical behaviour to occur. Rather, it recognizes that 'intentions' and 'motives' refer not to some kind of occult mental processes, but to what it is that permits the actions being observed to be described as actions of a particular sort. Intentions and motives are not 'behind' actions, functioning as their invisible mental 'cause'. Motives and intentions are intrinsically related to actions as part of their definition and meaning. For this reason Verstehen explanations do not depend on some mysterious kind of intuitive empathy which allows the social scientist to somehow put himself into the mind of the people he observes. Rather, they are explanations that seek to elucidate the intelligibility of human actions by clarifying the thinking by which they are informed and setting this in the context of the social rules and forms of life within which they occur. In doing this, Verstehen explanations aim to explicate the basic conceptual schemes which structure the ways in which the actions, experiences and ways of life of those whom the social scientist observes are made intelligible. Their aim is not to provide causal explanations of human life, but to deepen and extend our knowledge of why social life is perceived and experienced in the way that it is.

4 Theory and Practice

Just as a particular view of how theory guides practice is a defining characteristic of a positivistic conception of knowledge, so also the 'interpretive' model incorporates assumptions about the theory-practice relationship in its view of what constitutes valid theoretical accounts of human action and social life. For the purpose of interpretive social science is to reveal the meaning of particular forms of social life by systematically articulating the subjective-meaning structures governing the ways in which typical individuals act in typical situations.[14] Now when this kind of theoretical account is made available to the individual actors involved, it will reveal to them the rules and assumptions upon which they are acting, and hence 'enlighten' or 'illuminate' the significance of their actions. By so making the meaning of actions transparent to the individuals involved, interpretive social science creates the possibility of practical change in two ways. First, it serves to reduce problems of communication between those whose actions are being interpreted and those to whom the interpretive account is being made available. For, by showing what is going on in a particular situation, by revealing the ways in which the people in that situation make sense of what they are doing, interpretive accounts facilitate dialogue and communication between interested parties.

Secondly, interpretive social theory may influence practice by influencing the ways in which individual practitioners comprehend themselves and their situation. For an interpretive account, in trying to grasp the sense of individuals' lives and actions, may make use of concepts and understandings other than those used by the individuals themselves. As such, it may suggest to individuals alternative ways of interpreting their actions and defining their 'reality'. But to provide individuals with new concepts is not simply to offer them a new way of thinking. It is also to offer them the possibility of becoming more self-conscious about the basic pattern of thought in terms of which they usually make their own actions intelligible. It is by so providing individuals with the opportunity to reconsider the beliefs and attitudes inherent in their existing ways of thinking, that interpretive social theory can affect practice. Practices are changed by changing the ways in which they are understood.

Now this view of the relationship of theory to practice is not something that has been mechanically attached to the notion of interpretive theory. For just as positivistic conceptions of explanation and prediction imply that theory relates to practice through a process of technical control, so interpretive methods of validating knowledge entail that theory affects practice by exposing the theoretical context that defines practice to self-reflection. To be valid, an interpretive account must first of all be coherent: it must comprehend and coordinate insights and evidence within a consistent framework. For many interpretive researchers, this is enough. Their work is complete, they argue, when their account satisfies their own evaluative criteria and the evaluative criteria of the critical community of their fellow scientists. But a more stringent test may also be applied, either concretely or in principle: to be valid, the account must also be able to pass the test of participant confirmation. Researchers willing to take this more stringent test argue that an interpretive account must be recognized as a possibly true account of what is going on by those whose activities it describes. In other words, it is only when the theorists and those whose actions he observes come to agree that a theoretical interpretation of those actions is 'correct' that the theory can have any validity. Any claim to have successfully uncovered the individual's purposes and intentions, or the social rules providing the grounds for meaningful interactions between individuals, or the tacit assumptions inherent in certain situations, always requires that those acting in a situation agree that they can understand this situation in the way described. These purposes, intentions, meanings and assumptions are *their* purposes, intentions, meanings and assumptions, and whether or not a theoretical account has adequately acknowledged this can only be determined by them.

Because this kind of 'negotiation' between observer and observed is a necessary prerequisite for an account to be true, it follows that the validity of a theory is partially defined by its ability to remain intrinsically related to and compatible with the actor's own understanding. This does not mean that the actor's own account of what is going on and the 'interpretive' account must be identical or that one is in some sense superior to the other. It simply means that the interpretive account can be communicated to the actor and is commensurable with his own account. And this implies that the interpretive theory does not reinterpret the actions and experiences of individuals for its own purposes and in terms of its own conceptual frameworks, but rather provides a deeper, more extensive and systematized knowledge and understanding of the actor's own interpretations of what they are doing. It is the relationship of the truth criteria for this sort of theoretical knowledge to the actor's ordinary everyday understanding that constitutes the basis of the 'interpretive' view of the relationship of theory to practice.

5   The Interpretive Approach and 'the Practical'

Seen from the interpretive researcher's point of view, actions have meaning in relation to the understandings, purposes and intentions of the actor, and the actor's interpretations of the significance of the context of the action. The interpretive approach to social science aims to uncover these meanings and significances. For those who seek to act in more informed and enlightened ways, with wisdom and prudence, interpretive accounts offer opportunities to see more deeply under the surface of social life and human affairs. From the perspective of the social actor who wishes to act more rationally and more authentically, interpretive accounts provide opportunities to extend understandings, and also to extend the range and sophistication of the language for describing action, and thus to extend the capacity to communicate about action: to orient action and coordinate it with the right actions of others.

There has been a resurgence of interest in the kind of thinking which informs action from the perspective of the actor: Schwab's work on 'the practical' and 'practical deliberation' is of this kind.[15] Practical deliberation is needed when considering the alternative courses of action possible in a given situation and deciding which of these possible courses of action most fully expresses the purposes and commitments of the actor, given the present circumstances and constraints (including the perceptions and deliberation of other actors). Practical deliberation has its roots in the disposition of the actor to act truly, rightly, wisely and prudently — the disposition called *'phronesis'* by Aristotle. It expresses itself in *praxis* — informed action. The educated person, one might say, is interested only in this kind of committed, informed action. He or she lives by his or her commitments to the good.

Such a person will interpret the world reflectively, and will be conscious of the kinds of values to which he or she is committed, the value-commitments of others, and those fostered by contemporary culture. Perhaps such a person will write interpretive accounts of social life; but this question is not important in relation to what is at issue here. What is important is that such a person may be informed further by the accounts of social life available through a developed interpretive social science.

Interpretive social science, historically, aims to serve such readers. It aims to educate: to deepen insight and to enliven commitment. Its work is the transformation of consciousness, the differentiation of modes of awareness and the enlightenment of action. It expects critical reception (that is, it does not take the simplistic view that its truths are unified into single theories which will compel action along predetermined lines), and it aims to contribute to social life through educating the consciousness of individual actors. On this view, interpretive social science can feed practical deliberation and thus, if its significance is recognized, influence action indirectly; that is, through the mediation of the critical reflection of individual actors.

The account of the theory-practice relationship of interpretive social science is thus no one-way traffic of ideas into action; of practice from theoretical principles. The traffic is two-way: practical deliberation is informed not only by ideas but also by the practical exigencies of situations; it always requires critical appraisal and mediation by the judgment of the actor. In interpretive social science, each practical situation offers new experience to contribute to the actor's store of practical wisdom; equally, it offers new challenges to the expression of commitment to the good. These comments may serve to draw the contrast between the technical view of theory-practice relationship in positivist social science and the practical view of interpretive social science. Clearly, both have different views of the role and functions of social science vis-a-vis social life and social actors. Equally clearly, they make different assumptions about the nature of the social world of which social science is a part. The one attempts to stand above social life, taking the role of social engineering; the other sees itself within social life, as powerless to transcend it as it is to direct it. For interpretive social science, the only aim is enlightenment, and through enlightenment, rationality in a critical, moral and reflective sense.

6 Criticisms of Interpretive Social Science

In general terms, criticisms of the interpretive view of social science can be divided into two types. On the one hand, there are positivist-inspired objections to the basis foundations of interpretive theory that are usually presented in the form of evaluations based on positivist canons of rationality. These include the inability of the interpretive approach to produce wide-ranging generalizations, or to provide 'objective' standards for verifying or refuting theoretical accounts.[16]

The second kind of criticisms are those which accept that social activities must be understood in terms of their meanings and that such meanings derive from rules embodied in a social context. But these criticisms insist that the task of establishing correct interpretations of the intentions and meanings of social action does not exhaust the purpose of the social sciences. Indeed, they regard the limitation of the social sciences to the uncovering of actors' own 'definitions of the situation' and the subsequent assimilation of scientific understanding and ordinary everyday understanding as unnecessarily restrictive. These criticisms take many forms, but in general terms they reflect the belief that the interpretive approach by distinguishing between 'understanding' as the aim of interpretive social science and 'explanation' as the aim of natural science and by denying that scientific explanations have any place in the investigation of social phenomena, thereby excludes from social scientific enquiries the explanation of certain features of social reality which are of the utmost importance. In particular, it is argued that the interpretive model neglects questions about the origins, causes and results of actors adopting certain interpretations of their actions and social life, and neglects the crucial problems of social conflict and social change. Furthermore, it is argued that these defects entail that the interpretive view of the relationship of theory to practice is seriously flawed.

Because it emphasizes the way in which social reality is constructed out of a plurality of 'subjective meanings', the interpretive approach cannot help but neglect questions about the relationships between individuals' interpretations and actions and external factors and circumstances. But while it may be true that social reality is constructed and maintained through the interactions of individuals, it is also the case that the range of possible interpretations of reality that are open to individuals is constrained by the particular society in which they live. Social reality is not simply something that is structured and sustained by the interpretations of individuals — it also determines the kind of interpretations of reality that are appropriate for a particular group of individuals to possess. Social structure, as well as being the *product* of the meanings and actions of individuals, itself *produces* particular meanings, ensures their continuing existence, and thereby limits the kind of actions that it is reasonable for individuals to perform. It is appropriate, therefore, for social science to examine not only the meanings of particular forms of social action, but also the social factors that engender and sustain them. In pursuing this task, investigations may seek to discover what it is that causes individuals to act in certain ways by focusing on how certain kinds of social structure constrain particular social groups in a way that limits the range of actions open to them. This sort of enquiry being an enquiry into the preconditions that make particular interpretations of reality available, will not itself be interpretive. Rather, it will be a form of enquiry that seeks to reveal the historical and social causes of actions in a way that an interpretive explanation cannot. This kind of enquiry, it is argued, is not only legitimate: it is a necessary corrective to the passivity of a social science limited to providing interpretive accounts of social actions and meanings.

A second line of criticism aimed at the interpretive approach concerns the unintended consequences of social actions. For although it is clear that actions are always undertaken with certain intentions and purposes in mind, it is also clear that they have ramifications that were not intended, and of which the individuals concerned were not conscious. Furthermore, since such unintended consequences are unrelated to the intentions governing the actions that produced them, the individual actors concerned will be unaware of the results of what they are doing and unable to exercise any control over them. As such, they cannot be explained by reference to the intentions of the individual actors concerned.

Now some of these unintended consequences are 'functional', in the sense that they serve to maintain certain aspects of the wider social system by reinforcing the actions and interpretations of other social groups. In investigating this possibility, social science will need to construct theoretical accounts which attempt to explain the continuing existence of some institutionalized social activity, not by revealing the purposes that the actual participants believe them to fulfil, but rather by demonstrating the contribution that the unintended results of such activities make to the continuity and stability of the social system that produced and preserves them. And such explanations will be very different from the kind of accounts that an interpretive approach permits.

A third objection follows from the way in which the interpretive approach insists that any explanation of social action which is incompatible with the actors' own accounts is inadmissable. If this is so, then all those situations in which people's self-understanding of what they are doing is illusory or deceptive will be left unexplained. Yet clearly the ways in which people characterize their actions may be at variance with what they are really doing so that their understandings and explanations may be no more than rationalizations that obscure the true nature of their situation and mask reality in some important way. Explanations of how and why this occurs may take the form of a theoretical account that demonstrates how the understandings of individuals may be conditioned by 'false consciousness', and how certain social mechanisms operate to bind people to irrational and distorted ideas about their social reality. They may also try to reveal, at the social-structural level, the ideological character of group life by showing how social processes such as language and the processes of cultural production and reproduction shape our experience of the social world in specific ways and for specific purposes.

These kinds of explanations not only deny the validity of the individual's own explanation of what he is doing. They also offer alternative explanations which, were they made intelligible and acceptable to the individuals concerned, would prevent them from acting in the ways that they do. But explanations couched in the language of false consciousness and ideology are, by definition, not available to the individuals to whom they apply. Indeed, they are only possible if and when individuals cannot interpret their actions in this way, since to perceive their actions as conditioned by false consciousness or ideology would be to endow these actions with a totally different meaning and significance. But if this is so, then such explanations will necessarily be disconnected from the individuals' own interpretations and, from the perspective of the 'interpretive' approach, unacceptable. By emphasizing the importance of grasping the 'intelligibility' of the individuals' *own* meanings and actions, therefore, the interpretive approach offers no way of examining the ideological character that these meanings and actions possess, and the purposes they serve in social life. To penetrate this resistance to ideological explanations, interpretive social science would have to provide a mode of enquiry within which individuals' own interpretations can be critically reconsidered and reassessed.

If there is any truth in the claim that the interpretive approach fails to explain the relationship between people's interpretations of reality and the social conditions under which these interpretations occur, then it also offers an inadequate account of how theory relates to practice. For interpretive theories claim that by clarifying the meanings that individuals give to their actions, they overcome problems of communication between different social groups and thereby help people to change the way they think about what they or other social groups are doing. Now this suggests that to simply present an interpretive account, revealing the possibility of alternative definitions and conceptions, is sufficient grounds for expecting individuals to reinterpret their situation and change their actions. But this is to ignore the fact that conceptual changes do not occur simply because one interpretation is more rational or correct than any other. An individual's ideas and beliefs are not merely a set of true or false statements that have been adopted on the basis of purely rational considerations. Rather, they are intimately related to the individual's way of life, and, as such, they provide the sort of ideas and beliefs about oneself and others that are appropriate to the way one lives. It is precisely because an individual's identity is so closely related to the values, beliefs and attitudes inherent in the style of thought of the social group to which he or she belongs that any alternative interpretation of what he or she is doing will invariably be resisted. Far from changing individual's conceptions of themselves or others, any new interpretations will be perceived as an emotional threat to the individual's self-concept and discarded as 'unrealistic', 'ridiculous' or 'irrelevant'. Because it fails to deal with the question of why the possibility of change should be opposed in this way, the kind of practical effects that interpretive theories claim to produce will not occur.

The interpretive view of the theory-practice relationship is also unsound because it incorporates conservative assumptions about the relationship of social conflict to social change. This is so because it tends to assume that social conflicts are always the result of different social groups having conflicting interpretations of reality rather than contradictions in that reality itself. Such conflicts are, from the interpretive perspective, the manifestation of people's misunderstandings of the meaning of either their own or others' actions, and are overcome by revealing to those involved the faulty ideas and beliefs that they have. But, by implying in this way that social conflicts are the result of conceptual confusions which, once revealed, will demonstrate to people the rationality of their actions, the interpretive approach is always predisposed towards the idea of reconciling people to their existing social reality.

But not all of the conflicts and anxieties that people experience arise from their misunderstandings about their own or other people's practice. It may be that the 'faulty' beliefs that give rise to the conflict in the first place are a reflection of real conflicts and tensions endemic to the practice itself — that it is the social reality that is irrational and incoherent rather than the individual's conception of social reality. When such conflicts emerge, the interpretive approach encourages people to change the ways that they *think* about what they are doing, rather than suggest ways in which they should change what they *are* doing. Hence, although interpretive theories may be able to transform consciousness of social reality they can reveal no direct interest in providing methods for a crucial examination of social reality itself. Indeed, in so far as it regards the search for theories which incorporate standards for critically assessing the existing social order as somewhat misguided, the interpretive approach tends to remain indifferent to the need for social theory to be critical of the *status quo*.

7 Conclusion

Interpretive educational research, by stressing the ways in which the subjective interpretations of educational practitioners are constitutive of educational realities, challenges the positivist assumption of an objective reality that can be interpreted by causal explanations and universal laws. By so revealing the limitations of positivism, it undermines the self-understandings of those engaged in the natural scientific approach to educational research.

Despite their differences, however, both the 'interpretive' approach and positivist approach convey a similar understanding of educational researchers and of their relationship to the research act. In both approaches, the researcher stands outside the researched situation adopting a disinterested stance in which any explicit concern with critically evaluating and changing the educational realities being analyzed is rejected. Thus despite its insistence that educational realities are subjectively structured, rather than objectively given, the interpretive approach, like positivism, pursues the common methodological aim of describing social reality in a neutral, disinterested way.

Historically, this image of the theorist as somebody who must exclude all personal values and suppress all interest in the purposes and values of those whose actions are being analyzed, is quite recent. In many ways, it represents a reduction in the scope of legitimate theorizing to the single sphere of *theoria*, which in the Greek tradition was reserved for the contemplation of ultimate truths. The classical notion of a distinctive practical sphere in which theory is intrinsically concerned with guiding practice, rests, from the contemporary view, on a confusion of facts and values and, for this reason, is ruled out on methodological grounds. Yet, in so far as education is a practical value-laden activity, it seems that any educational theory worthy of the name cannot rest content with providing value-neutral theoretical accounts, but must be able to confront questions about practical educational values and goals. As one educational philosopher puts it:

> Where ... a practical activity like education is concerned, ... theory is constructed to determine and guide the activity ... The distinction ... between scientific theory and educational theory is the traditional distinction between knowledge that is organized for the pursuit of knowledge ... and knowledge that is organized for determining some practical activity. To try and understand the nature and pattern of some practical discourse in terms of the nature and pattern of some purely theoretical discourse can only result in its being radically misconceived.[17]

In many ways, resolving the tension between the practical discourse of education and the theoretical discourse of educational research is the central problem in relating educational theory and practice. It is this problem that provides the major theme of Chapter 4.

Further Reading

The case for educational sociology taking a new interpretive direction is to be found in two collections of essays — Young, M.F.D. (Ed.) *Knowledge and Control* and Filmer, P. *et al.*, *New Directions in Sociological Theory*. A good general account of the history of the 'interpretive' tradition is Outhwaites, *Understanding Social Life: The Method Called Verstehen*. A highly influential attempt to justify an interpretive view of the social sciences from within the neo-Wittgensteinian tradition of analytic philosophy is Peter Winch's, *The Idea of a Social Science*. A summary of the numerous criticisms made to the approach are to be found in Bernstein's, *The Restructuring of Social and Political Theory*, Part III, particularly pp. 156–69.

Notes

1 YOUNG, M.D.F. (Ed.) (1971) *Knowledge and Control: New Directions for the Sociology of Education*, London, Collier Macmillan.
2 See SCHUTZ, A. (1967), *The Phenomenology of the Social World*, Evanston, North-western University Press.
3 BERGER, P.L., and LUCKMAN, T. (1967), *The Social Construction of Reality*, London, The Penguin Press.
4 KEDDIE, N., 'Classroom knowledge', in YOUNG, M.F.D. (Ed.) (1971), *Knowledge and Control: New Directions for the Sociology of Education*, London, Collier Macmillan, pp. 133–60.
5 CICOUREL, A.V., and KITSUSE, J. (1963), *The Educational Decision-makers*, Indianapolis, Ind, Bobbs-Merrill Co.
6 OUTHWAITE, W. (1975), *Understanding Social Life: The Method Called Verstehen*, London, George Allen and Unwin. This book provides a useful historical introduction to the rise of interpretive methods.
7 For a good example of a book that criticizes functionalism and advocates a phenomenological perspective see FILMER, P. *et al.*, (1972), *New Directions in Sociological Theory*, New York, Collier Macmillan.
8 See, for example, PARLETT, M. and HAMILTON, D. 'Evaluation as illumination' in HAMILTON, D., *et al.*, (Eds) (1977), *Beyond the Numbers Game*, London, Macmillan, pp. 6–22.
9 The most influential text of this kind is WINCH, P. (1958), *The Idea of a Social Science*, London, Routledge and Kegan Paul.
10 WEBER, M. (1964), *The Theory of Social and Economic Organization*, New York, The Free Press, p. 88.
11 In this context, it is important to recall that Pavlov's ideas of conditioning, which later became so important to the development of behaviourist psychology, was based on an analogy between behaviour and reflexes — that is, on an analogy between action and a kind of behaviour which is not

influenced, so far as we know, by the meaning we attach to it.

12 AYER, A.J. (1964), *Man as a Subject for Science*, London, Athlone Press.

13 Historical and theoretical aspects of *verstehen* explanations are discussed in detail in OUTHWAITE, W. (1975), *Understanding Social Life: The Method Called Verstehen*, London, George Allen and Unwin.

14 Sometimes it attempts to do this through the study of 'deviants', like the insane, or others who press against the boundaries of the taken-for-granted: by studying how the boundaries of ordinary life may be challenged or changed, the interpretive scientist may throw light on the 'typical' and taken-for-granted.

15 SCHWAB, J.J. (1969), 'The practical: a language for curriculum', *School Review*, vol. 78, pp. 1–24.

16 See, for example, Nagel's criticisms in 'Philosophy and educational theory' (1969), *Studies in Philosophy and Education*, vol. 7, pp. 5–27.

17 HIRST, P.H. 'Educational theory', in TIBBLES, J.W. (1966), *The Study of Education*, London, Routledge and Kegan Paul, p. 40.

Chapter 4

Theory and Practice: Redefining the Problem

1 Introduction

The last two chapters have offered no more than a brief discussion of the two conceptions of theory that are commonly employed in educational research. Some of the conclusions to be derived from this discussion are more or less obvious. It is clear, for example, that different ways of understanding research are intimately connected to questions about how theory should be related to practice. Indeed, as the discussion unfolded, it became apparent that any adequate account of theory must take note of the relationship to practice that it implies.

Secondly, what emerges from the discussion of positivism is the naive way in which it takes the 'objective' character of reality for granted and then interprets that reality as something governed by inescapable laws. In consequence, it tends to confirm a spurious scientific respectability on prevailing 'commonsense' and offers no way of effecting practical change, other than through technical control. A major corrective to positivism provided by the interpretive approach is the recognition that the commonsense view of reality, far from being an 'objective' given, itself constitutes the major problem for theorizing and research. From the interpretive perspective, social reality is not something that exists and can be known independently of the knower. Rather, it is a subjective reality constructed and sustained through the meanings and actions of individuals. Positivist theories, by failing to recognize the importance of the interpretations and meanings that individuals employ to make their reality intelligible, fail to identify the phenomena to be explained. In consequence, the kind of theories that are produced are often trivial and useless, even though they may appear to be sophisticated and elaborate.

But achieving a correct understanding of individuals' meanings is only a necessary preliminary to social enquiries, and it is misguided to regard this as the whole substance of the theoretical enterprise. For the emphasis of the interpretive model on the subjective meanings of action tends to imply that social reality is nothing over and above the way people perceive themselves and their situation. But social reality is not simply structured and shaped by concepts and ideas. It is also structured and shaped by such things as historical forces and economic and material conditions. Moreover, these things also structure and affect the perceptions and ideas of individuals so that 'reality' may be misperceived as a consequence of the operation of various ideological processes. Uncovering these processes and explaining how they can condition and constrain interpretations of reality are vital requirements that are largely neglected by the 'interpretive' approach.

But perhaps the most important conclusion to be derived from the discussion so far is that any decision about the kind of theoretical perspective appropriate to educational research involves fundamental choices about the proper purpose which something called *educational* research should fulfil. Should it follow the natural sciences by providing a set of causal explanations that can be used to manipulate and control an educational situation? Or should it pursue the interpretive aim of revealing the different understandings of educational situations that various participants already possess, so that they can become more aware of what they normally take for granted? What, if anything, has emerged from the discussion so far is that neither of these answers seem to be really adequate and that some alternative understanding of educational theory and research is urgently needed.

The purpose of this chapter is to respond to this need by translating some of the insights and conclusions reached in previous chapters into more definite educational terms. In order to do this, the intention is to try and clarify some of the essential features that any coherent account of an *educational* science would need to incorporate. In pursuing this task the concern is not with describing the methods by means of which educational research could be conducted in a scientific manner. Rather, it is with the preliminary task of elucidating some of the formal elements that any adequate approach to educational research would need to incorporate. In doing this the intention is not only to point to some of the inadequacies in the two research epistemologies so far considered. It is also to pave the way for a discussion of the value of an alternative theory of social scientific enquiry for articulating a more coherent view of the nature of educational research and its relationship to educational practice.

2   The Idea of an Educational Science

Although it has long been believed that many of the intransigent problems of education could only be solved by enlisting the aid of the experimental methods of science,[1] experience has done little to support such optimism and contemporary opinion about the role of science in educational research is now deeply divided. These divisions have many facets and take many forms, but the central point at issue has been the question of whether the natural scientific model of enquiry has any place in educational research at all. As the previous chapters make clear, this dispute is but a particular instance of the more general conflict between positivist and interpretive approaches to social enquiry — a conflict which has dominated the entire history of the philosophy of the social sciences.

Now what is worth noting about the way in which this general controversy has been related to educational theory and research, is how the representatives of each of the two traditions share some common assumptions about how questions concerning the scientific status of educational research ought to be understood. For example, neither party seems to doubt that the two positions they represent more or less exhaust the range of possible options available for educational research to adopt. Despite all the arguments about whether educational research should be positivist and technical or interpretive and practical, the assumption that appropriate aims and structures for educational research must be derived from one or other of these two traditions remains largely unchallenged.

Similarly, interpretive arguments designed to reveal the limitations of a natural-scientific approach to educational research, invariably assume that the conceptions of science to which their opponents subscribe is adequate and correct. The sharp distinctions drawn in educational research between 'causal' and 'verstehen' explanations, 'nomothetic' and 'idiographic', 'subjective' and 'objective', are clear indications of how those on both sides of this intellectual divide adhere to a conception of science which ensures that scientific explanation and interpretative understanding are mutually exclusive categories.

Now the continuing adherence to these assumptions can be criticized on at least two counts. In the first place, any idea that educational research could become scientific if it were located within an already existing tradition of scientific enquiry, seems to stand in stark contrast to the Kuhnian view that, as a matter of historical fact, new theoretical activities do not develop by simply enlisting the aims and methods of some already established science. Rather, they emerge when those concerned with a specific field of enquiry adhere to a 'mode of community life' in which a body of theoretical knowledge can be developed to effectively resolve the particular problems of the field.[2]

The second line of criticism points to the ways in which the assumption that educational research must be *either* scientific *or* interpretive results in the avoidance of more fundamental questions concerning the possibilities of a research activity specifically directed towards a practical field like education. For example, to suggest that there must be an intrinsic connection between educational research and some existing conception of social scientific enquiry, is to leave the logically prior question of determining the distinctively educational features of the research untouched. Likewise, to accede to the view of science implicit in the methodologies employed in educational research overlooks the fact that there are various different conceptions of science and so neglects the need to specify the minimal conditions required for the scientific status of educational research to be secured. What, in short, these shared assumptions conceal is how it is only by first clarifying the *educational* character of research and, secondly, by clarifying the criteria for establishing its *scientific* character, that the question of the scientific status of educational research can be properly appraised. It is with the first of these tasks that the next section is concerned.

3   The Nature and Purpose of Educational Research

The task of characterizing 'educational research' can be approached in two quite different ways. On the one hand, it can be construed as requiring a neutral description of the wide range of methods and procedures employed by members of the educational research community. In fact, it is this interpretation of the task which the authors of most textbooks on educational research adopt in their opening chapters.[3] Alternatively, however, it may be regarded as an attempt to characterize the distinctive nature of educational research by explicating the criteria in terms of which a distinction can be drawn between research which is educational, and research which is not. Clearly, if there are no real differences between educational research and other kinds of research, then there are no real grounds for using this term to designate one form of research enquiry rather than any other. If, however, there are such differences, then these cannot be distilled from a descriptive survey of the work of educational research without first assuming an answer to the very question at issue. Answering questions about the nature of educational research, by reading off standards from the practices of those claiming to be undertaking this activity, is to prejudice the issue in a way favourable to those making these claims. For this reason, questions about the nature of educational research are not questions about the numerous ways in which this enterprise is practised, so much as questions about the criteria in terms of which each and any of these numerous practices can be assessed.

What, then, are the distinctive features of educational research? Clearly, different forms of research are not distinguished by their subject matter. Psychology, sociology, anthropology and philosophy, as well as education, may all take language as a common area of enquiry. Nor, since many forms of research employ similar methods and techniques, do these features of any research activity provide it with its distinctive character. Rather, a research activity is something that people *do* and as such is only made intelligible by reference to the overall purpose for which it is undertaken. This can be made clear by considering the following schema for clarifying the differences between theoretical and practical activities.[4]

Figure 1:   Langford's schema identifying practical activities

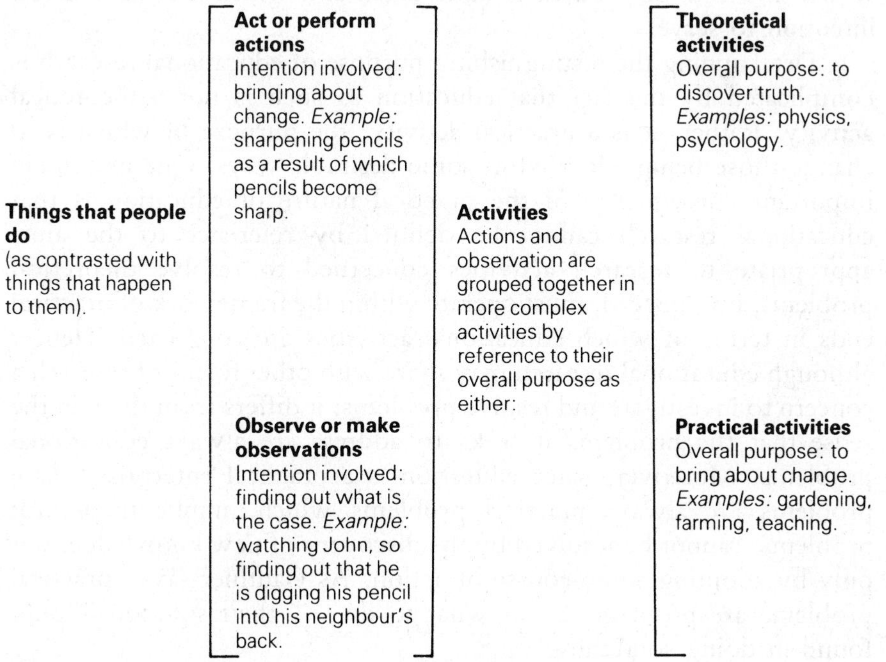

Things that people do
(as contrasted with things that happen to them).

Act or perform actions
Intention involved: bringing about change. *Example:* sharpening pencils as a result of which pencils become sharp.

Observe or make observations
Intention involved: finding out what is the case. *Example:* watching John, so finding out that he is digging his pencil into his neighbour's back.

Activities
Actions and observation are grouped together in more complex activities by reference to their overall purpose as either:

Theoretical activities
Overall purpose: to discover truth. *Examples:* physics, psychology.

Practical activities
Overall purpose: to bring about change. *Examples:* gardening, farming, teaching.

Commenting on this diagram, Langford argues that:

Many, though not all, of the things which people do form part of some more or less elaborate plan or pattern of activity in which the person is engaged. Individual actions and observations, each picked out by its own immediate goal or intention, form part of some more general, temporarily extended activity. The more general activity itself has an overall purpose, and the actions and observations which form its parts are seen as parts in virtue of their contribution to that purpose. (p. 5)

Looked at in this way, it is clear that particular research practices can only be understood as forming a part of a particular research activity, by seeing them as contributing to the end or purpose that distinguishes it as a research activity of a certain sort. To talk of theoretical research, therefore, is to talk of all those research activities that share the common aim of resolving theoretical problems in a particular way. To talk of different kinds of theoretical research, such as sociology and psychology, is to acknowledge some difference in the purpose that each of these activities seeks to pursue. Similarly, to talk of educational research is not to talk of any particular subject matter or methodological procedures, but to indicate the distinctive purpose for which this kind of research is undertaken and which it is its avowed intention to serve.

Determining the distinguishing purpose of educational research is complicated by the fact that education as such is not a theoretical activity. Rather, it is a practical activity, the purpose of which is to change those being educated in some desirable ways. One extremely important consequence of the practical nature of education is that educational research cannot be defined by reference to the aims appropriate to research activities concerned to resolve theoretical problems, but, instead, must operate within the framework of practical ends in terms of which educational activities are conducted. Hence, although educational research may share with other forms of research a concern to investigate and resolve problems, it differs from them in the sense that the problems it seeks to address are always educational problems. Moreover, since education is a practical enterprise, these problems are always practical problems which, unlike theoretical problems, cannot be resolved by the discovery of new knowledge, but only by adopting some course of action. As Gauthier says, 'practical problems are problems about what to do ... their solution is only found in doing something'.[5]

Now, although the fact that educational problems are practical is little more than a truism, the force of its implications for educational research is not always recognized. It is not always recognized, for example, that since problems may be *either* practical *or* theoretical but never both, educational problems are *never* theoretical. General or 'context-free' educational problems (for example, What should be taught to children? What should a 'core curriculum' contain?) are no more theoretical and no less practical than those which are more specific or concrete (for example, How should I assess the extent to which this group of thirteen-year-olds have learned quadratic equations?). In both of these cases of problem is not resolved by the discovery of knowledge, but by formulating and acting upon a practical judgment. Similarly, many theoretical problems that may appear at first sight to be educational problems, have no intrinsically educational character at all. Theoretical problems, both general and context free (for example, How do children learn? How do ruling classes maintain their hegemony through the operation of educational processes and institutions?) and specific and concrete (for example, Do middle-class pupils learn specific concepts more easily than working-class pupils?) may have some bearing on the practical decisions taken in response to educational problems. But they are not in *themselves* educational problems. Moreover, just as solutions to theoretical problems may be relevant in solving practical problems, so practical problems may arise in attempts to resolve theoretical problems. Clearly, the task of resolving theoretical problems is frequently impeded by practical difficulties which have to be overcome if this task is to be successfully accomplished. Just because these problems occur in the process of resolving theoretical problems does not alter their practical character, and, hence, does not alter the fact that theorists must actually *do* something if they are to be overcome.

At the outset, then, it is important to recognize that since it is the investigation of educational problems that provides educational research with whatever unity or coherence it may have, the testing ground for educational research is not its theoretical sophistication or its ability to conform to criteria derived from the social sciences, but rather its capacity to resolve educational problems and improve educational practice. For this reason, any account of the nature of educational research that simply transforms educational problems into a series of theoretical problems seriously distorts the purpose and nature of the whole enterprise. Indeed, to disregard or ignore the practical nature of educational problems in this way will so deprive them of whatever educational character they may have, as to ensure that any claim to be engaged in *educational* research, rather, say, than some form of social scientific research such as sociology or psychology, cannot be seriously maintained.

Confirmation of this can be gained by considering the source of the problems investigated by the social science disciplines. These are not determined by any of the practical activities to which social scientific theorizing may be addressed, but rather by the theoretical framework that structures and guides the conduct of social scientific research. What, for example, constitutes psychological or sociological problems about learning or language is determined not by the learner or the language speaker, but by the conceptual framework in terms of which these kinds of research are conducted.

Educational problems, however, because they arise out of practical educational activities, are not determined by the rules and norms governing the practice of the educational researcher. Rather, they occur when the practices employed in educational activities are in some sense inadequate to their purpose. They arise, in other words, when there is some discrepancy between an educational practice and the expectations in terms of which the practice was undertaken. Now the fact that educational problems occur because of this kind of non-fulfillment of expectations is informative; for to have expectations for a practice necessarily implies the possession of some prior beliefs and assumptions by virtue of which these expectations are explained and justified. Since, in this sense, those engaged in educational practices are already committed to some elaborate, if not explicit, set of beliefs about what they are doing, they already possess some theoretical framework that serves both to explain and direct their practices. Moreover, these expectations change, in response to the practical situations in which practitioners find themselves; that is, the beliefs that constitute their 'theoretical frameworks' are situationally embedded and shaped by particular histories of interactions in situations like and unlike the ones in which they find themselves. An educational problem, therefore, in denoting the failure of a practice, thereby implies a failure in the theory from which a belief in the efficacy of that practice is derived. By undermining the expectations of an educational practice, an educational problem undermines the validity of some logically prior theory or interpretation of an educational practice.

This same point can be made by reconsidering some of the issues discussed in the previous chapters. From the discussion of the 'interpretive' social sciences, for example, it is clear that when educational theorists set out to investigate educational situations, they will be confronted by a reality which is already permeated by the interpretations, beliefs and intentions of educational practitioners. What this means is that educational activities cannot be observed without reference to the shared educational values and beliefs of those engaged in educational pursuits. Again, following the discussion of Kuhn's account of science, it can be argued that the notion of 'paradigm' is very much applicable to a social institution like education. For just as a scientific paradigm provides a framework of assumptions which determine what is to constitute an approved scientific practice, so it is only against the background of a shared educational paradigm that educational practices can be made intelligible, not only to educational researchers, but also to educational practitioners as well. Only in terms of the intentions and beliefs provided by some paradigm can an educational practitioner understand his practice as a rational activity, and only within this framework of intentions and beliefs can the value which he places on these practices be made intelligible and justifiable. Furthermore, since the expected outcomes for educational practices are generated out of some educational paradigm, an educational problem indicates that at least some of the beliefs and assumptions it incorporates cannot be corroborated. In this sense, an educational problem constitutes a challenge to the paradigm's adequacy.

The major conclusions to be drawn from this account of the nature of educational problems and practices can be summarized in the following way. Since educational practitioners must already have some understanding of what they are doing and an elaborate, if not explicit, set of beliefs about why their practices make sense, they must already possess some 'theory' that serves to explain and direct their conduct. This entails that it is impossible for any researcher to observe an educational practice without any reference to the mode of understanding employed by the educational practitioner. The very identification of an educational practice depends on understanding the framework of thought that makes it count as a practice of that sort. However, although some elucidation of the interpretations of practitioners is a necessary feature of any research activity concerned to investigate educational problems, it is not sufficient. For to concede that educational problems arise out of the ideas and beliefs of educational practitioners is not to accept that those ideas and beliefs must be true. Practitioners' beliefs and preconceptions, although they may be constitutive of their practices, are also beliefs and preconceptions about the nature of the situations in which they are operating and the sort of consequence that their practices will have. As such, they always entail some minimal claims about the way things are that may turn out to be erroneous or false. Indeed, unless some distinction could be made between what practitioners think or believe they are doing and what they are doing, unless, that is, concrete realities impinge upon educational practices in ways not wholly determined by the practitioner's frame of mind, there would be no educational problems as such. It is precisely because there is some difference between what actually happens when teachers engage in educational practices, and their more or less accurate understanding of what is happening that educational problems occur. In this sense educational problems arise when expectations about practical situations are not congruent with the practical reality itself. In other words, an educational problem denotes a gap between a practitioner's theory and practice.

If educational problems arise because of gaps between a practice and the practitioner's theory about this practice, then it is clear that the notions of 'theory' and 'practice' can be interpreted very differently from the way in which they are normally understood in educational research. The purpose of the next section is to clarify these differences, and, by so doing, to suggest an alternative definition of theory and practice in education.

4 Theory and Practice: Redefining the Problem

It is apparent from the previous section that the notion of 'theory' can be used in various ways. It can, for example, be used to refer to the products of theoretical enquiries like psychology or sociology and, when used in this way, it is usually presented in the form of general laws, causal explanations, and the like. On the other hand, it can refer to the general theoretical framework that structures the activities through which these theories are produced. Used in this sense, it denotes the underlying 'paradigm' in terms of which a particular theoretical enterprise is practised. Phrases like 'psychological theory' or 'sociological theory' can therefore identify both the theoretical knowledge produced by those who engage in psychological enquiries (such as a theory of learning or a theory of social class) and also the particular theoretical framework that guides the activities of those engaged in psychological pursuits (such as behaviourism or functionalism). In effect, then, the 'theories' that arise out of activities like psychology are

no more than the formally stated outcome of practices (like psychological experimentation) that are themselves guided by 'theories' which
express how those who engage in these practices ought to proceed.

Now just as all theories are the product of some practical activity,
so all practical activities are guided by some theory. Teaching, for
example, although it is not concerned with the production of theories,
is similar to psychological experimentation in that it is a consciously
performed social practice that can only be understood by reference to
the framework of thought in terms of which its practitioners make
sense of what they are doing. Teachers could not even begin to
'practice' without some knowledge of the situation in which they are
operating and some idea of what it is that needs to be done. In this sense
those engaged in the 'practice' of education must already possess some
'theory' of education which structures their activities and guides their
decisions.

A 'practice', then, is not some kind of thoughtless behaviour
which exists separately from 'theory' and to which theory can be
'applied'. Furthermore, all practices, like all observations, have 'theory'
embedded in them and this is just as true for the practice of 'theoretical'
pursuits as it is for those of 'practical' pursuits like teaching. Both are
distinctive social activities conducted for distinctive purposes by means
of specific procedures and skills and in the light of particular beliefs and
values. The twin assumptions that all 'theory' is non-practical and all
'practice' is non-theoretical are, therefore, entirely misguided. Teachers
could no more teach without reflecting upon (and, hence, theorizing
about) what they are doing than theorists could produce theories
without engaging in the sort of practices distinctive of their activity.
'Theories' are not bodies of knowledge that can be generated out of a
practical vacuum and teaching is not some kind of robot-like mechanical performance that is devoid of any theoretical reflection. Both are
practical undertakings whose guiding theory consists of the reflective
consciousness of their respective practitioners.

The theories that inform theoretical pursuits like psychology, and
those that guide practical pursuits like teaching, share certain common
features. Both, for example, are the product of existing and ongoing
traditions and, as such, constitute the ways of thinking considered
appropriate to the institutional setting in which the respective activities
are undertaken. To talk of theorists and teachers, then, is to talk of
social communities whose members practise in conformity with a set
of beliefs, attitudes and expectations. While these two communities are
often different and institutionally separated, in practice they may

overlap to a greater or lesser degree, depending upon whose problems are being addressed and whether the *source* of the problem is dissatisfaction with a theory or with a practice. The fact that the guiding theory of a theoretical practice may be acquired in a more self-conscious way than that guiding an educational practice does not alter the fact that both are prescribed ways of thinking that are transmitted by a process of initiation.

Secondly, each mode of thought incorporates an interrelated set of concepts, beliefs, assumptions and values that allow events and situations to be interpreted in ways that are appropriate to their respective concerns. Psychological thinking, for example, may be structured around concepts like 'cognition', 'cognitive operations', 'semantic networks', and the like; while concepts such as 'teaching', 'learning' and 'enquiry method' are part of the conceptual background for educational discourse. Similarly, teachers, in explaining and justifying what they are doing, will reveal some commitment to various beliefs and assumptions about such things as how children learn and develop and the nature and value of certain kinds of knowledge. Theorists may also make assumptions about these things but they will, of course, be very different from those that teachers would adopt.

When 'theory' and 'practice' are looked at in this way, it becomes increasingly obvious that the kind of gaps between them that usually cause concern in educational research are not those occurring between a practice and the theory guiding that practice, but rather those that arise because it is assumed that 'educational theory' refers to theories *other than* those that already guide educational pursuits. The 'communication gap', for example, only arises when the language of educational theory is not the language of educational practice. Similarly, the gaps between educational theory and its practical application only exist because practitioners do not interpret or evaluate the theories that they are offered according to the criteria utilized by those engaged in theoretical pursuits.

Now the problem with this whole conception of educational theory is that it distorts, in several important respects, the relationship between theory and practice and the way in which gaps between them can occur. For example, to regard theory-practice gaps as problems of 'communication' or 'implementation' that are peculiar to practical activities like education, distorts the fact that a gap between theory and practice is the kind of practical problem that can also occur in the course of any theoretical undertaking. (For example, when a researcher interested in the comparative merits of progressive and traditional approaches to education uses tests which actually depend on a tradition-al view of education and therefore bias the objectivity of the compari-son.) Secondly, the assumption that these difficulties can somehow be identified and tackled 'in theory' and then 'applied' in practice tends to conceal how they are, in fact, generated out of the experience of practitioners and only emerge when the way in which these experiences are usually organized is found to be ineffective to their purpose. Thirdly, the view that the problems that these gaps create can be overcome by converting theoretical knowledge into rules of action overlooks the simple point that gaps between theory and practice, whether they occur for theoreticians or educators, are closed by the practitioners themselves formulating decisions in the light of the framework of understanding that they already possess. It also over-looks the fact that since it is only educational practitioners who actually engage in educational pursuits, it is the theory guiding *their* practices, rather than the theory guiding any theoretical practice, that constitutes the source of their educational principles, determines if and when any gaps between practice and these principles exist, and guides any decisions and actions that are taken to achieve their resolution.

The important points that need to be recognized, then, can be summarized like this. The gaps between theory and practice which everyone deplores are actually endemic to the view that educational theory can be produced from within theoretical and practical contexts different from the theoretical and practical context within which it is supposed to apply. Consequently, because this sort of view is so widespread, it is hardly surprising that the gaps thereby created are interpreted as impediments that can only be removed by finding ways of inducing teachers to accept and apply some theory other than the one they already hold. If, however, it is recognized that there is nothing to which the phrase 'educational theory' can coherently refer other than the theory that actually guides educational practices, then it becomes apparent that a theoretical activity explicitly concerned to influence educational practice can only do so by influencing the theoretical framework in terms of which these practices are made intelligible. 'Educational theory', on this view, is not an 'applied theory' that 'draws on' theories from the social sciences. Rather it refers to the whole enterprise of critically appraising the adequacy of the concepts, beliefs, assumptions and values incorporated in prevailing theories of educational practice.

This does not mean that the relationship of theory to practice is such that theory 'implies' practice, or is 'derived' from practice, or even 'reflects' practice. Rather, by subjecting the beliefs and justifications of existing and ongoing traditions to rational reconsideration, theory informs and transforms practice by informing and transforming the ways in which practice is experienced and understood. The transition is not, therefore, from theory to practice as such, but rather from irrationality to rationality, from ignorance and habit to knowledge and reflection. Furthermore, if educational theory is interpreted in this way, closing the gap between theory and practice is not a case of improving the practical effectiveness of the products of theoretical activities, but one of improving the practical effectiveness of the theories that teachers employ in conceptualizing their own activities. In this sense, reducing the gaps between theory and practice is the central *aim* of educational theory, rather than something that needs to be done *after* the theory has been produced, but *before* it can be effectively applied.

Once the relationship between theory, practice and problems is understood in this way, and once it is conceded that the investigation of educational problems is the only legitimate task for any coherent conception of educational research to pursue, then the strengths and weaknesses of both scientific and interpretive approaches can be more readily assessed. One of the strengths of the natural scientific approach is its aspiration to employ methodological principles designed to guard against the intrusion of bias, prejudice and ideology. Another is its claim that there may be factors operative in educational situations which remain opaque to the self-understandings of practitioners and cannot be explained by reference to their intentions and beliefs. Since these same methodological principles require, however, that the process of producing theoretical explanations be kept separate from the field to which they apply, the scientific approach mistakenly assumes that it is possible to resolve educational problems without influencing the frameworks of thought in terms of which these problems arise. To so assume that solutions to educational problems can be produced in a theoretical context other than the social and historical context in which they emerge, not only reveals a failure to appreciate the significance of the extensive theoretical powers that educational practitioners already possess. It also overlooks the simple point that educational problems are not resolved by converting theoretical solutions into technical recommendations which can be mechanically and passively applied. Rather, they are generated out of the experiences of practitioners and only emerge when the ways in which these experiences are usually organized are found to be inadequate. Because it is not directly concerned to help practitioners organize their experiences more adequately, the scientific conception of educational research is not really concerned with *educational* problems at all.

The 'interpretive' approach, of course, rejects the image of the practitioner as a consumer of scientific theories and recognizes instead that educational research must be rooted in the concepts and theories that practitioners have themselves acquired and developed to serve their educational purposes. It is, therefore, entirely correct to insist that educational research cannot rely on methods and techniques designed to produce scientific theories, but must instead adopt procedures for uncovering the theories in terms of which educational practices are conducted and made intelligible. If this connection between the theoretical accounts produced through research and the practitioner's own mode of thinking is not made, then the research will be divorced from the theoretical context in which educational practices are conducted and any *educational* character it may have will be hard to find.

Although this emphasis on uncovering the implicit theorizing of practitioners constitutes the major strength of the interpretive approach, its tendency to assume that this more or less exhausts the purpose of educational research constitutes its major weakness. For since educational problems occur only when the self-understandings of practitioners are inadequate, any research activity concerned to resolve these problems cannot rest content with a theoretical description of the practitioner's own meanings and interpretations. Rather, it must be able to make evaluative judgments about their validity and suggest alternative explanations that are in some sense better. This kind of research will not be interpretive. On the contrary, in so far as it recognizes the inadequacies of, and seeks to replace, the practitioner's own interpretations, the theories it generates will be incompatible with them. By limiting its task to the explication of the practitioner's own interpretations and by rejecting explanations incompatible with them, the interpretive approach offers no way of critically examining any defects that they may possess. Indeed, by refusing to recognize any evaluative criteria for assessing practitioners' interpretations and by failing to provide alternative explanations against which their existing interpretations can be judged, an interpretive approach to educational research excludes any concern with resolving educational *problems* at all.

Looked at in this way, it becomes increasingly clear that the inadequacies of natural scientific and interpretive approaches to educational research are such that the strengths of one are the weaknesses of the other. The scientific approach, by ignoring the fact that educational problems are always pre-interpreted, effectively eliminates their *educational* character. The interpretive approach, by insulating the self-understandings of practitioners from direct, concrete and practical criticism, effectively eliminates their *problematic* character. Any conception of educational research that takes its purpose seriously must, therefore, resist both the scientific tendency to assimilate practical educational problems to theoretical scientific problems, and the interpretive tendency to assimilate theoretical understanding to a descriptive record of practitioners' own understanding. What, in short, must be resisted is any suggestion that these two approaches to educational research constitute mutually exclusive and exhaustive possibilities.

More positively, it is clear that what is required is a view of educational research that is both 'interpretive' and scientific. 'Interpretive' in the sense that it generates theories that can be grasped and utilized by practitioners in terms of their own concepts and theories; 'scientific' in the sense that these theories provide a coherent challenge to the beliefs and assumptions incorporated in the theories of educational practice that practitioners actually employ. The findings assembled through research and any new theories it may offer will have little *educational* validity if they are unrelated to the theories and understandings of educational practitioners. And they will have little *educational* value if they do not enable practitioners to develop a more refined understanding of what they are doing and what they are trying to achieve. In this sense, the only legitimate task for any educational research to pursue is to develop theories of educational practice that are rooted in the concrete educational experiences and situations of practitioners and that attempt to confront and resolve the educational problems to which these experiences and situations give rise.

5 Educational Research and Science

Although the previous section suggests that it is misguided to believe that educational problems can be resolved by applying theoretical solutions produced by existing scientific disciplines, it would be equally misguided to infer from this that educational research cannot achieve the status of a scientific enterprise. Achieving this status is not simply a matter of importing methods and techniques from the established sciences. Rather, is it a question of determining whether educational problems can be confronted in ways which are consistent with the principles and rules that govern the conduct of scientific enquiry and in terms of which the conclusions of such enquiries can be given the status of scientific knowledge.

Although views about the nature of science are always contentious, the standard view in educational research is the hypothetico-deductive view that the distinctive features of scientific theories are their deductive validity and their empirical testability. As noted in Chapter 2,[6] deductive validity is achieved by ensuring that what a theory explains (the explanandum), can be validly deduced from the general statements and initial conditions adduced to explain it (the explanans). Empirical testability requires that the generalization incorporated in a scientific theory has the logical standing of an empirical hypothesis, the truth of which can be verified by measuring their deductive implications against observed results.

Some of the criticisms levelled at this view of scientific theories by those subscribing to what is often called the 'new philosophy of science' were discussed in Chapter 2. One of the original criticisms, made by Karl Popper[7], pointed to the fact that no number of true deductive inferences from a theory ever justified the conclusion that the theory was true. No matter how many instances of metals expanding when heated are observed, the truth of an unrestricted generalization, to the effect that 'all metals expand when heated', can still be doubted. However, argued Popper, while scientific theories cannot be verified by particular observations, they can be so falsified or refuted. For one instance of metal *not* expanding when heated conclusively refutes the theory that all metals expand when heated. In short, while true empirical deductions do not entail the truth of a theory, false empirical consequences necessarily refute it. Since, for this reason, only the falsity of a theory can be legitimately inferred from empirical tests, a theory is only testable, and hence only scientific, if some imaginable observation would refute it.

Popper's reformulation of the logic of scientific theories not only marked an important contribution to an understanding of the nature of science; it also led to some new ways of thinking about the purpose of the scientific method, the status of scientific knowledge and the nature of scientific progress. Thus it follows from the Popperian view that the crucial role of method is not to confirm, verify or prove scientific theories, but rather to challenge, evaluate and, if possible, refute the 'conjectures' normally advanced to explain some state of affairs. Moreover, if scientific theories can never be conclusively verified, then all scientific knowledge has a permanent provisional character and to try and prove a theory or justify a belief in its absolute truth is both misguided and unscientific. A justificatory rationality, that is, a rationality which allows for scientific theories and knowledge to be conclusively proved, is not possible. All that rationality permits is the acceptance of theories that can withstand criticism. In science, the purpose of reason is to be critical not justificatory.

Given this, it follows that science does not have any secure foundations on which a body of certain justified knowledge can be erected and hence that scientific progress cannot be a culminative process in which a corpus of true knowledge is painstakingly collected. Rather, scientific progress is more like an evolutionary struggle for survival in which competing theories are continuously being threatened with extinction and replacement by better, more 'fitter' theories. Furthermore, these better theories are not discovered by any distinctively scientific procedure, but arise out of the imaginative, creative, and sometimes speculative 'conjectures' put forward so as to overcome the errors in existing theories and resolve the problems that these errors cause. They are scientific only if, and when, they themselves become vulnerable to critical assessment and possible elimination; and they are better than those they have displaced just because they can withstand the range of confrontations with experience that their predecessors could not.

It is, at this point, that the Popperian view of science runs into serious difficulties. For if, as Popper suggests, theories can be conclusively refuted by bringing them into confrontation with single observations of counter-instances, then this assumes that it is possible to make theory-free observations which are true. Now, of course, this stands in stark contradiction to the view, shared by Popper, that observations are themselves always theory laden. But this means that theories can never be conclusively falsified because observation statements can never be theory-neutral and can never be conclusively true. In short, Popper's account requires that observation statements remain independent of theories, while at the same time conceding that this is not possible.

Philosophers of science have responded to this tension in the Popperian account in different ways. Those sympathetic to Popper's views have tried to refine and extend his account in ways which will overcome its internal difficulties.[8] Others have been more critical and have responded by rejecting the Popperian account in favour of some radically different alternative.[9] Despite the numerous disagreements between Popper's supporters and critics, however, what has emerged from their arguments and deliberations is a distinctive 'post-empiricists' philosophy which generates an image of science very different from the orthodox positivist account. Furthermore, there can be little doubt that this new philosophy of science constitutes a significant improvement over the traditional positivist philosophy and undermines many of its basic tenets. Some of the ways in which positivist assumptions are challenged by the new view of science are worth mentioning.

First, it repudiates the positivist idea that science is concerned with a quest for certainty and truth and argues instead that it is only by acknowledging the impossibility of absolute knowledge and the fallibility of all beliefs that genuine scientific progress is possible. Science is concerned not so much with gaining access to some absolute truth as with eliminating the prejudices and dogma that distort everyday commonsense thinking. In science, therefore, there is no indubitable 'given'. Rather, it develops by critically assessing commonsense knowledge and assumptions; by showing how the theories implicit in commonsense thinking lead to undesirable or unintended results, or by showing how some alternative theory either has certain advantages over commonsense understanding or offers a more adequate explanation of reality. 'In science,' says Popper, 'our starting point is commonsense and our greatest instrument for progress is criticism'.[10]

Secondly, the new philosophy of science rejects the image of the scientist as a spectator passively observing and recording the world of nature. Theories are created by individuals to explain their world rather than being discovered from the world. Furthermore, since all observations and language are impregnated with theories, the role of the scientist is not to produce theories so much as to examine and challenge the theories that are already embodied in language and commonsense.

Thirdly, in the light of this new image of science, it becomes increasingly clear that positivist philosophy, by focusing on the logic of the proof employed to demonstrate the truth of the theoretical end-products of scientific enquiry, failed to recognize the importance of the process of enquiry that science employs. For what distinguishes scientific knowledge is not so much its logical status, as the fact that it is the outcome of a process of enquiry which is governed by critical norms and standards of rationality. Thus, scientific 'objectivity' is not something that can be secured by mechanically applying some logical proof or by appealing to a realm of uninterpreted neutral 'facts'. 'Objectivity' involves not a naive belief in neutrality so much as a shared intersubjective agreement about the sort of norms of enquiry and standards of rationality which will ensure that theories can be critically assessed without the undue intervention of subjective bias and personal prejudice. In this sense, scientific objectivity is not that which corresponds to some neutral reality. Rather, 'objective' reality is itself that which corresponds to the intersubjective agreement of a community of enquirers whose deliberations are conducted in accordance with shared standards of rationality. 'Objectivity', therefore, is achieved when participants reveal a willingness to make their views and preconceptions available for critical inspection and to engage in discussion and argument that is open and impartial.

Finally, this recognition of the intersubjective dimension of scientific objectivity makes it clear that science cannot occur in a social vacuum. It always presupposes the existence of a critical community of enquirers which is open and pluralistic, where all are free to criticize the thinking of others and everyone can actively participate on equal terms. It also requires an appreciation of the historical and social contexts within which questions arise and possibilities for action are shaped and regulated. Furthermore, as some of the advocates of the new view of science have clearly recognized[11], such a self-critical, open scientific community itself depends on and seeks to support democratic ideals and a democratic form of social life. In this respect, they share Dewey's view that:

> ... Democracy as compared with other ways of life is the sole way of living ... which is capable of generating the science which is the sole dependable authority for the direction of further experience.... For every way of life that fails in its democracy limits the contacts, the exchanges, the communications, the interactions by which experience is ... enlarged and enriched.[12]

6 Towards a Science of Educational Research

From what has been said so far in this chapter it is clear that one of the major weaknesses of much educational research is its failure to offer adequate criteria for distinguishing research that is genuinely 'educational' from research of a purely 'theoretical' and, hence, non-educational character. Because of this oversight, the crucial point that the purpose of educational research is to develop theories that are grounded in the problems and perspectives of educational practice (rather than the problems and perspectives of some social scientific practice) has frequently been overlooked. A second failing of many contemporary discussions has been a failure to distinguish between questions about the extent to which existing social sciences can contribute to the solution of educational problems, and questions about the extent to which educational research can, or should, conform to scientific criteria of adequacy. The purpose of this concluding section is to indicate briefly some of the basic features of a theory of educational research which does not assume any intrinsic connection between the traditional methods and goals of the social sciences and the practical problems of education.

It has already been noted how educational practices are always conducted in the light of some conception of what is desirable and some understanding of what is possible. Hence, they incorporate beliefs and theoretical understandings about such things as the nature of an existing situation, the possibilities for change, and the most effective way to bring it about. At the same time they reflect certain values and principles, in terms of which desirable goals and chosen and acceptable means to their realization are justified.

Now, because these theoretical preconceptions are largely the product of habit, precedent and tradition, they are rarely formulated in any explicit way or informed by any clearly articulated process of thought. Indeed, a distinctive feature of the beliefs and values in terms of which everyday educational judgments are made is that their truth is regarded as self-evident so that they are accepted and adopted in an uncritical and non-reflective way. It is precisely this unquestioning attitude towards conventional educational thinking that ensures that any critical assessment of its merits can be systematically avoided.

Looked at in this way, it becomes apparent that a primary task for any research activity concerned to adopt a scientific approach to educational problems is to emancipate teachers from their dependence on habit and tradition by providing them with the skills and resources that will enable them to reflect upon and examine critically the inadequacies of different conceptions of educational practice. Hence, a first requirement of scientific educational research is for methodological strategies that do not simply test and refine 'scientific knowledge', but rather expose and eliminate the inadequacies of the beliefs and values that are implicit in educational practice and that are regarded as self-evidently true by educational practitioners. This does not mean that 'practical' ways of thinking must be abandoned in favour of some 'theoretical' mode of thought. What is being abandoned is an unreflective attitude so that a more critical, scientific attitude can be adopted towards established educational creeds. Hence, science does not *replace* existing theories of educational practice so much as *improve* them, by subjecting the beliefs and justifications which sustain them to criticism. For it is only by so challenging current educational certainties that the interpretations and judgments of educators will become more coherent and less dependent on the prejudices and dogma that permeate unreflective educational thinking. The point of educational research is, therefore, not merely to produce better theories about education or more 'effective' practices; educational research of the kind being advocated makes practice more 'theoretical' in that it is enriched by critical reflection and simultaneously remains 'practical', in the sense that it helps to make the judgments which inform educational practice more trenchant. In short, the purpose of educational research is to ensure that the observations, interpretations and judgments of educational practitioners can become more coherent and rational and thereby acquire a greater degree of scientific objectivity.

In determining the relevance and importance of science to educational research, therefore, a distinction needs to be made between educational research conceived on the one hand as a straightforward application of the scientific disciplines to educational problems, and on the other as the scientific investigation of the problems that arise out of educational practice. This is much more than a semantic distinction, for if the former interpretation is rejected in favour of the latter, then it is possible to deny that the aims and methods of the social sciences are necessarily the aims and methods of educational research; yet, at the same time, to recognize that they may provide important insights and sophisticated procedures for extending understanding of educational problems. Hence, educational research may have some need for the concepts, methods, theories and techniques of social scientific forms of research, but this only means that they constitute a fund of useful *resources*, rather than the *source* of educational theories and knowledge. Indeed, if educational research is wholly committed to the investigation of educational problems, then it will be based on a realization that the only genuine source of educational theories and knowledge is the practical experiences out of which these problems are generated, and that the proper concern of educational research is with formulating theories that are grounded in the realities of educational practice.

The idea that research should be more concerned with formulating 'grounded theory' has been explored in some detail by Glaser and Strauss[13] and some aspects of their position are worth mentioning. First, they show how social scientific research has become preoccupied with the testing and verification of existing theories and so neglected 'the prior step of discovering what concepts and hypotheses are relevant for the area one wishes to research'.[14] To remedy this situation they suggest that 'the generation of theory by logical deduction from *a priori* assumptions' be replaced by 'the discovery of theory from data systematically obtained from research'.[15] Only this kind of 'grounded theory', they maintain, will readily 'fit' the situation being researched, be understandable to 'significant laymen', and be suited to its supposed uses.

Secondly, they distinguish between two kinds of grounded theory: 'substantive' and 'formal'.

> By substantive theory we mean that developed for a substantive, or empirical area of . . . enquiry, such as . . . professional education. . . . By formal theory, we mean that developed for a formal or conceptual area of . . . enquiry, such as . . . socialization or social mobility.[16]

Thirdly, they argue that 'substantive theory faithful to the empirical situation cannot . . . be formulated merely by applying a few ideas from an established formal theory to the substantive area'.[17] Rather, relevant concepts, hypotheses and problems must be inductively developed from the 'raw data' provided by a study of the substantive area. Only then will it be possible to decide whether any formal theories are of use in furthering the formulation of adequate substantive theory.

If the proposal that educational research should adopt research strategies and methods that are appropriate to the development of 'grounded' substantive theories is taken seriously, then some important changes to existing research procedures would seem to be required. In the first place, it will need to be organized by an awareness of how any attempt to transform 'substantive' educational problems into a series of 'formal' theoretical questions merely deprives them of their essentially practical character and thereby misconceives the proper purpose of educational research. Hence, implicit in this view is a rejection of the belief that adequate educational theories can be produced by importing theories developed for areas of social scientific enquiry, such as 'motivation', 'learning', 'socialization' or 'deviance'. Instead, it has to be recognized that the task of educational research is to generate 'substantive' theories that are grounded in the complexities of practical reality and are not distorted by the imposition of 'formal' theories that effectively predetermine what the relevant research problems and categories are going to be.

Secondly, if research is to generate a body of theory that has as its focus of concern the resolution of educational problems, then the criteria according to which this theory is tested and assessed will need to be changed. In particular, the idea that existing and established social scientific theories are transformed into educational theories, simply because they are verified by data drawn from educational sources, needs to be resisted. So also must the practice of employing purely theoretical criteria to assess the value or validity of any educational theories that research may provide. Moreover, if educational research is rooted in an awareness of how educational theories are intrinsically related to educational practice, then it will be organized by a realization of the fact that the concrete practical experiences of teachers provide both the subject matter for theoretical enquiry and the testing ground on which the results of this enquiry must be based. Hence, it will be acknowledged that 'theory' only acquires a 'scientific' status when it suggests improved ways of understanding these experiences, and only acquires educational validity when these suggestions are tested and confirmed by practical experience. What this means is that the idea that theory can be devised and tested independently of practice and then used to correct, improve or assess any educational practice is rejected in favour of the diametrically opposite view that theory only acquires an educational character insofar as it can itself be corrected, improved and assessed in the light of its practical consequences. In this sense, it is practice that determines the value of any educational theory, rather than theory that determines the value of any educational practice.

A third requirement of the kind of research being envisaged is a recognition of how the problems it seeks to confront only arise for, and can only be resolved by, educational practitioners. As a result, it acknowledges that the success of research is entirely dependent on the extent to which it encourages teachers to develop a more refined understanding of their own problems and practices. Under this view, therefore, it is entirely inappropriate for researchers to treat teachers as objects for scientific inspection, or as clients who accept and apply scientific solutions. Rather, since the practical experience of teachers is the source of the problems under consideration, it must be recognized that the active participation of practitioners in the research enterprise is an indispensable necessity.

Interpreted in this way, educational research would be 'scientific' in the sense that it is subject to notions of cogency, rigour and critical reflection, and 'practical' in that it respects and preserves the actual context in which educational practices are conducted, educational problems emerge, and any solutions to them are tested. But to implement this conception of research is not an easy task, for it depends on researchers being prepared to merge their separate identities and collaborate with teachers in a common effort to resolve educational problems and improve educational practices. Indeed, from this perspective, teachers themselves must become educational reseachers, and professional researchers who are not teachers will only have a subsidiary role of supporting or facilitating teacher enquiry. This does not mean that educational research must be limited to 'practical' classroom matters. But what it does suggest is that educational research must look beyond a conception of social science as either scientific or interpretive and that some alternative epistemological basis is required. More particularly, it means that the proper development of educational research depends upon a model of educational science which is 'educational' in that it integrates theory and practice in its accounts of the nature of theory, and which is 'scientific' in that it regards the purpose of theory to be one of criticizing unsatifactory elements in practical thinking and of indicating how they may be eliminated. It is with the development of an epistemological framework within which such an educational science can be articulated, that the next chapter is concerned.

Further Reading

Examples of educational research textbooks that advocate a scientific approach abound. See, for example, N.J. Entwistle and J.D. Nisbet's *Educational Research in Action*. For a book which suggests a more interpretive approach to educational research see David Hamilton *et al.* (Eds) *Beyond the Numbers Game*.

As a problem for discussion and debate, the problem of relating educational theory and practice receives more attention than most. For a collection of articles dealing with the problem the two–volume book edited by Hartnett and Naish, *Theory and the Practice of Education*, is most worthwhile. For a general introduction to the new philosophy of science see A.F. Chalmers', *What is this Thing called Science?* More difficult is Lakatos and Musgrave (Eds), *Criticism and the Growth of Knowledge*. This is a collection of essays which discuss some of the implications of the views of Popper and Kuhn.

Notes

1 Probably the most influential of these was Alexander Bain whose book *Education as Science* appeared in 1879 (London, Kegan Paul). For a discussion of early arguments about the scientific status of educational research see SMITH, J.V. and HAMILTON, D. (Eds) (1980), *The Meritocratic Intellect: Studies in the History of Educational Research*, Elmsford, Pergamon, Aberdeen University Press.
2 KUHN, T.S. (1970), *The Structure of Scientific Revolutions*, (2nd edn.), Chicago, University of Chicago Press.
3 For a recent example see the opening chapters of BEARD, R. and VERMA, G. *What Is Educational Research?* Hants, Gower.
4 LANGFORD, G. (1973), 'The concept of education' in LANGFORD, G. and O'CONNOR, D.J. (Eds) *New Essays in the Philosophy of Education*, London, Routledge and Kegan Paul.
5 GAUTHIER, D.P. (1963), *Practical Reasoning*, London, Oxford University Press, chapter 1.
6 See chapter 2, section 4.
7 POPPER, K. (1969), *Conjectures and Refutations*, London, Routledge and Kegan.
8 See LAKATOS, I. (1970), 'Falsification and the methodology of scientific research programmes', in LAKATOS, I. and MUSGRAVE, F. (Eds) *Criticism and the Growth of Knowledge*, Cambridge, Cambridge University Press, pp. 91–195.
9 See, especially, KUHN, T.S. (1970), *The Structure of Scientific Revolutions*, (2nd edn)., Chicago, University of Chicago Press; and FEYERABEND, P.K. (1975), *Against Method: Outlines of an Anarchist Theory of Knowledge*, London, New Left Books.
10 POPPER, K.R. (1972), 'Two faces of common sense: an argument for common sense realism and against the common sense theory of knowledge', in *Objective Knowledge: An Evolutionary Approach*, Oxford, Clarendon Press.
11 See, especially, POPPER, K.R. (1966), *The Open Society and its Enemies*, London, Routledge and Kegan Paul.
12 DEWEY, J. (1939), *Freedom and Culture*, New York, G.P. Putnams and Sons, p. 102.
13 GLASER, B. and STRAUSS, A. (1967), *The Discovery of Grounded Theory*, Chicago, Aldine.
14 *Ibid.*, p. 2.
15 *Ibid.*, pp. 2–3.
16 *Ibid.*, p. 32.
17 *Ibid.*, p. 33.

Chapter 5

A Critical Approach to Theory and Practice

From the discussions of the previous three chapters, it is now possible to identify some of the formal requirements that any approach to educational theory needs to accept First, following the criticisms of positivism made in Chapter 2, it is apparent that *educational theory must reject positivist notions of rationality, objectivity and truth.* In particular, the positivist idea that knowledge has a purely instrumental value in solving educational problems and the consequent tendency to see all educational issues as technical in character needs to be firmly resisted. Secondly, following what was said in Chapter 3 about the importance of grasping the meanings that educational practices have for those who perform them, *educational theory must accept the need to employ the interpretive categories of teachers.* Indeed, the arguments of Chapter 3 suggest that for educational theory to have any subject-matter at all, it must be rooted in the self-understandings of educational practitioners.

However, the recognition that educational theory must be grounded in the interpretations of teachers, is not in itself sufficient. For while it may be true that consciousness 'defines reality', it is equally true that reality may systematically distort consciousness. Indeed, one of the major weaknesses of the interpretive model identified in Chapter 3 was its failure to realize how the self-understandings of individuals may be shaped by illusory beliefs which sustain irrational and contradictory forms of social life. For this reason, a third feature of any adequate approach to educational theory is that *it must provide ways of distinguishing ideologically distorted interpretations from those that are not. It must also provide some view of how any distorted self-understanding is to be overcome.*

Another related weakness of the 'interpretive' approach discussed in Chapter 3 is the failure to recognize that many of the aims and purposes that teachers pursue are not the result of conscious choice so much as the constraints contained in a social structure over which they have little, if any, direct control. A fourth requirement for educational theory, then, is that *it must be concerned to identify and expose those aspects of the existing social order which frustrate the pursuit of rational goals and must be able to offer theoretical accounts which make teachers aware of how they may be eliminated or overcome.*

The fifth requirement emerging out of the discussion in Chapter 4 is the need to recognize that educational theory is practical, in the sense that *the question of its educational status will be determined by the ways in which its relates to practice.* For this reason, educational theory cannot simply explain the source of the problems that practitioners may face. Nor can it rest content with trying to solve problems by getting teachers to adopt or apply any solutions it may produce. Rather, its purpose is to inform and guide the practices of educators by indicating the actions that they need to take if they are to overcome their problems and eliminate their difficulties. In this sense, educational theory must always be orientated towards transforming the ways in which teachers see themselves and their situation so that the factors frustrating their educational goals and purposes can be recognized and eliminated. Equally, it must be oriented towards transforming the situations which place obstacles in the way of achieving educational goals, perpetuate ideological distortions, and impede rational and critical work in educational situations.

A view of theory and research that incorporates these five requirements has been developed and articulated by a community of philosophers and social scientists who are usually referred to as the 'Frankfurt School'.[1] What, in general terms, unites these people is the belief that the all-pervading influence of positivism has resulted in a widespread growth of instrumental rationality and a tendency to see all practical problems as technical issues. This has created the illusion of an 'objective reality' over which the individual has no control, and hence to a decline in the capacity of individuals to reflect upon their own situations and change them through their own actions. An overriding concern of the Frankfurt School, therefore, has been to articulate a view of theory that has the central task of emancipating people from the positivist 'domination of thought' through their own understandings and actions.

This view of theory is usually labelled 'critical theory'[2] and the purpose of this chapter is to outline some of its central features. In doing this, it needs to be recognised that the term 'critical theory' can be interpreted in various ways. To some, critical theory is primarily an attempt to overcome some of the weaknesses of orthodox Marxism;[3] to others, it is part of a long-standing dispute about hermeneutic philosophy.[4] Yet others see it as an attempt to synthesise neo-Wittgensteinian philosophy with European philosophy.[5] In this chapter, primary emphasis is given to how critical theory has generated the idea of a *critical social science* and a view of the theory-practice relationship which is very different from that suggested by positivist and interpretive social sciences.

1 Critical Theory: the Background

One of the central aims of critical theory has been to reassess the relationship between theory and practice in the light of the criticisms of the positivist and interpretive approaches to social science which have emerged over the last century. Early critical theorists, such as Max Horkheimer, Theodore Adorno and Herbert Marcuse, were concerned with the dominance of positivist science and the degree to which it had become a powerful element in twentieth-century ideology. The success of research in the physical sciences led to attempts to emulate that success in the social sciences. The animate world was being treated as 'methodologically' equivalent to the inanimate, and the forms of reasoning appropriate for dealing with the inanimate world were being applied increasingly and impetuously to the human and social worlds. By the late 1920s, the early critical theorists could already see that the instrumental rationality of positivism had begun to generate a complacency about the role of science in society and about the nature of science itself. The role of science had become technical — feeding instrumental reasoning and providing the methods and principles for solving technical problems of producing given outcomes; and science itself had become doctrinaire, believing itself to have solved the essential problems of the nature of truth and diminishing the field of epistemology to the philosophy of science. Science, it was argued, had become 'scientistic', believing in its supreme power to answer all significant questions.

In the complacency of modern science, the critical theorists saw a great danger for modern society: the threat of the end of reason itself. Reason had been replaced by technique, critical thinking about society by scientistic rule following The very success of the natural sciences had created conditions under which the imaginative probings of scientists into the unexplained were turned into conformity with established ways of thinking. Science had become an ideology, a culturally produced and socially supported, unexamined way of seeing the world which shapes and guides social action. As such, science's role had become one of legitimating social action by providing 'objective facts' to justify courses of action. Questions of the values underlying these courses of action were believed to be beyond the scope of science and were thus left unexamined. Scientific results merely distinguished more effective courses of action from less effective ones and explained how outcomes occurred — not whether or not they should be allowed to occur. Far from being a relentless enquiry into the nature and conduct of social life, science was in danger of taking the forms of social life for granted and reflecting only on 'technical' issues.

The intellectual project of critical theory thus required recovering from early philosophy the elements of social thought which uniquely concerned the values, judgments and interests of humankind, and integrating them into a framework of thought which could provide a new and justifiable approach to social science. In undertaking this task, the critical theorists returned to the work of Aristotle and considered his conception of '*praxis*' as 'doing', rather than making. For Aristotle, the 'practical arts' like ethics, politics and education were not rigorous sciences. Rather, because of their practical intent and the nature of their subject matter, they had to rest content with a form of knowledge that was uncertain and incomplete. In these areas, theory referred exclusively to *praxis* and the disposition to be cultivated was *phronesis*; that is, a prudent understanding of what should be done in practical situations. With the rise of modern science, especially in the latter part of the nineteenth century, this classical conception of practical theory as a process for cultivating the character of the individual had been drastically altered, and what was once assumed to be a means of individual enlightenment had fallen prey to the methodological prohibitions of positivism. By the 1970s, 'theory' had begun to mean law-like generalizations which could be used to make predictions and, where appropriate variables could be manipulated, produce desirable states of affairs. In this sense, the sphere of the 'practical' had been absorbed into the sphere of the 'technical' and problems of 'right living' were transformed into the technical problem of regulating social arrangements in accordance with some predetermined values.

For the critical theorists, the principal loss incurred by this transformation was the replacement of a view of 'theory' which focused directly on the practical by a view of 'theory' in which access to practice is conceived as a technical process. As such, ethical categories were eliminated from the legitimate field of theoretical discourse, and the potential of reason to generate theories of enlightened action was no longer considered seriously. Rationality was now exhaustively defined in terms of a conformity to the rules of scientific thinking, and, as such, deprived of all creative, critical and evaluative powers.

At the same time, critical theorists acknowledged that not all of the effects of the expansion of science were negative. On the positive side, the introduction of a rigorous conception of objective knowledge into the study of human and social life was regarded as a major gain. Given this recognition of the important contribution of science, the principal dilemma for critical theory was to develop a conception of social science which would somehow combine the practical intentions informing the classical view of *praxis* with the rigour and explanatory power associated with modern science. Just as positivism had sought previously to rescue the social sciences from philosophy by insisting on a logical unity with the natural sciences, so critical theory sought to rescue the social sciences from the natural sciences by preserving the concerns of classical 'practical philosophy' with the qualities and values inherent in human life. Finding a meta-theory in terms of which this synthesis could be accomplished has been the primary task of one of the leading contemporary critical theorists, Jurgen Habermas. 'How', asks Habermas,

> . . . can we obtain clarification of what is practically necessary and at the same time objectively possible? This question can be translated back into our historical context: how can the promise of practical politics — namely of providing practical orientation about what is right and just in a given situation — be redeemed without relinquishing, on the one hand, the rigor of scientific knowledge, which modern social philosophy demands, in contrast to the practical philosophy of classicism? And on the other, how can the promise of social philosophy to furnish an analysis of the interrelationships of social life, be redeemed without relinquishing the practical orientation of classical politics?[6]

In attempting to elaborate coherent answers to these questions, Habermas has, in various works[7], developed the idea of a critical social science that can be located 'between philosophy and science'. It is with the formulation of this idea that the next section is concerned.

2 Habermas's Critical Social Science

In developing his theory of a critical social science, one of Habermas' principal targets is the positivist belief in the logical and methodological unity of the natural and social sciences. For Habermas, this is just one more example of 'scientism' — 'science's belief in itself' — which, by evaluating all knowledge in terms of natural scientific knowledge, makes it virtually impossible to comprehend science as just one form of knowledge among others. In order to show how this involves a reversal of the proper relationship between epistemology and science, and how it is science that should be justified by epistemology and not vice versa, Habermas critically examined the way in which this positivist understanding of knowledge is legitimized. In the course of his examination, he elaborated a theory of knowledge which seriously undermined 'scientism' in two specific ways. First, by trying to show how science offers just one kind of knowledge among others, Habermas seeks to refute any claims that science can define the standards in terms of which all knowledge can be measured. Secondly, in opposition to the claim that science offers an objective or neutral account of reality, Habermas tries to reveal how different kinds of knowledge are shaped by the particular human interest that they serve.

Habermas calls his theory of knowledge a theory of 'knowledge-constitutive interests'. It is so called because he rejects any idea that knowledge is produced by some sort of 'pure' intellectual act in which the knowing subject is himself 'disinterested'. Knowledge is never the outcome of a 'mind' that is detached from everyday concerns. On the contrary, it is always constituted on the basis of interests that have developed out of the natural needs of the human species and that have been shaped by historical and social conditions. Indeed, without the whole range of needs and desires incorporated in the human species, human beings would have no interest in acquiring knowledge at all.

For Habermas, then, knowledge is the outcome of human activity that is motivated by natural needs and interests. He calls them 'knowledge-constitutive interests' because they are interests which guide and shape the way knowledge is constituted in different human activities. According to Habermas, these 'knowledge-constitutive interests' are 'transcendental' or '*a priori*', in the sense that they are presupposed by any cognitive act and hence constitute the possible modes of thought through which reality may be constituted and acted upon.

Habermas contends that human knowledge is constituted by virtue of three knowledge-constitutive interests which he labels the 'technical', the 'practical' and the 'emancipatory'. The first of these, the *technical* interest, is the interest of human beings in acquiring knowledge that will facilitate their technical control over natural objects. The knowledge resulting from this interest is typically instrumental knowledge taking the form of scientific explanations. However, by saying that this kind of knowledge relates to a technical interest, Habermas does not mean that the pursuit of this knowledge is always motivated by a concern for its technical application. On the contrary, the form that this knowledge takes requires a 'disinterested' attitude. Moreover, he is quick to point out that the technical interest has produced much of the knowledge necessary for modern industry and production processes, and that this knowledge will remain necessary if humankind is to enjoy the material rewards of production. Habermas is not, therefore, concerned to denigrate technical knowledge, but only to reject any claim that it is the only type of legitimate knowledge.

In rejecting this claim, Habermas argues that knowledge of the symbolically structured domain of 'communicative action' is not reducible to scientific knowledge. To understand others requires grasping the social meanings constitutive of social reality. Drawing on the hermeneutic tradition, Habermas argues that the *Verstehen* methods provide knowledge which serve a 'practical interest' in understanding and clarifying the conditions for meaningful communication and dialogue. In this sense, the 'practical interest' generates knowledge in the form of interpretive understanding which can inform and guide practical judgment.

At the same time, however, Habermas maintains that the methods of the interpretive approach cannot provide an adequate basis for the social sciences. For, any reduction of the social sciences to the explication of subjective meanings fails to recognize that the subjective meanings that characterize social life are themselves conditioned by an objective context that limits both the scope of individuals' intentions and the possibility of their realization. By adopting an epistemology for the process of self-understanding that excludes critically questioning the content of such understanding, the interpretive approach cannot assess the extent to which any existing forms of communication may be systematically distorted by prevailing social, cultural or political conditions.

What this means is that the 'practical' interest in communication can only be adequately pursued when alienating conditions have been recognized and eliminated. There is, Habermas argues, a basic human interest in rational autonomy and freedom which issues in a demand for

the intellectual and material conditions in which non-alienated communication and interaction can occur. This emancipatory interest
requires going beyond any narrow concern with subjective meanings
in order to acquire an emancipatory knowledge of the objective
framework within which communication and social action occur. It is
with this emancipatory knowledge that a critical social science is
essentially concerned.

Habermas maintains that each of these knowledge-constitutive
interests takes form in a particular means of social organization or
'medium', and that the knowledge each interest generates gives rise to a
different science. The end result of Habermas' analysis is, therefore, a
three-tiered model of 'interests', 'knowledge', 'media' and 'science',
which can be represented diagrammatically in the following way:

Interest	Knowledge	Medium	Science
Technical	Instrumental (causal explanation)	Work	Empirical-analytic or natural sciences
Practical	Practical (understanding)	Language	Hermeneutic or 'interpretive' sciences
Emancipatory	Emancipatory (reflection)	Power	Critical sciences

'Critical social science', then, is the science which serves the
'emancipatory' interest in freedom and rational autonomy. But if, as
Habermas concedes, self-reflection and self-understanding may be
distorted by social conditions, then the rational capabilities of human
beings for self-emancipation will only be realized by a critical social
science that can elucidate these conditions and reveal how they can be
eliminated. Hence, a critical social science will seek to offer individuals
an awareness of how their aims and purposes may have become
distorted or repressed and to specify how these can be eradicated so that
the rational pursuit of their real goals can be undertaken. In this sense, a
critical social science will provide the kind of self-reflective understanding that will permit individuals to explain why the conditions under
which they operate are frustrating and will suggest the sort of action
that is required if the sources of these frustrations are to be eliminated.

Thus, Habermas's attempt to elaborate the idea of a critical social
science may be seen as an attempt to reconcile his recognition of the
importance of both 'interpretive' understanding and causal explanations. For example, although Habermas accepts the interpretive insight
that social life cannot be explained in terms of generalizations and
predictions, he also accepts that the source of subjective meanings lies

outside the actions of individuals and, hence, that the intentions of individuals may be socially constrained or redefined by external manipulative agencies. A critical social science, therefore, must attempt to move the 'interpretive' approach beyond its traditional concern with producing uncritical renderings of individuals' self-understandings, so that the causes of distorted self-understanding can be clarified, explained and eliminated. This interest in the elimination of conditions which distort self-understanding reveals that critical social science moves beyond the tendency of interpretive social science to rest content with illuminating, rather than overcoming, social problems and issues. By synthesizing interpretive and causal categories in this way, Habermas tries to produce a critical social science that can demonstrate why individuals have the distorted self-understandings that they do, and how they can be corrected.

In making use of causal explanations, however, Habermas is not returning to the positivist idea of social actions as some kind of natural events that occur outside the scope of human consciousness. Rather, the law-like regularities of positive social science are regarded as nothing other than evidence of structurally imposed constraints. The task of a critical social science is to dissolve these constraints by making the causal mechanisms underlying them transparent to those whom they affect. Critical theory, then, is not 'critical' simply in the sense of voicing disapproval of contemporary social arrangements, but in the sense that it attempts to distil the historical processes which have caused subjective meanings to become systematically distorted.

The *Verstehen* method is insufficient for this task because it provides no critical basis for rendering the nature of social life problematic. Nor, since it merely assumes the objective necessity of a given social reality, is the hypothetico–deductive method of natural science suitable. What is required, Habermas argues, is a method that will liberate individuals from the causal efficacy of those social processes that distort communication and understanding and so allow them to engage in the critical reconstruction of suppressed possibilities and desires for emancipation. Following Marx, Habermas argues that the method required for critical social science is that of *critique*. Marx had stated

> ... we do not anticipate the world dogmatically, but rather
> wish to find the new world through criticism of the old; ...
> even though the construction of the future and its completion
> for all times is not our task, what we have to accomplish at this

time is all the more clear: *relentless criticism of all existing conditions*, relentless in the sense that the criticism is not afraid of its findings and just as little afraid of conflict with the powers that be.[8]

Through this kind of criticism, argued Marx, humanity might liberate itself from the dictates and compulsions of established ways of thinking and the established forms of social life. In doing so, it could emancipate humanity from political oppression and the ways of thinking which legitimated it. In recognizing the importance of critique, critical social science focuses its attention on forms of social life which subjugate people and deny satisfactory and interesting lives to some while serving the interests of others. But it is particularly focused on the ways of thinking which support such subjugation, whether in the oppression of one class by another, or in the dominance of a way of thinking which makes such oppression seem unproblematic, inevitable, incidental, or even justified.

In introducing the Marxist concept of 'ideology critique' into critical social science, Habermas also draws heavily on the methodological procedures of psychoanalysis. In particular, he draws on the psychoanalytic method of self-reflection as a way of bringing to consciousness those distortions in patients' self-formative processes which prevent a correct understanding of themselves and their actions. In psychoanalysis, the aim of critique is not just for the theorist to be able to understand or explain the individual, but for the individual to be able, through his or her own transformed self-understanding, to interpret herself and her situation differently and so alter those conditions which are repressive. The purpose of critique, then, is to provide a form of therapeutic self-knowledge which will liberate individuals from the irrational compulsions of their individual history through a process of critical self-reflection.

While psychoanalysis seeks to uncover the cause of distorted understanding by revealing the history of an individual's self-formative process, critical social science seeks to locate the cause of the collective misunderstandings of social groups in ideology. Social groups, Habermas argues, are prevented from achieving a correct understanding of their situation because, under the sway of ideological systems of ideas, they have passively accepted an illusory account of reality that prevents them from recognizing and pursuing their common interests and goals. For this reason, critique is aimed at revealing to individuals how their beliefs and attitudes may be ideological illusions that help to preserve a social order which is alien to their collective experiences and needs. By demonstrating how ideological forces generate erroneous self-understandings, ideology critique aims to reveal their deceptive nature and so strip them of their power.

As well as revealing how ideology may conceal contradictions and inadequacies inherent in ideas and beliefs, ideology critique also attempts to show how these same ideas and beliefs contain some indication of the real interests of individuals and thereby imply some alternative self-conception based on their true meaning. In this sense, ideology critique attempts to show individuals how their erroneous self-understandings nevertheless intimate, in a disguised form, their real needs and purposes. A task of critical social science is to make the genuine self-conceptions implicit in the distorted ideas of individuals explicit, and to suggest how the contradictions and inadequacies in present self-understandings can be overcome. The essential features of a critical social science are, then, that it:

> ... is clearly rooted in concrete social experience, for it is ...
> explicitly conceived with the principal intention of overcoming
> felt dissatisfaction. Consequently, it names the people for
> whom it is directed; it analyzes their suffering; it offers enlight-
> enment to them about what their real needs and wants are; it
> demonstrates to them in what way their ideas about themselves
> are false and at the same time extracts from these false ideas
> implicit truths about them; it points to those inherently contra-
> dictory social conditions which both engendered specific needs
> and make it impossible for them to be satisfied; it reveals the
> mechanisms in terms of which this process of repression
> operates and, in the light of changing social conditions which it
> describes, it offers a mode of activity by which they can
> intervene in and change the social processes which are thwart-
> ing to them. A critical social theory arises out of the problems
> of everyday life and is constructed with an eye towards solving
> them.[9]

Habermas's attempt to develop this kind of critical social science was not without difficulties. One of the most persistent criticisms pointed to his failure to offer a detailed clarification of the epistemological basis of critical soical science and, in particular, to explicate the criteria of rationality in terms of which emancipatory knowledge generated by a critical social science could be validated or rejected. Put more provocatively, the requirement was for critical social science to show how its claims to be able to arrive at 'true' interpretations of social life were nothing than 'elitist' attempts to allow the critical social scientist to employ his own normative prejudices in order to arbitrate between false and correct understandings. One critic puts the problem like this:

> There appears to be a lack of symmetry in Habermas' analysis of those disciplines guided by a technical and a practical interest and those guided by an emancipatory interest. In the first two, Habermas is primarily interested in the *formal* conditions of the types of knowledge involved. To claim, for example, that the empirical-analytic sciences are guided by a technical interest . . . does not prejudice the issue of which theoretical schemes will be corroborated or falsified in the course of scientific enquiry. Again, to note the ways in which the historical-hermeneutic disciplines differ from the empirical analytic sciences . . . does not prejudice the issue of how we are to judge among compet- ing interpretations. . . . But an emancipatory interest and the disciplines supposedly guided by it, is not merely formal; it is substantive and normative. It dictates what ought to be the aim both of our study of society and of society itself — human emancipation. Habermas seems to be . . . smuggling in his own normative bias under the guise of an objective analysis of reason as self-reflection . . . critique . . . is a substantive normative theory which cannot be justified by an appeal to the formal conditions of reason and knowledge.[10]

The outstanding problem for Habermas, then, was to elucidate an epistemological framework in terms of which the theories of a critical social science can be shown to be 'better' or more 'correct' interpreta- tions that the ideologically infected interpretations they seek to replace. In short, the task was one of providing standards of rationality in terms of which a critical social science can justify its own procedures. Habermas's response was to turn to an analysis of language. In particular, he argued that the normative foundations which justify critical social science as a viable and rational enterprise can be derived from an analysis of ordinary speech and discourse.

In pursuing this argument, Habermas develops a theory of com- municative competence which, in a sense, is an ethical theory of self-realization. A defining quality of such theories is that they try to show how any adequate account of what human beings *are* provides answers to ethical questions about what they ought to become.

Philosophers as different as Aristotle, Hegel and Marx all argued that any distinction between 'what man is' and 'what he ought to be' (and hence between description and prescription) are misleading and confused. At any given historical moment, understanding 'what man is' is always a matter of grasping the underlying process imminent in man's present situation and in terms of which he strives to transform himself in order to realize his true 'potentialities' or 'essence'. Habermas's theory of communicative competence is an ethical theory of self-realization which transposes the source of human ideals onto language and discourse. For the purpose of Habermas's theory is to try and establish how, inherent in, and anticipated by, everyday human speech, there is a conception of an ideal form of life in which the sort of rational autonomy served by the emancipatory interest can be realized. In effect, therefore, the theory of communicative competence seeks to show how the normative justification for emancipatory knowledge is embedded in the structure of the communicative action which a critical social science is concerned to analyze and explore.

Central to Habermas's argument is a distinction between speech or 'communicative action' and discourse. Drawing on recent developments in the analytic philosophy of language, Habermas maintains that all speech implicitly presupposes the following of norms; that these norms are being followed and that these norms can be justified. When this consensus no longer pertains, then the presence of the norms which was taken for granted in speech is rendered problematic. It is in *discourse* that the presence or absence of the norms implicit in speech can be questioned. Thus Habermas says:

> Discourses help test the truth claims of opinions (and norms) which the speakers no longer take for granted. In discourse, the 'force' of the argument is the only permissible compulsion, whereas cooperative search for truth is the only permissible motive.... The output of discourse ... consists in recognition or rejection of problematic truth claims. Discourse produces nothing but argument.[11]

The claims which are naively accepted in speech, but made the subject of argumentation in discourse, involve four *validity claims*. These are, first, that what is stated is *true*; secondly, that the utterance is *comprehensible*; thirdly, that the speaker is *sincere*; and finally that it is *right* for the speaker to be performing the speech act. Since it is only discursively that these validity claims can be examined and tested, it follows that the purpose of discourse is to achieve, through argument alone, a rational reassessment of the validity claims initially accepted in speech. Any consensus arrived at within the framework of the appropriate discourse can, therefore, be regarded as a true consensus.

Now this conception of truth as consensual raises the question of why any consensus reached in this way should be regarded as rational consensus. Habermas's response is to argue that, inherent in all speech, is the idea of an 'ideal speech act' from which the sort of 'ideal speech situation' required for a rational consensus can be derived. Thus, he argues:

> ... the design of an ideal speech situation is necessarily implied in the structure of potential speech, since all speech, even intentional deception, is oriented towards the idea of truth ... In so far as we master the means for the construction of the ideal speech situation, we can conceive the ideas of truth, freedom and justice....[12]

The promise of an 'ideal speech situation', then, is anticipated by all speech and hence provides an image of the sort of conditions required to make any consensus reached in discourse rational and true.

These conditions are such that the true interests of the participants can emerge, that argument can proceed without any external pressures, and that the only compulsions are the compulsions of argument itself. In short, the ideal speech situation requires a democratic form of public discussion which allows for an uncoerced flow of ideas and arguments and for participants to be free from any threat of domination, manipulation or control. In other words, the emancipation from repressive distortions and the pursuit of rational autonomy which a critical social science seeks to foster are themselves anticipated in and presupposed by the 'communicative actions' such a science seeks to analyze and explain. Implicit in the object to which a critical social science is addressed, therefore, are the normative requirements in terms of which any science guided by an emancipatory interest can be justified. The pursuit of a form of life in which free and open communication is possible is not some arbitrary normative or political stance that is externally or mechanically attached to a critical social science. It is merely the explicit recognition of an ideal which is, as yet, unrealized, but which is promised by, and anticipated in, the very activity of language.

One implication of this discussion should not be missed: it is that the conditions for truth telling are also the conditions for democratic discussion. In a way, this has always been true of the aims of rational discussion in science: truth claims have always been regarded as open to challenge in free debate in which only the force of better argument prevails. But few academic discussions are truly open or free; in fact, they rarely approximate this ideal. But the linking of truth and social justice posited by Habermas is compelling. Thomas McCarthy, translator of a number of Habermas's works into English, summarizes this feature of Habermas's theory in the following passage:

> The very act of participating in the discourse, of attempting discursively to come to an agreement about the truth of a problematic statement or the correctness of a problematic norm, carries with it the supposition that a genuine agreement is possible. If we did not suppose that a justified consensus were possible and could in some way be distinguished from a false consensus, then the very meaning of discourse, indeed of speech, would be called into question. In attempting to come to a 'rational' decision about such matters, we must suppose that the outcome of our discussion will be the result simply of the force of the better argument and not of accidental or systematic constraints on discussion. Habermas' thesis is that the structure (of communication) is free from constraint only when for all participants there is a symmetrical distribution of chances to select and employ speech acts, when there is an effective equality of chances to assume dialogue roles. In particular, all participants must have the same chance to initiate and perpetuate discourse, to put forward, call into question, and give reasons for or against statements, explanations, interpretations, and justifications. Furthermore, they must have the same chance to express attitudes, feelings, intentions and the like, and to command, to oppose, to permit, and to forbid, etc. In other words, the conditions of the ideal speech situation must ensure discussion which is free from all constraints of domination. Thus, the conditions for ideal discourse are connected with conditions for an ideal form of life; they include linguistic conceptualizations of the traditional ideas of freedom and justice. 'Truth', therefore, cannot be analyzed independently of 'freedom' and 'justice'.[13]

By his own admission, Habermas's theory of communicative competence is not a finished product, but the beginnings of a theoretical task that stands in need of considerable development and detailed explication. The ideas introduced by Habermas should, therefore, be regarded as suggestive and tentative rather than as convincing and complete. At the same time, Habermas's work contains insights that seem crucial for any understanding of the relation of theory to practice; in particular, his attempt to produce a unified theory of knowledge, justice, action and rationality which can provide the grounds on which a social science with 'practical intent' can be constructed. It is this theme that is considered in the next section.

3 Theory and Practice

It is important to distinguish the notion of a *critical social science* from that of a *critical theory*. A critical theory is the product of a process of critique. In many, or even most instances, such a theory will be the outcome of a process carried out by an individual or group concerned to expose contradictions in the rationality or the justice of social actions. Many critical theories will be interpretations of social life created by individuals or groups concerned to reveal these contradictions. In this sense, critical theories may be the outcomes of interpretive social science, subject to criticism on the same grounds as other interpretive theories. Most particularly, they may be subject to the criticism that they transform consciousness (ways of viewing the world) without necessarily changing practice in the world.

The idea of a critical social science is developed by Habermas as a way of overcoming this limitation. A critical social science is, for Habermas, a social process that combines collaboration in the process of critique with the political determination to act to overcome contradictions in the rationality and justice of social action and social institutions. A critical social science will be one that goes beyond critique to critical praxis; that is, a form of practice in which the 'enlightenment' of actors comes to bear directly in their transformed social action. This requires an integration of theory and practice as reflective and practical moments in a dialectical process of reflection, enlightenment and political struggle carried out by groups for the purpose of their own emancipation.

Within a critical social science, therefore, the relationship between theory and practice cannot merely be one of prescribing practice on the basis of theory or of informing practical judgment. In fact, it has been the insistence on the priority of one or the other of these two elements (theory or practice) which has impeded a clear understanding of how the two relate to one another. In *Theory and Practice*, Habermas clarifies the relationship by discussing 'the organization of enlightenment', a social process through which theoretical ideas and practical exigencies are interrelated. To achieve this, he distinguishes the functions which mediate the relationship between theory and practice in critical social science in the following way.

> The mediation of theory and praxis can only be clarified if to begin with we distinguish three functions, which are measured in terms of different criteria: the formation and extension of critical theorems, which can stand up to scientific discourse; the organization of processes of enlightenment, in which such theorems are applied and can be tested in a unique manner by the initiation of processes of reflection carried on within certain groups toward which these processes have been directed; and the selection of appropriate strategies, the solution of tactical questions, and the conduct of political struggle. On the first level, the aim is true statements, on the second, authentic insights, and on the third, prudent decisions.[14]

A social science aimed at enlightening practice and practitioners must, then, distinguish between three functions in the mediation of theory and practice. These are, first, its theoretical elements ('critical theorems') and the manner by which they are developed and tested; secondly, its processes for the organization of enlightenment; and thirdly, its processes for the organization of action. Each has criteria by which it may be evaluated. To confuse them, or to evaluate the three by a single criterion, is to misunderstand the process of critical social science as a form of disciplined self-reflection aimed at enlightenment and improvement of the social and material conditions under which the practice takes place.

This confusion is a real possibility: positivist social science has made a shibboleth of 'truth' — as if it stood above social life, could be objectively ascertained, and could prescribe wise practice without understanding the human, social, economic, political, historical and practical constraints within which real practice occurs. Positivist social science thus uses the single criterion of 'truth' or 'objectivity' in arriving at conclusions about practical action. Interpretive social science on the other hand makes a shibboleth of practical judgment, which is informed by knowledge grounded in the actor's own understanding and circumstances. It thus uses the single criterion of authentic knowledge in arriving at conclusions about action: it aims to transform consciousness, but may not transform practice because it does not provide a systematic critique of the conditions under which the practice occurs.

Critical social science recognizes that social science is human, social and political. It is human in the sense that it involves active knowing by those involved in the practice of social life, and it is social in the sense that it influences practice through the dynamic social processes of communication and interaction. Inevitably, then, social science is political: what is done depends on the way social processes of knowing and doing in particular situations are controlled. Critical social science thus requires a political theory about social life and, equally importantly, about its own processes and their effects on social life. The political theory of critical social science is democratic and rests on Habermas's theory of communicative competence and, in particular, on the idea of rational communication in which decision-making is guided, not by considerations of power, but by the rationality of arguments for different courses of action.

The three separate functions mediating the relationship of theory and practice in critical social science may be distinguished in terms of their substance, the criteria by which they are evaluated, and the requisite conditions for each to be carried out successfully.

The first function of critical social science is the *formation and extension of critical theorems* which can stand up to scientific discourse. Critical theorems are propositions about the character and conduct of social life; for example, 'learning requires the active participation of the learner in constructing and controlling the language and activities of his or her learning', or 'cooperative teaching can only develop under conditions of continuing negotiation of the content and classroom practices through which the curriculum is expressed'. Here, the criterion is that the statements must be *true*; that is, critical theorems must be analytically coherent and stand up to examination in the light of evidence collected in relevant contexts. The examination of the truth of such propositions can only be carried out under the condition of *freedom of discourse*.

The second function is *the organization of processes of enlightenment* in which critical theorems are applied and can be tested in a unique manner by the initiation of processes of reflection carried on within the groups involved in the action and reflection on it. The organization of enlightenment is the organization of the learning processes of the group; in fact, it is a systematic learning process aimed at the development of knowledge about the practices being considered and the conditions under which they take place. The organization of enlightenment is a human, social and political activity; here, the criterion is that insights achieved must be *authentic* for the individuals involved and *communicable* within the group (that is, that they are mutually comprehensible). Processes for the organization of enlightment require that those involved *commit themselves wholly to appropriate precautions* and *assure scope for unconstrained communication* on the psychoanalytic model of therapeutic discourse. That is, they must aim at understanding achieved by practitioners on their own behalf (without illegitimate persuasion or coercion) and give everyone involved the opportunity to raise, question, affirm and deny validity claims (about comprehensibility, truth, sincerity and appropriateness) and test their own point of view in self-reflective discussion.

Concrete examples of the organization of enlightenment can be found in groups which are working together for understanding. In schools today, for example, we find school staff meetings constituted for the review and development of the school curriculum; they are constituted first as 'learning communities', with the primary task of learning about the nature and consequences of the curriculum. Once they have this task in hand, they may begin to organize themselves for action. But their first aim is enlightenment: organizing themselves to learn from the experience and context of the curriculum. Although few school review exercises actually reach these goals, to achieve genuine and undistorted enlightenment in the whole group review process they must engage the experience and understanding of all participants (authenticity), allow them to communicate openly and freely (mutual comprehensibility), and develop a common orientation to action. (This last element is an important aspect of language — that it orients group members to a common object.) A key aspect of this process will be that all present can really participate equally in raising questions, contributing suggestions, and so have equal opportunity to raise and test validity claims. After all, if each member cannot participate in the discussion fully, it will not be possible to assert that conclusions reached actually represent the best thinking of the group. If only a few participate, the understandings achieved will be the understandings of the few, and the claim that they are the understandings of the whole group will be hollow.

The third function is the *organization of action* (or, as Habermas puts it, 'the conduct of the political struggle'). This involves the selection of appropriate strategies, the solution of tactical questions, and the conduct of the practice itself. It is the 'doing' which will be reflected upon in retrospect and which is prospectively guided by the fruits of previous reflection. The criterion by which the organization of action may be judged is that *the decisions must be prudent*; that is, that the decisions are such as to ensure that those involved can carry out the activity without exposing themselves to unnecessary risks. This requires that those involved in the action are involved in the practical discourse and decision-making process which lead to the action, and that they participate on the basis of their *free commitment* to the action. '... here too, and especially here,' writes Habermas, 'there is no privileged access to truth'.[15]

To return to the previous example, the organization of action may be identified when a school staff meeting begins to put its learnings from the organization of enlightenment into practice. For the organization of enlightenment, it will have constituted itself so that its discourse was rational and authentic: so that people could speak openly and freely, so that, as individuals, they could understand what was being said so that there would be mutual understanding through the language used, and so that they could develop a common orientation towards action. Now as the staff begins to decide what to do, further, and different, criteria become relevant. Not only must it constitute itself for open discourse, it must also constitute itself to survive the step to action. As real decisions are taken, the self-interests of some on the staff will be served at the expense of the self-interests of others, and self-interests of the staff may come into conflict with self-interests outside the group (those of students or parents, for example). In the real situation, the decision to act one way rather than another will threaten the integrity of the group. Action must be decided carefully and prudently: members must not only agree to abide by democratic group decisions, but also to underwrite them by their free commitment to decisions. This will only be possible if the organization of enlightenment has really been an open and rational process and if the process of group decision-making has been democratic. Clearly, to achieve common commitment of this kind, action must be prudent. Otherwise the group may find itself committed to action which will undermine the prospects for success of its joint project.

It is evident from these three functions of critical social science that its epistemology is constructivist, seeing knowledge as developing by a process of active construction and reconstruction of theory and practice by those involved; that it involves a theory of symmetrical communication (a process of rational discussion which actively seeks to overcome coercion on the one hand and self-deception on the other), and that it involves a democratic theory of political action based on free commitment to social action and consensus about what needs to be and should be done. In short, it is not only a theory about knowledge, but also about how knowledge relates to practice.

It is also clear that critical social science is about social praxis (informed doing, or strategic action) and that it is a form of social science to be carried out by self-reflective groups concerned to organize their own practice in the light of their organized self-reflection. It is, perhaps, in this last feature that we see the clearest distinction between critical social science and positivist or interpretive social science. Critical social science is a process of reflection which requires the participation of the researcher in the social action being studied, or rather, that participants become researchers. The disinterested, 'objective' researcher of natural science and the empathetic observer of interpretive science may help in the organization of self-reflection, but they are 'outsiders' and, as such, they see only the exterior of the action, whether as a social system or as a re-enacted experience. But, as Habermas (1974) puts it:

> The vindicating superiority of those who do the enlightening over those who are to be enlightened is theoretically unavoidable, but at the same time it is fictive and requires self-correction: in a process of enlightenment there can only be participants.[16]

How, then, does critical social science measure up to the five formal requirements of an educational theory outlined at the beginning of this chapter? Firstly, a critical social scientific approach to educational research rejects the positivistic notion of rationality, objectivity and truth, seeing truth as historically and socially embedded, not as standing above or outside history and the concerns of participants in real social situations. Moreover, it does not have a technical interest in problem solving, but sees the conduct of social science itself as an opportunity for the emancipation of participants.

Secondly, critical social science depends upon the meanings and interpretations of practitioners: the terms in critical theorems must be grounded in the language and experience of a self-reflective community and meet the criteria of authenticity and communicability. Thirdly, social science institutes critical processes of self-reflection (the organization of enlightenment) whose purpose is to distinguish ideas and interpretations which are ideological or systematically distorted from those which are not, and distorted self-understandings from those which are undistorted. Fourthly, critical social science employs the method of critique to identify and expose those aspects of the social order over which participants have no control and which frustrate rational change, and both its critical theorems and its strategic organization of action are directed at eliminating, or overcoming, constraints on rational change. And finally, critical social science is practical, being directed towards helping practitioners inform themselves about the actions they need to take to overcome their problems and eliminate their frustrations.

4 Conclusion

This chapter has passed quickly over the territory of critical theory and Habermas's critical social science and, as a result, has been unable to set out many of its key tenets in detail. In consequence, it is difficult to assess all of the many criticisms of the approach, especially since they frequently involve sophisticated philosophical issues.[17] Nevertheless, there are some criticisms which are worth mentioning. First, there is a strong counter-attack against the position of Habermas from advocates of interpretive social science, especially in the hermeneutics of Hans-Georg Gadamer.[18] Essentially, the argument is that hermeneutic understanding is not so limited as Habermas and others have claimed and that traditional interpretive methods are the most appropriate ones for understanding social life. Secondly, there are arguments advanced to suggest that there are some crucial ambiguities in Habermas's position; for example, regarding the status of knowledge-constitutive interests.[19] Are they merely contingent empirical interests, or are they transcendental and beyond human history? If merely contingent, they are social products which may be subject to change (and thus not fundamental). If they are transcendental, they enjoy a status which he is unwilling to allow, as is demonstrated in his criticisms of Kant's transcendental categories. According to one critic, Habermas is himself guilty of introducing purely categorical distinctions for the purposes of his argument in demolishing the categorical distinctions of others.[20]

Finally, there are very general criticisms that Habermas's work does not concretely exemplify critical social science, but instead merely discusses its possibility. In the conclusion to his discussion of critical social science, Bernstein puts the point like this:

> If one is to fulfill the promise of developing a critical theory that
> has practical intent, then it is not sufficient to recover the idea of
> self-reflection guided by an emancipatory interest. It is not

sufficient to develop a critique of ideology and contemporary society which exposes the powerful tendencies to suppress practical discourse and force all rationality into the form of instrumental reason. It is not sufficient even to show that a critical theory can serve to further enlightenment and affect a transformation in political agents.... All the preceding is necessary but the very idea of practical discourse — of individuals engaged in argumentation directed towards rational will formation — can easily degenerate into a 'mere' ideal, unless and until the material conditions required for such discourse are concretely realized and objectively realized. Habermas ... does not offer any real understanding of how this is to be accomplished ... in the final analysis the gap still exists ... between the idea of such a critical theory ... and its concrete practical realization.[21]

Bernstein has identified a problem which is the source of considerable frustration to those who look in vain to Habermas's work for the *praxis* of critical theory: its use in real social action. If Habermas condemns the unproductiveness of theoretically driven research which does not authentically engage social action and social actors, why does he fail to produce concrete examples of relevant critical social scientific work? Habermas has responded to such criticism with further developments in his theories, but the question of moving from the *idea* of a critical social theory to its concrete realization remains. For educational theory, the problem is to articulate a conception of educational research which could bring about the emancipatory aims and purposes that are characteristic of a critical social science.

Some of the features of an approach to educational research that is informed by critical theory are obvious enough. For example, in this kind of research, the relationship of the researcher to the research act would be understood quite differently from that required in either positivist or interpretive approaches. In positivist educational research it will be recalled that the researcher is merely an instrument by which research is undertaken; he stands outside the progress of science as an objective or disinterested observer. The interpretive researcher, by contrast, is an individual who adopts the position which Mannheim describes as 'disciplined subjectivity' so as to acquire a vantage-point from which events can be reconstructed and interpreted; the activity of the researcher is within social life, and the interpretations reached become part of intellectual history. Nevertheless, the interpretive researcher affects the development of history only 'accidentally', as it were, when the interpretations he or she produces become part of the language of their time and influence the decisions made by others. In any critical approach to education research, however, a new role for the researcher is discovered whereby his or her participation in the development of knowledge is comprehended as social and political action which must be understood and justified as such.

It is also clear that the relationship between theory and practice would be understood very differently. Earlier chapters described how, in the positivist approach, theory is regarded as a source of disinterested principles which give a guide to effective action and, once the aims of action are decided, may be taken to prescribe for action (in the sense that the most effective means to a given end can be defined). Interpretive approaches do not prescribe for action; on the contrary, interpretations merely inform teachers about the nature, consequences and contexts of past actions, and require that practitioners use their own practical judgment in deciding how to act. What this and the previous chapter offer is an approach to the question of theory and practice in which the interpretations of actors play a central role, but where more than practical judgment is required. Indeed, from a critical perspective, the teacher needs to develop a systematic understanding of the conditions which shape, limit and determine action so that these constraints can be taken into account. And this is seen to require the active participation of practitioners in collaborative articulation and formulation of the theories imminent in their own practices, and the development of these theories through continuing action and reflection.

Joseph Schwab distinguishes between the first and second of these three approaches in his discussion of the 'practical'.[22] The first he called the 'theoretic' approach; the second he called the 'practical'. Following Habermas, this third approach might be described as 'emancipatory'. And, following the way it emphasizes the organization of 'action', it might also be described as 'action research'. The view that emancipatory action research could be a way of relating the perspectives of critical social science to educational research provides the starting point for the next chapter.

Further Reading

For an historical account of the development of the 'Frankfurt School' of critical theory, see Martin Jay, *The Dialectical Imagination: A History of the Frankfurt School and the Institute of Social Research 1923–50.* Part IV of Richard Bernstein's book, *The Restructuring of Social and Political Theory* gives a briefer account of the history and some of the main themes of critical theory. A general introduction may be found in David Held's book, *Introduction to Critical Theory: from Horkheimer to Habermas.* For an introduction to the text of Habermas in particular, see Thomas McCarthy's, *The Critical Theory of Jurgen Habermas.*

Habermas's own work is challenging and displays an extraordinary breadth of scholarship. Major works available in English include *Toward a Rational Society, Knowledge and Human Interest, Legitimation Crisis, Theory and Practice,* and a collection of essays, *Communication and the Evolution of Society.*

Notes

1 The 'Frankfurt School' is so called because its founders were initially based in Frankfurt, although they moved to the United States for the Second World War years. For an interesting account of the main ideas and history of the School, see JAY, M. (1973), *The Dialectical Imagination: The History of the Institute for Social Research and the Frankfurt School, 1923–1950,* Boston, Little, Brown and Co.
2 For one of the earliest expositions of this kind of theory see HORKHEIMER, M. (1972), 'Traditional and critical theory' in *Critical Theory,* New York, The Seabury Press, p. 188.
3 See, for example, CONNERTON, P. (Ed.) (1975), *Critical Sociology: Selected Readings,* Harmondsworth, Penguin.
4 For an interesting discussion of the place of critical theory in the hermeneutic tradition see BLEICHER, J. (1980), *Hermeneutics as Method, Philosophy and Critique,* London, Routledge and Kegan Paul.
5 The relationship between hermeneutics, philosophy and ordinary language philosophy is discussed in THOMPSON, J.B. (1981), *Critical Hermeneutics,* Cambridge, Cambridge University Press.
6 HABERMAS, J. (1974), *Theory and Practice,* tr. John Veirtel, London, Heinemann, p. 44.
7 See, particularly, *Knowledge and Human Interest; Theory and Practice; Communication and the Evolution of Society.*
8 MARX, K. (1967), *Writings of the Young Marx on Philosophy and Society,* ed. and tr. by EASTON, L.D. and GUDDAT, K.H. New York, Anchor Books, p. 212.
9 FAY, B. (1977), *Social Theory and Political Practice,* London, George Allen and Unwin, p. 109.
10 BERNSTEIN, R.J. (1979), *The Restructuring of Social and Political Theory,* London, Basil Blackwell.
11 HABERMAS, J. (1973), 'A postscript to knowledge and human interest', *Philosophy of the Social Sciences,* vol. 3, p. 168.

12 HABERMAS, J. (1970), 'Towards a theory of communicative competence', *Inquiry*, vol. 13, p. 372.
13 McCARTHY, T. (1975), in his introduction to his translation of *Legitimation Crisis*, Boston, Beacon Press, p. xvii.
14 HABERMAS, J. (1974), *op. cit.*, p. 32.
15 *Ibid.*, p. 34.
16 *Ibid.*, p. 40.
17 For a discussion of some of these issues, see BERNSTEIN, R.J. (1976), *The Restructuring of Social and Political Theory*, London, Basil Blackwell.
18 GADAMER, H. (1975), *Truth and Method*, London, Sheed and Ward.
19 BERNSTEIN, R.J. (1976), *op. cit.*, p. 222.
20 *Ibid.*, p. 223.
21 *Ibid.*, p. 225.
22 SCHWAB, J.J. (1969), 'The practical: a language for curriculum', *School Review*, vol. 78, pp. 1–25.

Chapter 6

Towards a Critical Educational Science

---

1 Introduction

Concluding his article 'A preface to critical theory', James Farganis argues:

> ... the problem of how to establish an emancipatory or critical
> social science remains. How does one move from the theoretical
> critique to the necessary action that will bring about the desired
> end? Since critical theory professes a unity of theory and
> practice, the question is a legitimate one.[1]

The question may or may not be legitimate; it is certainly
revealing. One must surely move from Habermas's theoretical critique
to action by resolving to act on it. But this is not a matter of asking for
further instructions about what one is to do, it is a matter of deciding to
enact a critical social science. The purpose of this chapter is to answer
Farganis's question not for the case of a critical social science in general,
but for a critical *educational* science. It does so by arguing for a form of
educational research which is not research *about* education but research
for education.

2 Critical Educational Science as Research *for* Education

In previous chapters, the burden of the argument has been that
positivist and interpretive approaches to educational research are inade-
quately justified and that educational research must adopt the forms of
critical social science. The decisive break between critical educational
research and the dominant positivist and interpretive modes was

succinctly formulated by Marx in his *Eleventh Thesis on Feuerbach:* 'philosophers have only interpreted the world in various ways ... the point is to change it'[2]. Thus, a critical educational science has the aim of *transforming* education; it is directed at educational change. The aims of explanation (characteristic of the positivist view of educational research) or understanding (characteristic of the interpretive view) are merely moments in the transformative process, rather than sufficient ends in themselves. The point is made by Josef Bleicher in his contrast between a species of interpretive research he calls 'hermeneutic philosophy' and a form of critical research he calls 'critical hermeneutics':

> ... hermeneutic philosophy attempts the mediation of tradition and is thereby directed at the past in the endeavour to determine its significance for the present; critical hermeneutics is directed at the future and at changing reality rather than merely interpreting it.[3]

Previous chapters have shown that different modes of educational research involve different views of the relationship between educational theory and educational practice and embody different views of educational change. Although these views of change relate to the nature and findings of particular research studies, when applied to whole traditions in educational research they also refer to competing views of *educational reform* and the place of institutionalized educational research in the process of reform. Thus, positivism views educational reform as technical; interpretive research views it as practical. A critical educational science, however, has a view of educational reform that is participatory and collaborative; it envisages a form of educational research which is conducted by those involved in education themselves. It takes a view of educational research as critical analysis directed at the *transformation* of educational practices, the educational understandings and educational values of those involved in the process, and the social and institutional structures which provide frameworks for their action. In this sense, a critical educational science is not research *on* or *about* education, it is research *in* and *for* education. From this perspective, we may return to the view of critical social science put by Fay and already quoted in the last chapter:

> (Critical social science) ... is clearly rooted in concrete social experience, for it is ... explicitly conceived with the purpose of overcoming felt dissatisfaction. Consequently, it names the people for whom it is directed; it analyzes their suffering; it

offers enlightenment to them about what their real needs and wants are; it demonstrates to them in what way their ideas about themselves are false and at the same time extracts from these false ideas implicit truths about them; it points to those inherently contradictory social conditions which both engender specific needs and make it impossible for them to be satisfied; it reveals the mechanisms in terms of which this process of oppression operates and, in the light of changing social conditions which it describes, it offers a mode of activity by which they can intervene in and change the social processes which are thwarting them. A critical social theory arises out of the problems of everyday life and is constructed with an eye towards solving them.[4]

Similarly, Comstock writes:

Critical social research begins from the life problems of definite and particular social agents who may be individuals, groups or classes that are oppressed by and alienated from social processes they maintain or create but do not control. Beginning from the practical problems of everyday existence it returns to that life with the aim of enlightening its subjects about unrecognized social constraints and possible courses of action by which they may liberate themselves. Its aim is enlightened self-knowledge and effective political action. Its method is dialogue, and its effect is to heighten its subject's self awareness of their collective potential as the active agents of history.... Critical research links depersonalized social processes to its subjects' choices and actions with the goal of eliminating unrecognized and contradictory consequences of collective action.[5]

If these statements, about critical social science in general, are rephrased for an educational science, a view emerges of a critical educational science which aims at involving teachers, students, parents and school administrators in the tasks of critical analysis of their own situations with a view to transforming them in ways which will improve these situations as *educational* situations for students, teachers and society.[6] In this sense, critical educational science is not unlike the process of conscientization, described by Freire as

... the process in which people, not as recipients, but as knowing subjects, achieve a deepening awareness both of the sociohistorical reality which shapes their lives and of their capacity to transform that reality.[7]

A critical educational science must then be a participatory science, its participants or 'subjects' being the teachers, students and others who create, maintain, enjoy and endure educational arrangements. These arrangements have individual and social consequences which include both enlightenment and alienation, social solidarity and social division, the empowerment of persons and the authoritarianism of contemporary society. Through critical educational science, participants explore such contradictions and seek to resolve them.

In considering the character of a critical social science, Habermas[8] makes it clear that the research knowledge generated by critical social science is not, by itself, compelling for social action. There must also be 'processes of enlightenment' by which participants in a situation reach authentic understandings of their situation, and a 'practical discourse' in which decisions are taken by participants about appropriate courses of action which are agreed to be wise and prudent. He says:

> Critique understands that its claims to validity can be verified only in the successful process of enlightenment, and that means in the practical discourse of those concerned.[9]

It has seemed to some researchers that they can stand outside the educational situations they aim to transform, as critics whose job is to enlighten others. They interpret the necessary independence of mind of the critic in terms of a division of labour, with their own roles as 'outsiders' being defined and procedurally guaranteed by institutional and theoretical separation from the 'insiders' whose work they study.[10] This is an important and helpful role, but it is not sufficient for educational research of a critical social scientific kind. What locks the scientific discourse and the processes of enlightenment of the research task into the task of transforming educational situations is a concrete commitment to the improvement of education. If research is to achieve the concrete transformation of real educational situations, then it requires a theory of change which links researchers and practitioners in a common task in which the duality of the research and practice roles is transcended. Habermas puts the point this way:

> ... the theory that creates consciousness can bring about conditions under which the systematic distortions of communication are dissolved and a practical discourse can then be

conducted; but it does not contain any information which prejudges the future action of those concerned. The psychoanalyst does not have the right, either, to make proposals for prospective action: the patient must make his own conclusions as far as his actions are concerned.[11]

The full task of a critical educational science requires participants to collaborate in the organization of their own enlightenment, the decision-making by which they will transform their situations, and continuing critical analysis in the light of consequences of those transformations which can sustain the engagement of scientific discourse, processes of enlightenment and practical action. But these are tasks primarily for the participants in educational situations who, by their practices, construct and constitute these situations as educational, transform them by transforming their own practices, and live with the consequences of the transformations they make. The 'outsider' researcher may interpret or inform these practices, but does not constitute them, has limited power to transform them, and rarely lives with the consequences of any actual transformations that occur.

We may thus prefer to reject Comstock's description of the role of the critical researcher vis-a-vis participants:

> Practically, (critical social research) requires the critical investigator to begin from the intersubjective understandings of the participants of a social setting and to return to these participants with a program of education and action designed to change their understandings and their social conditions.[12]

The source of programmes of education and action designed for enlightenment must surely be *participants themselves*, not 'critical investigators'. Habermas likens the role of critical social science (in relation to groups committed to self-reflection and transformation of the conditions of their action) to the role of psychoanalysis.[13] In doing so, he raises the possibility that the critical investigator is like a social-political version of the psychoanalyst. But he is aware of the danger of creating a new priesthood of social analysts. As he says: 'in a process of enlightenment there can only be participants'.[14]

In practical terms, this can only mean two things: on the one hand, it means that 'outsiders' helping to establish processes of self-reflection in schools must become participants in the schools themselves; and, on the other, it means that school communities must become, and see themselves as becoming, participants in a general social project by

159

which education and educational institutions may be critically transformed in society at large.

The tasks of a critical educational science cannot be divorced from the practical realities of education in particular schools and classrooms, nor from the political reality that schools themselves are concrete historical expressions of the relationship between education and society. Without concrete, practical grounding in research processes which may create critical communities of teachers, students and others, educational research is forced to justify itself in much more general terms (aiming to influence 'policy-makers' or changing the conditions of legitimation of certain educational programmes). Unless engaging specific political movements in education, it runs the risk of treating the actors it is intended to influence or enlighten as a reified and abstract category or class ('policy-makers', 'educationists' . . . even 'teachers' in general). Much critical research in education today falls prey to this reification and fails to 'name the people from whom it is directed' (as Fay put it). When it does so, it becomes a species of interpretive research, lacking practical commitment because it does not employ a self-subsuming theory of educational, social and political change.

The antidote to this reification of educational actors and educational situations is concrete engagement in the task of educational transformation. This antidote can be realized in collaborative work in the transformation of the concrete settings and institutions of education. Put simply, the contribution of educational research to educational practice must be evident in actual improvements of concrete educational practices, of the actual understandings of these practices by their practitioners, and in the improvement of the concrete situations in which these practices occur. In relation to this last arena for improvement, we must remember that educational situations are constituted as such not in terms of such things as bricks and mortar, financial resources, the use of time, and organizational arrangements. More importantly, they have their educational character because people act in them in certain ways which they understand as educational. Practices constitute educational situations and, in particular, the practices of teachers, administrators, and students, parents and others whose actions are themselves partly shaped in reaction to the practices of institutional education. To improve actual educational situations, therefore, we must transform the interacting webs of practices that constitute them.

This emphasis on practice and its transformation will not be surprising to those familiar with the development of social theory and philosophy since Marx's challenge in the famous *Eleventh Thesis on Feuerbach*. At that time he also wrote:

> The materialist doctrine that men are products of circumstances and upbringing and that, therefore, changed men are products of other circumstances and changed upbringing, forgets that it is men that change circumstances and that the educator must himself be educated.

To change circumstances and people was a simultaneous task, a dialectical process, not a riddle of chicken and egg. He wrote:

> The coincidence of the changing of circumstances and the changing of human activity can be conceived and rationally understood only as revolutionizing practice.

Michael Matthews, commenting on Marx's conception of practice as the 'germ' of his epistemology, reiterated this thrust, and emphasized Marx's achievement in transcending the old materialist doctrine:

> Marx offered a new version of materialism. Specifically, it was *historical* materialism; a materialism which saw practice or conscious human activity as mediating between mind and matter; between subject and object. It was something which by its mediation altered both society and nature. Consciousness arises out of and is shaped by practice, and in turn is judged in and by practice.[15]

The last clause — 'and in turn is judged in and by practice' — is at the heart of the argument about educational research and its critical contribution to the improvement of education. This theme is addressed repeatedly in those recent writings on educational research[16] which argue that it must be judged by its contribution not only to transforming the thinking of practitioners but also, and simultaneously, by its contribution to the transformation of education itself. For educational researchers who remain *outside* the educational contexts being studied, this implies new relationships between researchers and practitioners: collaborative relationships in which the 'outsider' becomes a 'critical friend' helping 'insiders' to act more wisely, prudently and critically in the process of transforming education. The success of the work of such 'critical friends' is to be measured in the extent to which they can help those involved in the educational process to improve their own educational practices, their own understandings, and the situations and institutions in which they work. On this view, the success of educational research conducted by outsiders is to be measured not in terms of what they expropriate from the experience and work of teachers for the research literature, but in terms of their contribution to the improvement of education in the real and concrete situations in which those teachers work.

The more significant implication of this view of critical educational science, however, concerns teachers themselves. Clearly, a critical educational science requires that teachers become researchers into their own practices, understandings and situations. While there is a role for 'critical friends' in helping teachers and others involved in education to conduct critical research, the primary work of educational research must be participatory research by those whose practices constitute education. To show how those whose work constitutes education itself can also develop forms of work which can constitute a reformed practice of educational research, it will be useful to introduce the idea of educational action research.

3   The Definition and Character of Action Research

Action research is simply a form of self-reflective enquiry undertaken by participants in social situations in order to improve the rationality and justice of their own practices, their understanding of these practices, and the situations in which the practices are carried out. In education, action research has been employed in school-based curriculum development, professional development, school improvement programmes, and systems planning and policy development. Although these activities are frequently carried out using approaches, methods and techniques unrelated to those of action research, participants in these development processes are increasingly choosing action research as a way of participating in decision-making about development.

In terms of method, a self-reflective spiral of cycles of planning, acting, observing and reflecting is central to the action research approach. Kurt Lewin, who coined the phrase 'action research' described the process in terms of planning, fact-finding and execution:

> Planning usually starts with something like a general idea. For one reason or another it seems desirable to reach a certain objective. Exactly how to circumscribe this objective and how to reach it is frequently not too clear. The first step, then, is to examine the idea carefully in the light of the means available.

Frequently more fact-finding about the situation is required. If this first period of planning is successful, two items emerge: an 'overall plan' of how to reach the objective and a decision in regard to the first step of action. Usually this planning has also somewhat modified the original idea. The next period is devoted to executing the first step of the overall plan. In highly developed fields of social management or the execution of a war, this second step is followed by certain fact-findings. For example, in the bombing of Germany a certain factory may have been chosen as the first target after careful consideration of various priorities and of the best means and ways of dealing with this target. The attack is pressed home and immediately a reconnaissance plane follows with the one objective of determining as accurately and objectively as possible the new situation. This reconnaissance or fact-finding has four functions: it should evaluate the action by showing whether what has been achieved is above or below expectation; it should serve as a basis for correctly planning the next step; it should serve as a basis for modifying the 'overall plan'; and finally, it gives the planners a chance to learn; that is, to gather new general insights, for instance, regarding the strength and weakness of certain weapons or techniques of action. The next step again is composed of a circle of planning, executing, and reconnaissance or fact-finding for the purpose of evaluating the results of the second step, for preparing the rational basis for planning the third step, and for perhaps modifying again the overall plan.[17]

Lewin documented the effects of group decision in facilitating and sustaining changes in social conduct, and emphasized the value of involving participants in every phase of the action research process. He also saw action research as based on principles which could lead 'gradually to independence, equality and cooperation' and effectively alter policies of 'permanent exploitation' which he saw as 'likely to endanger every aspect of democracy'.[18] Lewin saw action research as being essential for the progress of 'basic social research'. In order to 'develop deeper insights into the laws which govern social life', mathematical and conceptual problems of theoretical analysis would be required, as would 'descriptive fact-finding in regard to small and large social bodies'. 'Above all', he argued, basic social research 'would have to include laboratory and field experiments in social change'.[19]

Lewin thus presaged three important characteristics of modern action research: its *participatory* character, its *democratic* impulse, and its *simultaneous contribution to social science and social change*. In each of these three areas, however, action researchers of the 1980s would take exception to Lewin's formulation of the significance of action research. First, they would regard group decision-making as important as a matter of principle, rather than as a matter of technique; that is, not merely as an effective means of facilitating and maintaining social change, but also as essential for authentic commitment to social action. Second, contemporary exponents of action research would object to the notion that participants should, or could, be 'led' to more democratic forms of life through action research. Action research should not be seen as a recipe or technique for bringing about democracy, but rather as an embodiment of democratic principles in research, allowing participants to influence, if not determine, the conditions of their own lives and work, and collaboratively to develop critiques of social conditions which sustain dependence, inequality or exploitation. Third, contemporary action researchers would object to the language in which Lewin describes the theoretical aims and methods of social science ('developing deeper insights into the laws that govern social life' through mathematical and conceptual analysis and laboratory and field experiments). This language would now be described as positivistic and incompatible with the aims and methods of any adequate social or educational science.

Lewin developed the idea of action research in investigating social practices like production in factories, discrimination against minority groups, or habits of food buying in the middle 1940s. According to Lewin, action research consists of analysis, fact-finding and concep-tualization about problems; planning of action programmes, executing them, and then more fact-finding or evaluation; and then a repetition of this whole circle of activities; indeed, a spiral of such circles.[20] Through the spirals of these activities, action research creates conditions under which learning communities may be established; that is, communities of enquirers committed to learning about and understanding the problems and effects of their own strategic action, and the improve-ment of this strategic action in practice.

Participants in a National Invitational Seminar on Action Research held at Deakin University, Geelong, Victoria in May 1981, agreed on a definition of educational action research which is presented here in a slightly edited form:

> Educational action research is a term used to describe a family of
> activities in curriculum development, professional develop-

ment, school improvement programs, and systems planning and policy development. These activities have in common the identification of strategies of planned action which are *implemented*, and then systematically submitted to *observation, reflection and change*. Participants in the action being considered are integrally involved in all of these activities.[21]

In this definition, the Lewinian notion of the spiral is preserved in the notions of planning, acting, observing and reflecting. Participation, too, long recognized by Lewin and his colleagues as an essential aspect of the action research process, remains an essential feature. But the definition also gives central importance to the notion of *strategic action*. Action research, it is claimed, is the research method of preference whenever a *social practice* is the focus of research activity. It is to be preferred to positivistic research which treats social practices as functions of determinate systems, and to purely interpretive approaches which treat practices as cultural-historical products. In fact, social practices are essentially risky enterprises requiring judgments about their prudence, and as such they cannot be justified solely by reference to theoretical principles nor justified purely retrospectively by reference to their cultural and historical location.

There are two essential aims of all action research: to *improve* and to *involve*. Action research aims at improvement in three areas: firstly, the improvement of a *practice*; secondly, the improvement of the *understanding* of the practice by its practitioners; and thirdly, the improvement of the *situation* in which the practice takes place. The aim of *involvement* stands shoulder to shoulder with the aim of *improvement*. Those involved in the practice being considered are to be involved in the action research process in all its phases of planning, acting, observing and reflecting. As an action research project develops, it is expected that a widening circle of those affected by the practice will become involved in the research process.

What are the minimal requirements for action research? It can be argued that three conditions are individually necessary and jointly sufficient for action research to be said to exist: firstly, a project takes as its subject-matter a social practice, regarding it as a form of strategic action susceptible of improvement; secondly, the project proceeds through a spiral of cycles of planning, acting, observing and reflecting, with each of these activities being systematically and self-critically implemented and interrelated; thirdly, the project involves those responsible for the practice in each of the moments of the activity, widening participation in the project gradually to include others affected by the practice, and maintaining collaborative control of the process. Some of the work that now passes for action research in education does not meet these criteria. Some will develop towards meeting all of the requirements; some will be 'arrested' action research and falter before completing its development. Still other work will fail to meet these requirements and cannot seriously lay claim to the title 'action research' at all.

Lewin's early action research work was concerned with changes in attitudes and conduct in a number of areas of social concern and his ideas were carried quickly into education.[22] However, after a decade of growth, educational action research went into decline. Although some educational action research work continued in the United States, in 1970 Nevitt Sanford[23] argued that its decline was attributable to a growing separation of research and action, of theory from practice. As academic researchers in the social sciences began to enjoy unprecedented support from public funding bodies, they began to distinguish the work of the theorist-researcher from that of the 'engineer' responsible for putting theoretical principles into practice. The rising tide of post-Sputnik curriculum development, based on a research-development-diffusion (RD and D) model of the relationship between research and practice, legitimated and sustained this separation. Large-scale curriculum development and evaluation activities, based on the cooperation of practitioners in development and evaluation tasks devised by theoreticians, diverted legitimacy and energy from the essentially small-scale, locally organized, self-reflective approach of action research. By the mid-1960s, the technical research development and diffusion (RD and D) model had established itself as the pre-eminent model for change.

The initial resurgence of contemporary interest in educational action research arose from the work of the 1973–76 Ford Teaching Project in Britian, under the direction of John Elliott and Clem Adelman.[24] This project involved teachers in collaborative action research into their own practices, and its central notion of the 'self-monitoring teacher' was based on Lawrence Stenhouse's[25] views of the teacher as a researcher and as an 'extended professional'. There are a number of reasons why this project led to a resurgence of interest. First, there was the demand from within an increasingly professionalized teacher force for a research role, based on the notion of the extended professional investigating his or her own practice. Second, there was the perceived irrelevance to the concerns of these practitioners of much contemporary educational research. Third, there had been a revival of interest in 'the practical' in curriculum, following the work of Schwab[26] and others on 'practical deliberation'. Fourth, action research was assisted by the rise of the 'new wave' methods in educational research and evaluation with their emphasis on participants' perspectives and categories in shaping educational practices and situations. These methods place the practitioners at centre stage in the educational research process and recognize the crucial significance of actors' understandings in shaping educational action. From the role of critical informant helping an 'outsider' researcher, it is but a short step for the practitioner to become a self-critical researcher into her or his own practice. Fifth, the accountability movement galvanized and politicized practioners. In response to the accountability movement, practitioners have adopted the self-monitoring role as a proper means of justifying practice and generating sensitive critiques of the working conditions in which their practice is conducted.[27] Sixth, there was increasing solidarity in the teaching profession in response to the public criticism which has accompanied the post-expansion educational politics of the 1970s and 1980s; this, too, has prompted the organization of support networks of concerned professionals interested in the continuing developments of education even though the expansionist tide has turned. And, finally, there is the increased awareness of action research itself, which is perceived as providing an understandable and workable approach to the improvement of practice through critical self-reflection.

A range of practices have been studied by educational action researchers and some examples may suffice to show how they have used action research to improve their practices, their understandings of these practices, and the situations in which they work.

For several years, John Henry at Deakin University has worked with teachers concerned to explore the problems and effects of enquiry teaching in science.[28] Through close analysis of transcripts of their own teaching, the teachers involved discovered how their normal practices of classroom interaction, emphasizing didactic talk and closed questioning, actually operated to deny students the opportunity to raise their own questions and to develop independence of the teacher in their learning. Instead, the teachers' usual teaching practices were predicated on maintaining classroom control through controlling classroom talk. The teachers learned to change the form of their classroom questioning, and to provide resources which encouraged students to raise questions in a framework of classroom activity which would give them opportunities to answer the questions they had raised. Not only did they change their practices of questioning, however: they also changed the way they understood classroom questioning. They understood it in terms of classroom control as well as in terms of sharing knowledge. They began to understand more deeply how their questioning practices could create or deny opportunities for students to engage actively in the learning process. These teachers also changed the situations in which they worked, though not without some personal struggle. Their classrooms changed physically (there were more resources to support students' independent enquiries) and socially (students came to have more control over their own classroom behaviour, and teachers and students began to negotiate the learning activities of the classroom).

The teachers who worked with John Henry collaborated in their own learning process (in some projects, several teachers in an individual school were involved, in others, teachers from different schools worked together). They used the self-reflective spiral of action research to make initial observations and analyze their current teaching practices, then planned ways they wanted to change and observed the problems and effects of the changes they introduced, then reflected on their observations to decide how next to act in the process of improving their practice. By the end of a number of cycles of action research, they began to achieve marked differences in their classroom practices which they regarded as clear improvements in the education available in their classrooms, and they were able to report on the improvements they had made.

A group of teachers worked with Stephen Kemmis and others at Deakin University in exploring the problems and effects of strategies for remedial reading teaching in the junior secondary school.[29] They began by describing about ten different strategies that could be employed by remedial reading teachers, and by analyzing the problems of remedial reading teaching that they wanted to address. The group decided to make a closer analysis of four of the strategies (uninterrupted, sustained, silent reading; the formation of consultative groups of teachers in schools; contract learning; and team teaching). Different teachers collected data on the strategies of interest to them, and attempted to improve their implementation of the strategies in the light of the data they collected. Their practices changed as they sharpened their understandings of the problems and effects of each strategy, and there were changes in the situations in which they worked (for example, in involving more teachers in responding to the needs of children with reading problems, changing the school day to place greater emphasis on the development of reading, or establishing teams of regular classroom teachers and specialist 'remedial' teachers to bring the remedial teaching into the regular classroom). In particular, these teachers began to understand how some strategies for remedial reading teaching actually divorced reading skills from the learning contexts for which they were required; how some strategies preserved and strengthened the labelling of some students as 'remedial' students rather than helping them to overcome their difficulties; how some strategies deskilled students by taking them out of the classroom learning context in which they needed to develop substantive knowledge and skills and thus maintained their poor performance in classroom work; and how some strategies denied rather than created conditions under which teachers could work together to help students develop needed reading skills across the curriculum.

In a project which involved teachers from several schools in developing a school-controlled approach to in-service education, several teachers explored the issue of negotiating classroom rules with students.[30] Faced with discipline problems in the classroom, they involved students in setting rules for classroom behaviour, and came to develop a shared sense of responsibility for maintaining a classroom climate conducive to learning. Teachers and students together came to understand how their own classroom practices created a climate for others, and how teacher-centred classroom control actually worked to deny student responsibility for classroom climate. The success of the strategy of negotiating classroom rules was so marked that a number of teachers in the school took it up, and the general view of the school on classroom control and teachers' responsibilities for it began to change.

In the same project, a teacher explored the problems and effects of descriptive, non-competitive assessment as an alternative to competitive numerical grading. The project began with work in an 'alternative' programme for low-achieving year 10 students. The teacher reasoned that these students had a low sense of their own worth which had been reinforced by competitive grading in which they seemed always to do poorly by comparison with their classmates. In order to implement the strategy of descriptive, non-competitive assessment, the teachers in the class established a system in which a class meeting determined learning tasks for the whole class, and divided responsibilities for the task among the class group. For each task, clear and explicit requirements were agreed, and students could determine individually, collectively and with their teachers whether requirements were met when the tasks were completed. By gathering data on classroom participation, on the quality of work done and on the amount of work actually completed by students, the teachers were able to modify their own practices. They also came to understand how students could take responsibility for their learning and succeed in their own terms. Their classroom situation was dramatically different from the one these teachers established in their early work with this 'alternative' group. The strategy was sufficiently successful that they began to implement it in other classes with some success, and there was a suggestion that the process might be employed more widely in the school. Despite the strong argument they mounted for changing the school's assessment policy on the basis of the evidence they collected, however, other teachers who had not been involved in the action research process remained unconvinced, and the general assessment policy was not changed. The situation did not change as radically as the teachers involved had hoped, but they learned something about the change process itself: that they needed to involve others in the learning process they had gone through, and to involve them early.

A variety of other accounts of action research studies, especially action research by teachers, could be given. Several collections of teacher action research have now been published which show something of its richness and diversity.[31] Studies of action research conducted by students are also beginning to emerge.[32]

Perhaps one slightly more extended account of an action research project would be helpful in forming an image of how action research works in practice. We have used this example because it is widely available.[33]

The example is Jo-Anne Reid's study of negotiating the curriculum. It recounts an investigation into the problems and potential of curriculum negotiation in a year 9 English class in a Perth, Western Australia, secondary school. The study involved Reid, an advisory teacher (normally working as a consultant to other teachers) in an investigation into the role of language in learning in the classroom.

A National Working Party of the Role of Language in Learning had been established in 1977 by the Curriculum Development Centre in Canberra, and had provided an opportunity for a coordinated exploration of issues related to the role of language in learning by advisers and teachers around Australia. Of particular concern to the Working Party was the notion that students learn through using language; it followed, then, that teaching and learning strategies which recognized and extended children's own language could more surely engage children in particular learning tasks and more surely contribute to learning by recognizing what the children already knew (as this was expressed in and mediated through their own language). From this proposition, the slogan 'negotiating the curriculum' was fashioned. In a negotiated curriculum, teachers would invite students to reflect on what they already knew about a topic, to decide what else they would like to know about it, to consider ways they might find out what they wanted to know, to implement plans to find out more after negotiation with peers and teachers, and to evaluate the success of their enquiries by reflection on what they had learned in the light of their initial aims and plans. (These steps in the process of curriculum negotiation bear strong similarities to those of the spiral of self-reflection in action research.) The teacher would function in these enquiries as a stimulus for students, provoking reflection; as a resource, providing ideas and information when it seemed helpful; and as a constraint, limiting the scope of enquiries by relating individual student plans to one another (to create opportunities for student collaboration) and to areas in which the teacher was willing and able to function as a resource.

As an English teacher, Jo-Anne Reid was aware of the work of the National Working Party, and she believed that its general principles about the relationship between students' language and their learning were right and appropriate. They were also practicable. She was interested to explore them further for herself in the classroom, however, and, in particular, to explore the idea of curriculum negotiation. She thus 'borrowed' a class of thirty-four year 9 students for sixteen periods (over eight weeks in 1979). This would allow her to explore curriculum negotiation for herself, as one of a group of English teachers and consultants exploring the role of language in learning and curriculum negotiation in Perth at that time.

Curriculum negotiation involves giving students a voice in the choice and development of learning opportunities in the classroom: both the 'what' and the 'how' of curriculum. As a stranger to the class, Reid needed a topic area which could interest the students rapidly; it was the International Year of the Child, so Reid chose the topic 'Kids in schools',

> on the assumption that this was one situation that everybody in
> the class would
> (a) have direct experience of;
> (b) have formed personal opinions on;
> (c) be able to relate directly to themselves, and therefore;
> (d) find a non-threatening area to examine with a stranger.[34]

In the spirit of negotiating the curriculum, Reid was thus constituting the class as a reflective and self-reflective community of participant-researchers.

By choosing an enquiry topic which the students could relate to directly, Reid created conditions under which they could reflect on their own experience (and, as the work progressed, on their own processes of reflection and enquiry), and was able to create a convergence between her educational aim of fostering reflection among students and her own (self-educational) aim of self-reflection on strategies for curriculum negotiation.

Reid was thus creating conditions in which five separate levels of reflection were being organized:

(i)   students' substantive reflection on the topic of 'kids in schools';

(ii)   students' self-reflection on the processes by which they pursued their investigation of the topic (which also, by the way, allowed them to explore their insights about what they found out about 'kids in school' as they came to bear on their own processes of investigation in the exercise);

(iii)   Reid's reflection on the practices involved in negotiating the curriculum in this specific case (Reid as teacher);

(iv)   Reid's reflection on these practices as educational practices within the broader framework of strategies for English teaching with which she was concerned as an advisory teacher in English (Reid as advisory teacher); and

(v)   Reid's self-reflection on her own processes of reflection and enquiry (Reid as teacher-researcher).

At each of these levels, participants were collaboratively involved in reflection and self-reflection (planning, acting, observing and reflecting together).

It is clear from the account this far that Reid was fulfilling the conditions of *participation* and *collaboration* characteristic of critical social science.

Following the model of curriculum negotiation, Reid asked the students to list what they knew about school, and then to list what they didn't know but wanted to find out. She then asked them to decide how to find answers to the questions they had posed for themselves, through discussion and group decision.

Throughout the process, the students kept journals recording their activities and progress, as did Reid herself. These data provided a documentary record but also provoked and recorded self–reflection about the processes all were engaged in. The collection of this evidence promotes the attitude of self–reflection (distancing) as well as providing material for it. Keeping a journal helps participants to become what Bev Beasley[35] called 'reflexive spectators' who reflect on their actions and transform their ideas and their future action in the light of reflection.

In these ways, the study was beginning to develop a *critical* perspective: it was creating the conditions under which the participants could consider their own interests (as students, teacher, etc.) and perhaps, how they related to wider social interests.

Perhaps also, the topic 'kids in school' (for the students) and 'the negotiated curriculum' (for Reid and the other teachers and advisers she worked with) began to provoke an *emancipatory* interest in how schools and teaching are shaped and formed (that is, in ideological questions), and in how they might be made better (through changing conditions of communication, decision–making and educational action). It is difficult to say whether or how far this emancipatory intent developed on the basis of Reid's report, but clearly the topics invited self–reflection along these lines.

There is no doubt, however, that the study was *practical*: for students and teacher alike, it engaged them in considering their own practices, and in modifying their practices in the light of their reflection and self–reflection. For students, it provided an opportunity to think about their learning practices and the conditions of their learning; for Reid as a teacher, it provided an opportunity to reflect on the practices of negotiating the curriculum; for Reid as advisory teacher, it provided an opportunity to reflect on curriculum negotiation in relation to other teaching practices in English; for Reid as teacher-researcher, it provided an opportunity to reflect on action research as a way of improving teaching.

The study involved several cycles of planning, acting, observing and reflecting, with reflection providing a basis for planning what to do next.

The study produced several sets of 'findings':

(i)   At the level of the students' investigation of 'kids in school', it produced insights for students which they presented to students at a nearby primary school;

(ii)   at the level of student self-reflection on the enquiry process, it produced conclusions about their own participation in the process, and evaluations of enquiry as an approach to learning;

(iii) at the level of reflection about negotiating the curriculum as a strategy (Reid as teacher), it produced insights about the problems and prospects of the approach.

These first three sets of 'findings' are quite explicit in the report. Two further levels are present, but implicit:

(iv) at the level of reflection on English teaching and the role of language in learning, the report contains reflections on the nature of students' writing and talk in the context of the negotiated curriculum; these comments presume an interested and critical community of fellow English teachers;

(v) at the level of self-reflection on the action research process, the report provides information and commentary for others interested in teacher-research (for example, comments about data-gathering techniques and the difficulties encountered: problems of audio-taping, problems with the regularity of journal-writing, and problems of ensuring time for reflection).

We have not been explicit about the findings of Reid's study: it is a story she tells herself. The example does show, however, how one teacher learned about her educational practices by changing them, and by observing systematically and reflecting carefully on the problems and effects of the changes she made.

4 Conclusion

This chapter began with the idea of a critical social science, explored it in the particular context of educational research and proposed the idea of a critical educational science. It argued that the practice of critical educational science cannot be derived from theory alone; it also involves a commitment on the part of educational researchers inside and outside the educational process to the improvement of education. It also requires participation by those whose practices constitute education in researching education. Clearly, it involves teachers in researching education, and it can also involve students, parents, school administrators and others. The conditions of its success are in the improvement of actual educational practices, the improvement of the understandings of those involved in the educational process, and the improvement of the situations in which those practices are carried out. Through a discussion of the nature and history of educational action research and by describing some practical examples, an initial case was made for suggesting that educational action research meets these conditions. It is to a more detailed analysis of educational action research as a critical educational science that we now turn.

Further Reading

The volume *Knowledge and Values in Social and Educational Research* edited by E. Bredo and W. Feinberg provides a useful collection of papers concerned with the three main approaches to educational research discussed in this book. It presents several classical papers about each approach to research methodology, some examples, and strong introductory commentaries for each of its main sections. The papers in the last section, on critical research, are especially relevant to the concerns we have addressed in this chapter. For a more general discussion of Marxist epistemology and education, the book *The Marxist Theory of Schooling: A Study of Epistemology and Education* by Michael Matthews provides a helpful introduction to major issues both in relation to general concerns about education and in relation to the problem of theory and practice. Brian Simon's paper 'Educational research: Which way?', initially his Presidential address to the British Educational Research Association in 1977 (published in 1978), discusses the problem of intelligence testing from a historical materialist viewpoint. It makes a powerful argument about the way educational research can relate to educational practice.

The 'classical' text for educational action researchers is Stephen Corey's *Action Research to Improve School Practices*. The text which has provided the basis for much of the contemporary interest in educational action research is Lawrence Stenhouse's *Introduction to Curriculum Research and Development*.

A set of recent anthologies, books and monographs will extend the reader's familiarity with the field in recent years. Kemmis, *et al. The Action Research Reader* presents key papers from the history of action research and gives examples of teacher action research written by teachers themselves. Jon Nixon has edited an impressive collection of British teachers' accounts of their own action research projects in *A Teacher's Guide to Action Research*. John Elliott and others report action research in the context of school accountability in their report of the British Social Science Research Council Cambridge Accountability Project entitled *School Accountability*.[36] Gwyneth Dow has edited an interesting collection of Australian accounts of teacher research in *Teacher Learning*.[37] Garth Boomer and others present an important collection of action research studies concerned with the role of language in learning and the negotiation of curriculum with students in the book *Negotiating the Curriculum*.

Robin McTaggart and Stephen Kemmis have produced a brief guide to planning and conducting action research studies called *The Action Research Planner*.[38]

Notes

1 FARGANIS, J. (1975), 'A preface to critical theory', *Theory and Society*, vol. 2, no. 4, p. 504.
2 MARX, K. (1941), 'Theses on Feuerbach', in ENGELS, A. (Ed.) *Ludwig Feuerbach*, New York, International Publishers.
3 BLEICHER, J. (1980), *Hermeneutics as Method, Philosophy and Critique*, London, Routledge and Kegan Paul, p. 233.
4 FAY, B. (1977), *Social Theory and Political Practice*, London, George, Allen and Unwin, p. 109.
5 COMSTOCK, D. (1982), 'A method for critical research', in BREDO, E. and FEINBERG, W. (Eds) *Knowledge and Values in Social and Educational Research*, Philadelphia, Temple University Press, pp. 378–9.
6 A compelling example of critical educational analysis undertaken by a group of students is recounted in SCHOOL OF BARBIANA (authors), (1971) *Letter to a Teacher* Harmondsworth, Penguin Education Special. The book is a chilling indictment of 1950s educational provision for the children of Italian peasants, and reveals a lucid critical understanding of education and a lucid understanding of the practices which constituted a defensible critical alternative to state provision for these children.
7 FREIRE, P. (1970) *Cultural Action for Freedom*, Cambridge, Mass., Center for the Study of Social Change, p. 27.
8 In HABERMAS, J. (1972) *Knowledge and Human Interests* (trans. SHAPIRO, J.J.), London, Heinemann; and his (1974) *Theory and Practice* (trans. VIERTEL J.), London, Heinemann.
9 HABERMAS, J. (1974), *op. cit.*, p. 2.
10 For an example of this view, see POPKEWITZ, T. (1984) *Paradigm and Ideology in Educational Research*, Lewes, Falmer Press.
11 HABERMAS, J. (1974), *op. cit.*, pp. 38–9.
12 COMSTOCK, D. (1982), *op. cit.*
13 For example, HABERMAS, J. (1974), *op. cit.*, p. 29.
14 *Ibid.*, p. 40.
15 MATTHEWS, M. (1980), *The Marxist Theory of Schooling: A Study of*

Epistemology and Education, Brighton, Harvester, p. 86.

16 For example, SIMON, B. (1978), 'Educational research: Which way?', *Research Intelligence*, vol. 4, no. 1, pp. 2–7; BROADFOOT, P. (1979), 'Educational research through the looking glass', *Scottish Educational Review*, vol. 11, no. 2, pp. 133–42; CODD, J. (1983), 'Educational research as political practice', paper presented to the annual meeting of the Australian Association for Research in Education, Canberra, November.

17 LEWIN, K. (1952), 'Group decisions and social change', in SWANSON, G.E., NEWCOMB, T.M. and HARTLEY, F.E., (Eds) *Readings in Social Psychology*, New York, Holt.

18 See, for example, LEWIN, K. (1946) 'Action research and minority problems', *Journal of Social Issues*, vol. 2, pp. 34–6 (reprinted in KEMMIS, S., *et al.* (Eds.) (1982) *The Action Research Reader*, Geelong, Victoria, Deakin University Press, pp. 32–7).

19 LEWIN, K. (1952), *op. cit.*

20 *Ibid.*, p. 35.

21 See, BROWN, L. *et al.* (1981) 'Action research: notes on the national seminar', School of Education, Deakin University (mimeo).

22 COREY, S. (1953), *Action Research to Improve School Practices*, Columbia University, New York, Teachers' College.

23 SANFORD, N. (1970), 'Whatever happened to action research?', *Journal of Social Issues*, vol. 26, pp. 3–23 (reprinted in KEMMIS, S. *et al.*, (1982), *op. cit.*).

24 See, for example, ELLIOTT, J. (1976–7), 'Developing hypotheses about classrooms from teachers' practical constructs: An account of the Ford Teaching Project', *Interchange*, vol. 7, no. 2, pp. 2–20 (reprinted in KEMMIS, S. *et al.*, (1982) *op. cit.*).

25 STENHOUSE, L. (1975), *Introduction to Curriculum Research and Development*, London, Heinemann.

26 SCHWAB, J.J. (1969), 'The practical: A language for curriculum', *School Review*, vol. 78, pp. 1–24.

27 See, for example, ELLIOTT, J. *et al.* (1981) *School Accountability,* London, Grant McIntyre.

28 HENRY, J. (1985), *A Critical Analysis of Action Research-Based In-service Education: Four Case Studies*, unpublished Ph.D. thesis, Geelong, Victoria, Deakin University.

29 KEMMIS, S. (1982), 'The remedial reading group: A case study in cluster-based action research in schools', in KEMMIS, S. *et al.* (Eds) *The Action Research Reader*, Geelong, Victoria.

30 FENTON, J. *et al.* (1984), *School-controlled In-service Education* (a report of the Wimmera school-controlled in-service education project), Horsham, Education Department of Victoria (mimeo).

31 Examples include BOOMER, G. (Ed.) (1983), *Negotiating the Curriculum*, Sydney, Ashton Scholastic; NIXON, J. (Ed.) (1981), *A Teachers' Guide to Action Research*, London, Grant McIntyre; and KEMMIS, S. *et al.* (Eds) (1982), *op. cit.*

32 See, for example, COVENTRY, G. *et al.* (1984) *Student Perspectives on Truancy*, Melbourne, Victorian Institute of Secondary Education,

(mimeo); and HENRY, C. (1985) *Enduring a Lot: A Report to the Human Rights Commission on the Effects of Schools on Students with non-English Speaking Backgrounds*, Geelong, Victoria, Deakin University, (mimeo).

33 REID, J. 'Negotiating the curriculum' in both KEMMIS, S. *et al.* (Eds) (1982), *op. cit.* and BOOMER, G. (Ed.) (1983), *op. cit.*

34 *Ibid.* (p. 128 in KEMMIS, S. *et al.* (1982)).

35 BEASLEY, B. (1981), 'The reflexive spectator in classroom research', paper presented at the annual meeting of the Australian Association for Research in Education, Adelaide, November.

36 ELLIOTT, J. *et al.* (1981) *School Accountability*, London, Grant McIntyre.

37 DOW, G. (Ed.) (1982) *Teacher Learning*, Melbourne, Routledge and Kegan Paul.

38 McTAGGART, R. and KEMMIS, S. (1982), *The Action Research Planner*, Geelong, Victoria, Deakin University Press.

Chapter 7

Action Research as Critical Educational Science★

1 Introduction

Chapter 5 began by identifying five formal requirements that any coherent educational science must be able to meet and concluded that these requirements may be satisfied by Habermas's notion of a critical social science. Chapter 6, therefore, discussed the notion of a critical *educational* science arising from the general conception of a critical social science, and explored the idea of educational action research as a form of research *for* education which offered a way of enacting a critical educational science. The purpose of this chapter is to further explore this idea by examining educational action research in relation to the five requirements of an educational science that have been identified.

This will entail, first, indicating how action research rejects positivist notions of rationality, objectivity and truth in favour of a dialectical view of rationality. Second, it will entail indicating how action research employs the interpretive categories of teachers by using them as the basis for 'language frameworks' which teachers explore and develop in their own theorizing. Third, it will entail showing how action research provides a means by which distorted self-understandings may be overcome by teachers analyzing the way their own practices and understandings are shaped by broader ideological conditions.

Fourth, it will involve considering how action research, by linking reflection to action, offers teachers and others a way of becoming aware of how those aspects of the social order which frustrate rational change

★ We are indebted to Shirley Grundy who assisted substantially in the development of some of the ideas presented in this chapter.

may be overcome. Finally, it involves returning to the question of theory and practice, to show that self-critical communities of action researchers enact a form of social organization in which truth is determined by the way it relates to practice.

2 A Dialectical View of Rationality

The 'objects' of action research — the things that action researchers research and that they aim to improve — are their own educational practices, their understandings of these practices, and the situations in which they practice. Unlike positivist educational researchers, action researchers do not treat these 'objects' as 'phenomena' by analogy with the objects of physical science, as if practices, understandings or social situations were independent of the researcher-practitioner, and determined by universal physical laws. Nor do action researchers regard their practices, understandings or situations as 'treatments' by analogy with the objects of agricultural research, as if education were a purely technical process of achieving higher 'yields' of educational attainment.

Some philosophical objections to the positivist view of educational science and its associated view of the relationship between theory and practice were outlined in Chapter 2. An additional reason why action researchers cannot regard the 'objects' of action research as determined, independent, external 'phenomena' is because they recognize that their educational practices, understandings and situations are their own — that they are deeply implicated in creating and constituting them as educational. Nor do action researchers take a technical or instrumental view of the relationship between theory and practice. The problems of education are not simply problems of achieving known ends; they are problems of acting *educationally* in social situations which typically involve competing values and complex interactions between different people who are acting on different understandings of their common situation and on the basis of different values about how the interactions should be conducted.

Neither can action researchers accept the interpretive view of educational practices, understandings and situations. Where positivists are inclined to reduce these things to physicalistic descriptions of behaviour and the conditions which determine it, interpretivists are inclined to construe educational practices and situations solely as expressions of practitioners' intentions, perspectives, values and understandings, and thus to fall prey to a rationalist theory of action which suggests that ideas alone guide action, and that changed ideas can produce different social or educational action. The interpretive researcher aims to understand practices and situations by seeking their significance in the ideas of actors. As was argued in Chapter 3, this view of social or educational science fails to account for the external conditions which distort and constrain actors' understandings, and fails to provide actors with ways of identifying these distortions and ways of overcoming the constraints on their action. Action researchers therefore reject the account of the relationship between theory and practice given by interpretive research because they reject the view that transformations of consciousness are sufficient to produce transformations of social reality.

Nevertheless, action researchers accept that transformations of social reality cannot be achieved without engaging the understandings of the social actors involved. They accept that understanding the way people construe their practices and their situations is a crucial element in transforming education, but not that this understanding provides a sufficient basis for achieving such transformations.

In the last Chapter, we considered Matthews's view that 'consciousness arises out of and is shaped by practice, and in turn is judged in and by practice'.[1] This statement encapsulates a very different view of rationality to the views we have so far considered. It is also central to all Marxist and non-Marxist theories of knowledge which take the view that knowledge is the outcome of human activity that is motivated by natural needs and interests, and that takes place in a social and historical context. According to those views, human activity has its meaning and significance only by virtue of its being understood by social actors as activity of a certain kind, whether by actors themselves as social agents, by the people with whom they interact, or by scientific observers. It is interpreted in terms of language categories whose meaning is established through the social process of learning to mean in social interaction. Hence, the possibility of expressing a true statement only exists by virtue of shared language which, as Wittgenstein[2] pointed out, is in turn only possible on the basis of shared forms of social life. Truth and action are thus interdependent, and exist in a social matrix within which meanings are constructed and actions can be given meaning. But coming to mean does not happen in a vacuum. It is a process which takes place in and through history, even if only the history of a small group or only over a short period of time. To understand any human activity of any general significance at all requires seeing it in an historical, as well as a social, framework.

Equally, language itself has a history, and to understand any supposed truth or any truth claims requires setting it in the framework by which language came to mean, and to allow us to mean, the particular thing being claimed.

Action research, being concerned with the improvement of educational practices, understandings and situations, is necessarily based on a view of truth and action as socially-constructed and historically-embedded. First, it is itself an historical process of *transforming* practices, understandings and situations — it takes place in and through history. Any action research study or project begins with one pattern of practices and understandings in one situation, and ends with another, in which some practices or elements of them are *continuous* through the improvement process while others are *discontinuous* (new elements have been added, old ones have been dropped, and transformations have occurred in still others). Similarly, understandings undergo a process of historical transformation. And the situation in which the practices are conducted will also have been transformed in some ways.

Second, action research involves relating practices and understandings and situations to one another. It involves discovering *correspondences* and *non-correspondences* between *understandings and practices* (for example, by counterposing such categories as rhetoric and reality or theory and practice), between *practices and situations* (for example, by counterposing practices against the institutional permissions and constraints which shape them), and between *understandings and situations* (for example, by counterposing the educational values of practitioners and their self-interests as these are shaped by institutional organizational structures and rewards). The action researcher, in aiming to improve practices, understandings and situations, is therefore aiming to move more surely into the future by understanding how her or his practices are socially-constructed and historically-embedded, and by seeing the situations or institutions in which she or he works in an historical and social perspective.

Action research is also a deliberately *social process*. It focuses on the social practices of education, on understandings whose meaning is shareable only in the social processes of language and social situations, including educational institutions. Not only does it involve the action researcher in recognizing the social character of educational practices, understandings and situations; it also engages the action researcher in extending the action research process to involve others in collaborating in all phases of the research process.

In adopting a view of truth and action as socially-constructed and historically-embedded, action research is not distinctive: interpretive educational researchers adopt a similar view. But action researchers are distinct from interpretive researchers in adopting a more activist view of their role; unlike interpretive researchers who aim to understand the significance of the past to the present, action researchers aim to transform the present to produce a different future. While interpretive researchers are relatively passive, action researchers are deliberately activist. While positivistic educational researchers may often be described as 'objectivist', emphasizing the objective status of knowledge as independent of the observer, and interpretivist educational researchers may be described as 'subjectivist', emphasizing the subjective understandings of the actor as a basis for interpreting social reality, critical educational researchers, including educational action researchers, adopt a view of rationality which is *dialectical*. Hence, they recognize that there are 'objective' aspects of social situations which are beyond the power of some particular individuals to influence at a particular time and that to change the way people act it may be necessary to change the way these constraints limit their action. At the same time, they recognize that people's 'subjective' understandings of situations can also act as constraints on their action, and that these understandings can be changed. In fact, what is an 'objective' set of constraints for one person (for example, institutional rules which prevent her or him from taking certain courses of action) may be a 'subjective' constraint for another (who never thought of taking a particular course of action which happens to be contrary to institutional rules). The action researcher attempts to discover how situations are constrained by 'objective' and 'subjective' conditions, and to explore how both kinds of conditions can be changed.

For example, if someone argues that there is no time for a certain important topic to be covered in the school timetable, the action researcher will argue that the ('objective') constraint of time is only apparent; in fact, the issue of time is an issue about how people choose to use their time, and that either the timetable should be changed, or the important topic should be included in a subject already in the timetable. On the other hand, if someone argues that certain students do poorly in certain subjects because their home background has not given them the background knowledge or skills to handle the subject (a 'subjective' constraint), then the action researcher will argue that it is the business of the school to create learning conditions which overcome this lack of background. In short, the action researcher attempts to see the interplay between so-called 'objective' and so-called 'subjective' constraints on knowledge and action, and to achieve a perspective from which the contributions of both sets of factors can be understood in constraining social reality.

A dialectical view of rationality recognizes the partial, one-sided contributions of the 'objectivist' and 'subjectivist' positions, rejecting the determinism and physicalism of the first and the relativism and rationalist theory of action of the second. The dialectical view does recognize, however, that there are 'objective' constraints on social thought and action which are beyond the control of particular individuals or groups. Equally, it recognizes that there are 'subjective' constraints which people could change if they knew more or understood the world differently, but which do limit their potential for changed thought and action.

The dialectical view of rationality employed by action researchers places particular emphasis on the dialectical relationships between two pairs of terms which are normally thought of as opposed and mutually-exclusive: theory and practice and individual and society. How theory and practice are dialectically related has already been discussed. The dialectical relationship of individual and society is closely related to this discussion: theory and practice, or thought and action, are socially-constructed and historically-embedded. Individual thought and action have their meaning and significance in a social and historical context, yet, at the same time, themselves contribute to the formation of social and historical contexts. This *double dialectic* of theory and practice, on the one hand, and individual and society, on the other, is at the heart of action research as a participatory and collaborative process of self-reflection. Action research recognizes that thought and action arise from practices in particular situations, and that situations themselves can be transformed by transforming the practices that constitute them and the understandings that make them meaningful. This involves transformations in *individual* practices, understandings and situations, and transformations in the practices, understandings and situations which *groups* of people constitute through their interaction. The double dialectic of thought and action and individual and society is resolved, for action research, in the notion of a *self-critical community* of action researchers who are committed to the improvement of education, who are researchers *for* education.

Chapter 6 referred to the Lewinian notion of a self-reflective spiral of cycles of planning, acting, observing, reflecting then replanning, further action, further observation and further reflection. This self-reflective spiral demonstrates a further dialectical quality of action research: the dialectic of retrospective analysis and prospective action.

The 'action' moment of the cycle is a probe into the future — the taking of a step which reflection alone cannot justify. It also requires a commitment, based on practical judgment, to act in order to achieve certain hoped-for consequences. But action always entails the risk that one's judgment or the judgment of a collaborating group will be wrong and that things will turn out in ways other than was expected. The action research process involves a sequence of such practical judgments and practical actions. The improvement of educational practices, understandings, and situations depends on a spiral of cycles which bring action under programmatic control: the first action step is incorporated into the self-reflective framework of the first cycle; the first cycle is incorporated into a spiral of such cycles. As the action research process gets under way it becomes a *project* aiming at a transformation of individual and collective practices, individual and shared understandings, and the situations in which participants interact. From these particular projects, a *programme* of reform emerges — each project embodies particular practices of collaborative self-reflection, employs particular understandings of the process of self-reflection (a theory of critical social or educational science), and establishes a particular form of social situation for the purposes of self-reflection (what Habermas calls 'the organization of enlightenment'). The establishment of a widening circle of self-reflective communities of action researchers in this way foreshadows and engenders a different form of social organization — perhaps the kind of social organization Habermas had in mind in his book *Toward a Rational Society*.[3]

In action research, a single loop of planning, acting, observing and reflecting is only a beginning; if the process stops there it should not be regarded as action research at all. Perhaps it could be termed 'arrested action research'. Two kinds of arrested action research are evident in contemporary educational research and evaluation. The first is mere problem-solving, in which a problem is identified on the basis of some diagnosis or reflection, a plan is made, action is taken, and some final observation is made to check that the problem has been 'solved'. The second case is that species of evaluation exercises employing an instrumental aims-achievement model of evaluation in which the initial action-research-like cycle does not develop into a participatory and collaborative process of deepening reflection, more controlled and critical practice, and the establishment of more educationally defensible situations and institutions.

The essential epistemological problem to be considered in relation to the self-reflective spiral of action research is the problem of relating *retrospective* understanding to *prospective* action. Clearly, action research requires a different epistemology from positivist and interpretive approaches, both of which have difficulty relating retrospective explanation or understanding to prospective action. Positivistic research relies on a notion of prediction based on scientific laws established in past situations and expressed as controlled intervention, as its basis for informing future action. Interpretive research relies on a notion of practical judgment based on the understandings of the practitioner derived from the observation of previous situations. Action research involves both controlled intervention and practical judgment, but gives them both a limited place in the notion of the self-reflective spiral of action research which is arranged as a *programme* of controlled intervention *and* practical judgment conducted by individuals and groups committed not only to understanding the world but to changing it.

The essentially dialectical relationship between retrospective explanation or understanding and prospective action can be understood in terms of Marx's 'revolutionizing practice', Habermas's 'conduct of political struggle', or Freire's formula of 'problematization — conscientization — praxis'.[4] It may, however, be understood in the context of educational action research, as an organized programme of educational reform. At the level of the particular self-reflective spiral of a particular action research project, the tension between retrospective understanding and prospective action is enacted in each of the four 'moments' of the action research process, each of which 'looks back' to the previous moment for its justification, and 'looks forward' to the next moment for its realization, as represented in Figure 2.

Figure 2:   The 'moments' of action research

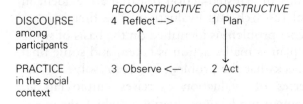

In the self-reflective spiral, the plan is prospective to action, retrospectively constructed on the basis of reflection. Action is essentially risky, but is retrospectively guided by past reflection on which basis the plan was made and prospectively guided towards observation and the future reflection which will evaluate the problems and effects of the action.

Observation is retrospective on the action being taken and prospective to reflection in which the action will be considered. Reflection is retrospective to the actions so far taken and prospective to new planning.

The self-reflective spiral links reconstruction of the past with construction of a concrete and immediate future through action. And it links the discourse of those involved in the action with their practice in the social context. Taken together, these elements of the process create the conditions under which those involved can establish a programme of critical reflection both for the organization of their own enlighten-ment and for the organization of their own collaborative action for educational reform.

This view of the self-reflective spiral of action research locates the process in history, casting the actors in the process as historical agents who understand from the outset that their consciousness arises from and is shaped by their historical practice, that their consciousness will in turn be judged in and by their practice. Through the action research process, action researchers thus become aware of themselves as both the products and producers of history. In this sense, action research gives concrete meaning to Marx's statement:

> The materialist doctrine that men are products of circumstances
> and upbringing and that, therefore, changed men are products
> of other circumstances and changed upbringing, forgets that it
> is men that change circumstances and that the educator himself
> must be educated.

In making this statement, Marx was objecting to the view that social reality was determined by objective conditions alone, a view closely associated with positivist educational science. In taking a view of their historical agency, which also recognizes that they are the products of history, action researchers can transcend the positivist view of rational-ity, with a view which consciously and dialectically interrelates *theory and practice, individual and society* and *retrospective understanding and prospective action*. In this sense, the self-reflective spiral of action research does not merely reject the positivist view; it also enacts a view of rationality as dialectical, as constructed in social practices, and as embedded in history.

3   The Systematic Development of Teachers' Interpretive Categories

The second requirement identified in Chapter 5 for any educational science was that it must employ the interpretive categories of teachers. Clearly, action research engages these categories in focusing on the improvement of practitioners' own *understandings* of their practices by involving practitioners in the systematic development of their understandings, both in the context of the practices themselves and also in the context of explicitly sharing and examining these understandings through communication between collaborating action researchers.

One of the things that makes action research 'research' is that it aims at the systematic development of knowledge in a self-critical community of practitioners. Lawrence Stenhouse had this to say about 'research':

> I see academia as a social system for the collaborative production of knowledge through research. Research is systematic enquiry made public. It is made public for criticism and utilization within a particular research tradition. . . .[5]

It may or may not be that 'academia' adequately produces knowledge which educational practitioners can use in the development of their own practice. In Chapter 6 we argued that the institutional separation of researchers from practitioners in much educational research actually mitigates against the development of educational practice by splitting the research task of researchers from the educational tasks of practitioners. Sanford[6] makes a similar point about social research in general to argue that action research can bridge the gap between research and practice. In several places[7], Stenhouse has argued strenuously for teacher-research on the grounds that improving educational practice requires engaging teachers' understandings of their own work, claiming, in one place, that 'using research means doing research'. Clearly, this does not entail only that teachers be reflective and critical users of research knowledge produced by other researchers; it entails in addition that teachers must establish self-critical communities of teacher-researchers which systematically develop the educational knowledge which justifies their educational practices and the educational situations constituted by these practices. This means that it is not only the systematic development of teachers' ideas or understandings which is essential to the development of education and educational research; it also requires the systematic development of educational *theory* by teachers who, as self-critical communities of educational researchers, establish their own critical and self-critical research tradition as an integral part of their attempt to develop education itself.

There are some who argue that teachers always operate according to 'implicit' or 'tacit' 'theories', even though they may not be conscious of their theories. On this view, teachers can be understood as acting *as if* they were following a set of principles. This description of 'having a theory' is unacceptable; much teacher action is the product of custom, habit, coercion and ideology which constrain action in ways that the teachers themselves do not recognize, as ways in which they would not deliberately choose if their sources in custom, habit or coercion were recognized. It is a misuse of the notion of 'theory' to assert that it is something which one can hold 'implicitly' or unconsciously. Indeed, for the concept of 'theory' to have any power at all requires that it is something consciously held by the person whose theory it is reputed to be, and that it is the product of reflection rather than mere habit, custom or coercion.

Action research is concerned with the development of educational theory of this kind. It is concerned not only to engage the understandings and interpretive categories of individuals; it is also concerned to explore how these interpretive categories relate to practice and to the systematic development of critical educational theories. In order to address this issue it will be useful to consider the relationship between personal knowledge, practice and *praxis*.

While practical experience can be gained through unsystematic reflection on action, a rational understanding of practice can only be gained through systematic reflection on action by the actor involved. The knowledge developed by action researchers about their own practices is of this kind; it includes what Michael Polanyi calls 'personal knowledge'. Such knowledge, he says, cannot be termed either 'subjective' or 'objective':

> Insofar as the personal submits to the requirements acknowledged by itself as independent of itself, it is not subjective; but insofar as it is an action guided by individual passions, it is not objective either. It transcends the disjunction between subjective and objective.[8]

Personal knowledge acquires this unique character through rational reflection on experience and the criterion by which it is judged is *authenticity*. When personal knowledge arises out of one's own rational reflection upon one's own considered action, it may be regarded as authentic. This implies that the actor alone can be the final arbiter of the truth of an interpretation of a considered action and, hence, that the correctness of the interpretation of an action is not a matter to be decided by external reference to rules or principles or theories. It does not imply, however, that the actor can be impervious to the interpretations others may make of his or her own action or understanding; these are only compelling for the actor to the extent that they are understood by the actor to be relevant to his or her own authentic knowledge. The criterion of authenticity thus acts as a defence against the politics of persuasion in educational research; the actor can only be expected to alter his or her own understanding of a situation to the extent that he or she understands others' interpretations as relevant.

Personal knowledge can be developed through rational discourse between action researchers and other people with whom they interact. The development of self-critical communities of action researchers actually puts the individual in a situation in which such discourse is required. Personal knowledge also develops in and through practice. 'Practice', in its commonsense meaning, is usually understood to refer to habitual or customary action. But it also means 'the exercise of an act', referring back to its origins in the Greek notion of *praxis*, meaning 'informed, committed action'. The action researcher distinguishes between practice as habitual or customary, on the one hand, and the informed, committed action of *praxis*, on the other. One way to describe the general aim of a critical educational science and of educational action research would be to say that both are interested in a critical revival of practice which can transform it into *praxis*, bringing it under considered critical control, and enlivening it with a commitment to educational and social values. The action researcher is interested in theorizing practice in the sense of setting practice in a critical framework of understanding which makes it rational, appropriate and prudent.

Praxis has its roots in the commitment of the practitioner to wise and prudent action in a practical, concrete, historical situation. It is action which is considered and consciously theorized, and which may reflexively inform and transform the theory which informed it. *Praxis* cannot be understood as mere behaviour; it can only be understood in terms of the understandings and commitments which inform it. Moreover, *praxis* is always risky; it requires that the practitioner makes a wise and prudent practical judgment about how to act in *this* situation. As Gauthier[9] remarks, 'practical problems are problems about what to do ... their solution is only found in doing something'.

The significance of *praxis* is that it is a response to a real historical situation in which an actor is compelled to act on the basis of understanding and commitment. Further, the actor and others can judge the correctness of the practical judgment actually made in praxis: they can observe and analyze the actual historical consequences of the action. *Praxis*, as the action taken in action research, is thus both a 'test' of the actor's understandings and commitments and the means by which these understandings and commitments can be critically developed. Since only the practitioner has access to the understandings and commitments which inform action in *praxis*, only the practitioner can study *praxis*. Action research therefore cannot be other than research into one's own practice.

It is for this reason that action research is essentially participatory; it is collaborative when groups of practitioners jointly participate in studying their own individual *praxis*, and when they study the social interactions between them that jointly constitute aspects of the situations in which they work. In action research projects organized by Elliott and Adelman[10] and John Henry[11], teachers have deliberately developed 'language frameworks' which allow them to describe particular problems and issues in their own teaching and to evaluate their teaching in the light of their understandings and their commitments. In these particular examples, the language frameworks have concerned enquiry teaching, 'open' and 'closed' questioning, and student dependence and independence. Using the language frameworks, teachers individually analyzed and critically evaluated their own practice; they also used the frameworks to discuss their understandings and their practices with one another. The explicit development of these language frameworks demonstrates how teachers have used action research projects to develop the interpretive categories they employ in understanding their own practice. In doing so, they draw the distinction between speech and discourse central to Habermas's theory of communicative competence. They do not simply talk about their practice (speech); they institute discourses about practice, in which the comprehensibility of utterances, their truth, the sincerity of speakers and the rightness of actions can all be examined.[12] In this way, action researchers come to develop their own educational theories from its basis in personal knowledge, through its expression in *praxis*, to its systematic development in the discourse of self-reflective communities of action researchers.

If it is only practitioners who can research their own *praxis*, a problem seems to arise about whether their research can ever be unbiased. The charge is often made that action research is always biased because it involves the researcher in analyzing his or her own practices. This seems to suggest that the 'findings' of action research are unreliable, perhaps the result of self-deception, or of ideological distortion.

Of course, this way of construing the problem of 'bias' suggests that there is some 'value-free' or 'neutral' medium in which *praxis* could be described and analyzed in ways which are unrelated to the values and interests of those doing the observing. This is an illusion created by the image of a value-free, 'objective' social science which, by definition, could not be a science of human *praxis*. Any science of human *praxis* must embody values and interests, both as objects of enquiry and as knowledge-constitutive interests for the science itself. The study of *praxis* (informed, committed action) is always *through praxis* (action with and for the critical development of understanding and commitment); it embodies *praxis* in the form of an interest in improving *praxis*. Moreover, this way of construing the problem fails to take seriously the claim of critical educational science that the very purpose of critical self-reflection is to expose and identify self-interests and ideological distortions. The practitioner sets out deliberately to examine where his or her own practice is distorted by taken-for-granted assumptions, habits, custom, precedent, coercion or ideology. The action researcher sets out to improve particular practices, understandings and situations by acting in a deliberate and considered way in which understandings and values are consciously expressed in *praxis*. Moreover, by observing the action taken and the consequences of the action, the action researcher deliberately arranges things so that these understandings and commitments can be critically examined. As was indicated in relation to the self-reflective spiral, the action researcher deliberately analyzes the correspondences and non-correspondences between understandings, practices and the structure of educational situations, and searches for contradictions within and between them.

In short, action research is a deliberate process for emancipating practitioners from the often unseen constraints of assumptions, habit, precedent, coercion and ideology. Of course any particular project only achieves these results in a very partial and limited way; to imagine that it could be otherwise is to seek a scientific vantage point beyond the reach of history and human interests.

4 Ideology-Critique

Chapter 5 introduced the notion of ideology-critique and suggested that it was in some senses parallel to the psychoanalytic process by which people uncover the causes of distorted self-understanding by revealing the history of their own self-formative processes. Critical social science similarly seeks to locate the collective misunderstandings of social groups in ideology. Ideological forces generate erroneous self-understandings; ideology-critique aims to reveal how these deceptions occur.

Educational action research, employing a dialectical view of rationality as socially-constructed and historically-embedded, sets out to locate the actions of the actor in a broader social and historical framework. It treats the actor as the bearer of ideology as well as its 'victim'. By changing his or her own practices, understandings or situations, action research reminds the practitioner that he or she is, in some small way, changing the world.

Ideology is the means by which a society reproduces the social relations that characterize it. Regarded as a corpus of ideas or a pattern of thinking, it is the cognitive residue of the practices of social, cultural and economic relationships which sustain society. More dialectically, ideology is created and sustained through definite practices of work, communication and decision-making. Ideology is created and laid down in these practices and, therefore, may be transformed by transformation of these practices. To transform the ideology of our present society, characterized by forms of work which do not provide access for all to an interesting and satisfying life, forms of communication which do not aim at the achievement of mutual understanding and rational consensus among people, and forms of decision-making which do not aim for social justice in which people participate democratically in making the decisions affecting their lives, we must transform our current practices of work, communication and decision-making.

The criteria of rationality (in communication), justice (in decision-making) and access to an interesting and satisfying life (in relation to work) provide benchmarks against which practices of communication, decision-making and work can be evaluated. Action researchers can examine their own educational practices to discover the ways in which they are distorted away from these values; they can also examine the situations and institutions in which they practice to see how they are constituted so as to prevent more rational communication, more just and democratic decision-making, and productive work which provides those involved with real access to an interesting and satisfying life.

The third requirement of an educational science was to provide a way of distinguishing ideas which are distorted by ideology from those which are not and to show how such ideological distortions can be overcome. Educational action research meets this requirement by engaging teachers and others in the practical process of ideology-critique, and in so doing provides a vehicle through which action researchers can identify and explore the contradictions of their own practices, understandings and situations. As such, it allows them to identify those institutionalized patterns of practice which limit the achievement of more rational communication, more just decision-making and access to an interesting and satisfying life for all.

5 From the Organization of Enlightenment to the Organization of Action

The fourth requirement of an educational science was that it should be able to expose those aspects of the social order which frustrate rational change, and to offer theoretical accounts which allow teachers and others to become aware of how they may be overcome. The way in which action research meets this requirement can be clarified by discussing the relationship between educational practices and educational institutions, the participatory and collaborative character of action research and the role of 'facilitators' in the action research process. It can be further demonstrated by showing how different forms of action research offer different amounts of scope for educational change and by examining the relationship between educational action research and educational reform. The overall reason for discussing these matters is to show how action research moves from the passivity of interpretive social science to a critical stance which is committed not only to understanding the social world but also to changing it.

Chapter 5 presented Habermas's argument that the organization of action was not justified by appeal to retrospective interpretations of social life alone; it also required the creation of democratic conditions for the formation of the will to act: participants need to be able to decide freely, on the basis of collaborative practical discourse, what courses of action they should adopt in their attempts to change social reality. It is necessary, therefore, to say something about the conditions under which these participants are galvanized into action for the transformation of social reality.

Institutions are patterns of social relationships formalized into organizational structures; they are created and recreated by practices which sustain them and they are reproduced or transformed either by maintaining or transforming the practices which constitute them. So understood, institutions are malleable. They can be changed by political pressure from 'above' or by social pressure from 'below'. In either case, they are changed by changing the practices of the people who constitute them. For example, policies of educational authorities are implemented by changes in administrative procedures which modify the practices of those in the system. New practices determined by educational practitioners at the school level make new demands on old administrative procedures. Under this pressure, the procedures may be modified and new policies may come into being to legitimate the new practices.

New policies and practices are products of their history. In time, contradictions in policy may be revealed either within the language of policy, or between policy and practice. Similarly, contradictions in practice may be revealed, as one set of practices comes into conflict with another in the practical reality of an educational programme or curriculum. For example, the move to 'informal education' seemed both theoretically proper and practically successful until contradictions were revealed: informal relationships between teachers and students often made invisible the hidden curriculum which domesticated students to unchanged demands of institutionalized schooling, especially in relation to the assessment of student learning. Teachers now treated students as persons, but they did not change their view of learning and knowing; students felt accepted but still experienced the classroom as a place which did not value their knowledge unless it met teachers' definitions of knowledge.[13] As this contradiction between the practices of treating students as valued persons and of valuing only particular kinds of student knowledge has become more evident, the institution of informal education has come under critical review.

Alasdair McIntyre defined practices in terms of the values they embody:

> (A practice is) . . . any coherent and complex form of socially
> established cooperative human activity through which goods
> internal to that activity are realized, in the course of trying to
> achieve those standards of excellence which are appropriate to,

and partially definitive of, that form of activity, with the result that human powers to achieve excellence, and human conceptions of the ends and goods involved, are systematically extended.[14]

He goes on to say:

Practices must not be confused with institutions. Chess, physics and medicine are practices; chess clubs, laboratories, universities and hospitals are institutions. Institutions are characteristically and necessarily concerned with ... external goods. They are involved in acquiring money and other material goods; they are structured in terms of power and status, and they distribute money, power and status as rewards. Nor could they do otherwise if they are to sustain not only themselves, but also the practices of which they are the bearers. For no practices can survive any length of time unsustained by institutions ... institutions and practices characteristically form a single causal order in which the ideals and the creativity of the practice are always vulnerable to the acquisitiveness of the institution, in which the cooperative care for common goods of the practice is always vulnerable to the competitiveness of the institution.[15]

Education is a practice sustained in society by the institution of schooling and, therefore, is always vulnerable to the acquisitiveness and competitiveness of schooling as an institution. Thus, there is a permanent tension between education and schooling which requires that teachers and others maintain a critical vigilance about the extent to which schooling is undermining rather than sustaining the values definitive of educational practices.

A critical educational science aims to identify and expose the contradictions between educational and institutional values. For example, when forms of assessment are used to distribute students into different categories so they can be given different opportunities for further learning, assessment may run counter to educational values. That it is possible to treat assessment simply as a device for categorizing students to increase the efficiency of schooling, rather than as an educational issue concerning the lives of students, is a demonstration of the power of the ideology we know as 'meritocracy'. Meritocratic ideology does not just refer to the idea that people should be rewarded with power, status and access to material goods on the basis of merit; it also refers to the assessment practices by which such an outcome is actually achieved.

Action research not only attempts to identify contradictions between educational and institutional practices, it actually creates a sense of these contradictions for the self-critical community of action researchers. It does so by asserting an alternative set of values to the bureaucratic values of institutions. The self-critical community of action researchers undertakes to practice values of rationality in communication, justice and democratic participation in decision-making, and fulfilment in work, both in relation to the educational process itself and in relation to the self-educational process of action research. It thus creates conditions under which its own practice will come into conflict with irrational, unjust and unfulfilling educational and social practices in the institutional context in which the action research is carried out.

The organization of enlightenment in action research thus gives rise to conditions under which the organization of action can take place as an attempt to replace one distorted set of practices with another, undistorted set of practices. Such action is always political action; new practices always challenge established institutional interests. They express a realignment of tendencies towards empowerment and emancipation, on the one hand, as against tendencies towards the entrenchment of sectional self-interests, on the other. At every moment, of course, any action research project will contain some balance of both of these tendencies. Since it is undertaken by a particular group with particular self-interests of its own, and under particular historical conditions of relative power or powerlessness, it is always subject to distortion by these self-interests. By aiming to involve others in its progress, however, it can expand the community of self-interests it represents, and can prefigure an ideal situation in which community self-interests coincide with the emancipatory interest in freeing all people from ideological constraints.

Action research can thus establish conditions under which it can identify and expose those aspects of the social order which frustrate rational change, and provide a basis for action to overcome irrationality, injustice and deprivation. It does so by creating conditions in which the self-critical communities of action researchers commit themselves to rational communication, just and democratic decision-making and access to an interesting and satisfying life for all. In enacting these values in its own practices, the action research group confronts institutional values and practices which are distorted by ideology. This is no abstract confrontation between one set of ideals and another; it is a specific and concrete confrontation between one form of practice and another. It has a specific focus and demands a specific response. It invites coordinated, directed and strategic action.

Action research not only creates conditions under which practitioners can identify aspects of institutional life which frustrate rational change; it also offers a theoretical account of why these constraints on rational change should be overcome, by offering *and enacting* an emancipatory theory in the form of the theory by which action research itself is justified. It also offers a theory of *how* the constraints of ideology can be overcome. This can be made clear by considering the participatory and collaborative character of action research, by which action researchers are authentically engaged, as individuals, in the process of enlightenment, and democratically involved, as members of collaborating groups, in the process of organizing action.

One way to open up this issue is to consider *whose* experience is represented and refined in different kinds of educational research. In the case of positivist educational research, the experience of teachers is appropriated and objectified in the language and concepts of the educational researcher. In the process, it is stripped from its roots in the personal knowledge and histories of the practitioners themselves and remade within the conceptual framework of the researcher. The interpretive researcher, by contrast, attempts to reconstruct the life-worlds of participants but, nevertheless, appropriates and reinterprets them within the researcher's framework of understandings. In both cases, the researcher systematically dislocates knowledge of the action being studied from its history in the self-understandings and commitments of participants. As such, it creates and maintains a separation of knowledge from action. A critical educational science takes it as central that this institutionalized separation of knowledge from action (in a division of labour between researchers and researched, or researchers and practitioners) must be overcome; it aims at the transformation of action through the *self*-critical transformation of practitioners.

Educational action research engages, extends and transforms the self-understandings of practitioners by involving them in the research process. Far from appropriating practitioners' self-understandings and formulating them within theoretical or interpretive frameworks shaped by the concerns and interests of outside observers, action research involves practitioners directly in theorizing their own practice and revising their theories self-critically in the light of their practical consequences. Thus, a critical educational science must be participatory: 'In the process of enlightenment', writes Habermas, 'there can be only participants'.[16] Action research is research into practice by practitioners for education and those involved in the practices which constitute education. It thus contrasts with forms of research undertaken by external researchers whose aim is to explain, interpret or inform practice 'from the outside'. Where external researchers control the generation of knowledge about educational processes, their prescriptions for practice require verification in the self-reflection of practitioners themselves. Since practitioners do not control the processes by which this research knowledge and its prescriptions are critically evaluated, however, it must either be taken on trust or be regarded as authoritative. In fact, the institutions of science operate ideologically to legitimate such knowledge — to convince practitioners that it is indeed authoritative because of the scientific processes by which it is produced. In Chapters 2 and 3 we saw how fragile these claims to scientific authority actually are and how they misconstrue the relationship between theory and practice. In Chapter 4, we saw that a correct understanding of the relationship between education theory and educational practice requires the development of practitioners' own theories of their own educational practices. In short, the only theory that can be compelling for a practitioner's own practice is the theory developed in his or her own self-reflection. Other theories may be provocative, interesting, plausible or arresting but they only become compelling when they are authentically understood and critically evaluated in the self-reflection of the practitioner.

Because educational action is *social* action, however, the participatory element of action research extends beyond individual engagement in the process. Understanding the nature and consequences of social action requires understanding the perspectives of others involved in and affected by the action. Action research therefore precipitates *collaborative involvement* in the research process, in which the research process is extended towards including all those involved in, or affected by, the action. Ultimately, the aim of action research is to involve all these participants in communication aimed at mutual understanding and consensus, in just and democratic decision-making, and common action towards achieving fulfillment for all.

In action research, all those involved in the research process should come to participate equally in all its phases of planning, acting, observing and reflecting. In this, action research is democratic: it recognises that conditions for investigating the truth of knowledge-claims are also the conditions for democratic participation in critical discussion.[17] We have seen (in Chapter 6) that Lewin[18] regarded action research as a democratic form of social research; Habermas has extended and articulated the justification for critical social science as democratic. The account of educational action research as critical educational science given here simply synthesizes these claims.

Collaborative participation in theoretical, practical and political discourse is a key feature of educational action research. There are occasions when such discourse is essentially solitary, only prefiguring public discussion. Many individual teacher-researchers are forced to accept this solitary reflection because they lack the interest and support of colleagues. Bev Beasley[19] discusses the importance of individual self-reflection in a paper on 'the reflexive spectator'; the action researcher must in any case clarify her or his own understandings as a basis for thoughtful interaction with others. There are dangers associated with solitary self-reflection, though, which Habermas recognized:

> The self-reflection of a lone subject ... requires a quite paradoxical achievement: one part of the self must be split off from the other part in such a manner that the subject can be in a position to render aid to itself. ... (Furthermore), in the act of self-reflection the subject can deceive itself.[20]

The collaborative nature of action research thus offers a first step to overcoming aspects of the existing social order which frustrate rational change: it organizes practitioners into collaborative groups for the purposes of their own enlightenment, and in doing so, it creates a model for a rational and democratic social order. The practice of collaborative educational action research envisages a social order characterized by rational communication, just and democratic decision-making, and fulfilling work. Moreover, it focuses the attention of participants on their own educational action with the intention of reforming it so that educational practices, understandings and situations are no longer marred by contradictions or distorted by ideology. Action research as an organization for the self-education of those involved in the action research process thus suggests directions for the transformation of education generally.

One of the problems in educational action research is that people involved in education do not 'naturally' form action research groups for the organization of their own enlightenment. The institutionalization of education in schooling, and the institutionalized separation of educational research from educational practice simultaneously operate to legitimate forms of education and educational research which appear to require no special efforts towards the justification of practice in critical self-reflection. To revive the sense that education is indeed problematic, and that educational action requires justification, some intervention is necessary. But this places the person who intervenes in a special category which is paradoxical, given the commitment of critical educational science and educational action research to participatory, collaborative forms of critical self-reflection. It appears to elevate the person intervening to the status of someone with superior knowledge to impart to potential participants in the action research process. In addressing this issue, Habermas states:

> The vindicating superiority of those who do the enlightening over those to be enlightened is theoretically unavoidable, but at the same time it is fictive and requires self-correction.[21]

Those who intervene in the life of groups concerned with education to establish communities of action researchers are frequently regarded as 'manipulators' who are in fact responsible for the action taken by these groups. Since the fact that they are so labelled is practically troublesome, it is necessary to pause in this discussion of how groups move from the organization of enlightenment to the organization of action in order to examine how, in different types of action research, outsiders take different responsibilities in relation to the action taken by action research groups.

It is common for 'outsiders' to be involved in the organization of action research, providing material and moral support to action-researching teachers. The relationships established between outside 'facilitators' and action researchers can, however, have a profound effect on the character of the action research undertaken. To varying degrees, they influence the agenda of issues being addressed in the action research process, the data-gathering and analytic techniques being employed, the character of reflection, and the interpretations reached on the basis of the evidence generated by the study.

Some of what passes for action research today fails to meet the requirements so far outlined for action research: it is not concerned with the systematic investigation of a social or educational practice, it is not participatory or collaborative, and it does not employ the spiral of self-reflection. For example, those studies which simply involve educational researchers in field experimentation in which they provide the impetus for setting up the practices to be studied are not properly to be regarded as action research. 'Applied' research conducted by academic or service researchers is similarly not action research: these researchers merely coopt practitioners into gathering data *about* educational practices for them.

When 'facilitators' work with teachers and others in establishing teacher-research projects, they often create circumstances under which project control is not in teachers' hands. Different kinds of 'facilitator' roles establish different kinds of action research, which may be distinguished in terms of Habermas's knowledge-constitutive interests as 'technical', 'practical' or 'emancipatory' action research.

At worst, facilitators have coopted practitioners into working on externally-formulated questions which are not based in the practical concerns of teachers. To the extent that this is action research at all, this form may be described as *technical* action research. It employs techniques like the techniques of group dynamics to create and sustain investigation of issues raised by the outsider, and it frequently concerns itself almost solely with the efficiency and effectiveness of practices in generating known outcomes. Such studies may lead to improvement in practices from the viewpoint of outsiders, and even from the perspectives of participants themselves. But they run the risk of being inauthentic for the practitioners involved, and may create conditions under which teachers or others accept the legitimacy of practices on the authority of the 'facilitator' rather than by authentic analysis of their own practices, understandings and situations. The aim of technical action research is efficient and effective practice, judged by reference to criteria which may not themselves be analyzed in the course of the action research process. Moreover, the criteria may be 'imported' into the situation by the facilitator, rather than emerging from the self-reflection of practitioners.

Technical action research occurs when facilitators persuade practitioners to test the findings of external research in their own practices, but where the outcome of these tests is to feed new findings into external research literatures. In such situations, the primary interest is in the development and extension of research literatures rather than the development of practitioners' own practices on the basis of their own collaborative and self-reflective control.

It should be said in defence of this kind of action research that it can produce valuable changes in practice — but the value may be in the eyes of the observer rather than practitioners themselves. Moreover, technical action research studies may encourage practitioners to begin more intensive analyses of their own practices: for example, action research studies which begin by asking questions about the effects of gender on classroom interaction may, as well as replicating well-known findings in the research literature, also help teachers to see how their own practices are shaped by ideological conditions in society at large. Finally, technical action research studies may assist teachers to develop skills in self-monitoring which they can use in their own analyses of their practices, understandings and situations.

In *'practical'* action research, outside facilitators form cooperative relationships with practitioners, helping them to articulate their own concerns, plan strategic action for change, monitor the problems and effects of changes, and reflect on the value and consequences of the changes actually achieved. This is sometimes called a 'process consultancy' role. In such cases, outsiders may work with individual practitioners or work with groups of practitioners on common concerns but without any systematic development of the practitioner group as a self-reflective community. Such action research may be labelled 'practical' because it develops the practical reasoning of practitioners. It is to be distinguished from technical action research because it treats the criteria by which practices are to be judged as problematic and open to development through self-reflection, rather than treating them as given.

In practical action research, participants monitor their own educational practices with the immediate aim of developing their practical judgment as individuals. Thus, the facilitator's role is Socratic: to provide a sounding-board against which practitioners may try out ideas and learn more about the reasons for their own action, as well as learning more about the process of self-reflection. Practical action research may be a stepping-stone to emancipatory action research in which participants themselves take responsibility for the Socratic role of assisting the group in its collaborative self-reflection.

The form of action research which best embodies the values of a critical educational science is *emancipatory* action research. In emancipatory action research, the practitioner group takes joint responsibility for the development of practice, understandings and situations, and sees these as socially-constructed in the interactive processes of educational life. It does not treat teacher responsibility for classroom interaction as an individual matter, but, on the contrary, takes the view that the character of classroom interaction is also a matter for school determination and decision-making. In certain areas, the whole school may want to determine policies on how classroom interaction should be conducted, for example, by adopting a common policy on respect for students' knowledge in teaching, or on common assessment practices for the school. This involves an understanding of the dialectical relationship between individual and group responsibility, in which neither individuals nor the group are the sole arbiters of policy or practice, and in which a process of collaborative action research is employed in an open-minded, open-eyed way to explore the problems and effects of group policies and individual practices.

In emancipatory action research, educational development is understood as a joint enterprise which expresses a joint commitment to the development of educational *practices* as forms of interaction which, taken together, form the fabric of social and educational relationships; common educational *theories* which, taken together, express the under-standings of those involved about the educational process, and which direct critical reflection towards the issues needing to be addressed for the further development of education; and the common *situation*, in which the work of individual classrooms informs and is informed by the curriculum and the educational policy of the whole school. In emancipatory action research, the practitioner group itself takes re-sponsibility for its own emancipation from the dictates of irrationality, injustice, alienation and unfulfillment. It explores such things as habits, customs, precedents, traditions, control structures and bureau-cratic routines in order to identify those aspects of education and school-ing which are contradictory and irrational. The group recognizes its responsibilities in maintaining and transforming the practices and understandings that characterize the common situation and which allow it to be changed. It also recognizes the limitations of its power to change these things by its own action, but determines directions for action which can realize more completely the educational values to which it is committed.

Thus, emancipatory action research includes the impulses and forms of practical action research but extends them into a collaborative context. The critical impulse of emancipatory action research towards the transformation of educational institutions is expressed not only in individual critical thinking but in the common critical enterprise of changing selves in order to change the institutions those selves generate through their joint practices of communication, decision-making, work and social action. Here again, we return to the notion that the double dialectic of theory/practice and individual/institution is at the theoretical core of emancipatory action research.

The role of facilitator in a generally collaborative group is one which can, in principle, be taken by any member of the group; an out-sider taking such a role persistently would actually undermine the group's collaborative responsibility for the process. However, outsiders can legitimately take a kind of facilitatory role in establishing self-reflective communities of action researchers. Werner and Drexler[22] describe the role of the 'moderator' who helps practitioners to problematize and modify their practices, identify and develop their own understandings, and take collaborative responsibility for action to change their situations. In short, the 'moderator' can help to form a self-critical and self-reflective community, but, once it has formed, it is the responsibility of the community itself to sustain and develop its work. Any continuing dominance of a 'moderator' will be destructive of the collaborative responsibility of the group for its own self-reflection.

There are reasons for concluding that technical action research is of value only within a relatively circumscribed domain. There is a sense, however, in which technical action research has significance within the framework of emancipatory action research, as, for example, when an individual explores the problems and effects of assessment strategies in his or her own teaching in order to contribute to group reflection about a school assessment policy. But this technical action research should find its value in the development of individual commitment to the formation of a rationally-debated, democratically-decided school policy to which the individual contributes as a member of the self-reflective community. In short, the technical character of the action research is transcended by its location within the community context. Similarly, practical action research remains necessary within the context of emancipatory action research as the expression of individual self-reflection which contributes to community self-reflection both by extending and by challenging the formation of common practices, theories and institutional structures.

Emancipatory action research is an empowering process for participants; it engages them in the struggle for more rational, just, democratic and fulfilling forms of education. It is 'activist' in the sense that it engages them in taking action on the basis of their critical and self-critical reflection, but it is prudent in the sense that it creates change at the rate at which it is justified by reflection and feasible for the participants in the process. It is not critical enough or radical enough for some: it only produces reform at the rate at which it is practically-achievable, not at the rate that some would like; and it produces less radical change than some would like, though it does produce changes in concrete practices, understandings and situations which earn the commitment of practitioners in their own self-reflection. The empowerment which action research produces is significant because action research initiates processes of the organization of enlightenment and the organization of change and realizes them in the concrete practices of groups of practitioners who are committed to the critical improvement of education. It is theoretically-significant because it realizes a form of critical educational science in concrete historical practices, and it is practically-significant because it provides one model of how an emancipatory human interest can find concrete expression in the work of practitioners and how it can produce improvements in education through their efforts.

The organization of enlightenment is, in one sense, a step towards the organization of action and action itself. But this is a rationalistic description of their relationship, suggesting that reflection finishes before action begins. In the action research process, reflection and action are held in dialectical tension, each informing the other through a process of planned change, monitoring, reflection and modification. Action research acknowledges that human practices, understandings and institutions are malleable: that they change with changing social and historical conditions. It deliberately explores the power and limitations of practices, understandings and situations by changing them and learning from the effects of change. In this way, it enables practitioners to become aware of how aspects of the social order which frustrate rational change may be overcome.

Of course, in considering how practitioners may help to bring about rational educational change it has to be acknowledged that educational institutions are shaped by social pressures, practices and policies outside practitioner control. Changing educational practices and institutions, therefore, not only requires the involvement of practitioners in changing their practices, but also in confronting the constraints on their action. Thus, action researchers, by becoming critically-informed about their participation in the maintenance and transformation of education, constitute a critical force. They represent a challenge to established authority, and frequently meet resistance at the classroom level, and the school level and from administrative authorities beyond the school, such as examination boards and educational departments and from communities who expect education today to be like education in previous times. These conflicts and confrontations can be difficult for action research communities to handle: they may find themselves exposing unexpected interests and unexpectedly naked demonstrations of coercive power. They learn prudence and caution quickly.

The strength of reaction to considered change often surprises action researchers; they often feel as though the process has suddenly 'become political', or that they are brought up against non-educational obstacles and obstinate administrators who either refuse to recognize educational arguments or dismiss them as 'pure idealism'. This should not be at all surprising. Schooling exists not only to serve the values of education, but also to serve particular social interests and the institutionalized self-interests of particular groups. The conflict between educational values and other social and cultural values can be very real. Changing schooling to realize educational values more fully may well reduce its effectiveness in realizing other social and cultural values.

What needs to be remembered, then, is that educational practices are social practices; educational reform is social reform. It must be understood in a social, cultural, political and economic context. In order to sustain educational reform in the service of educational values, practitioners must develop not only educational theories but also social theories. A critical educational theory prefigures a more general critical social theory. Educational action researchers must be socially realistic as well as educationally committed. They need to develop forms of social organization in which the power of their educational arguments can be discursively tested and examined in practice.

6 The Unity of Theory and Practice: Criticism and Praxis in Self-reflective Communities

Some critical social theorists argue that the enterprise of criticism is essentially theoretical and that criticism limited to the possibilities of practice will always limit the prospects of a radical critique of education and society. In short, it is argued, too great a 'practicality' (for example, an educational action research which concentrates its energies in the reform of particular, local, immediate practices) will anchor the possibilities of criticism too closely to the conditions of the status quo. There is something to commend this viewpoint. Education today needs to meet the challenges of alienated students, low morale among teachers, uncoordinated and frequently unstimulating curricula. Bureaucratized school structures in contemporary schooling mock the educational rhetoric of concern for students and of concern for rationality, justice and access to an interesting and satisfying life for all in and through education. In short, the reality of contemporary schooling does little to reassure us that it is guided by educational values and it is not difficult to find sympathy with critical theorists who argue that major transformations of schooling are urgently needed. When it comes to the practical point of deciding what one is to *do* in order to transform contemporary schooling towards educational values, however, these critics are frequently led either towards a powerless and irresponsible radicalism which demands change but cannot furnish realizable strategies to achieve it, or towards a radical triumphalism which believes that, in seizing power, it could remake social reality by command. The first is a counsel of hopelessness, the second is a counsel of hope; both are mere whistling in the dark. While criticism remains essentially a theoretical enterprise, it remains divorced from the fortunes of practice. It can no longer be judged in terms of the practical resolution of contradictions but only in its own terms as theoretical discourse. At worst, it becomes an exercise in erudition which requires no practical transformations of social reality to demonstrate its power; it speaks to practice entirely from without. Insofar as it speaks to practitioners, it offers them only the responses of hopelessness and cynicism; insofar as it speaks to policy-makers it offers them only the usual promise that a new programme can 'fix' schooling. The celebration of theory in such criticism reinforces the cultural image of theory as the province of the theorist unsullied by practice, and practice as the labour some perform to realize the ideas of others. A theory-led critical approach thus threatens to undermine the very conditions it claims to promote: conditions for the *self*-critical transformation of irrational, unjust, coercive and unfulfilling social structures.

The fortunes of a critical educational science, like those of any critical social theory must be linked to its practical achievements. To be sure, criticism must make use of the sharpest and most rigorous critical discourse available, but it must be more than discourse alone. Powerful criticism depends upon the capacity of practitioners to participate in a concretely-relevant theoretical discourse, to arrange the conditions for the organization of their own enlightenment, and to organize themselves for the practical struggle to change education. Thus, the participation of practitioners in the project of critical educational science is not merely a theoretical necessity; it is also a practical necessity. The promise of a critical educational science can only be redeemed through the dialectical unity of theory and practice. The problem for a critical science of education is to achieve this unity of a theory organized for enlightenment with a practice which achieves it.

The unity of a critical theory and a critical practice is not, therefore, the unity of a theory of education on the one side and a practice of criticism or theorizing on the other. It is the unity of an educational theory with an educational practice. Educational action research is a practice which embodies certain educational values and simultaneously puts those values to the test of practice. The nature of educational values must be debated by action researchers not only as a theoretical question, but as a practical question of finding forms of life which express them.

Thus, the project of a genuine critical educational science requires a dialectical unity of educational theory and educational practice. Habermas's critical social science emphasizes the role of the organization of enlightenment both in relation to the development of scientific discourse *and* in relation to the organization of action. Emancipatory action research similarly relates critical educational theorizing to a critical educational practice in a process which is simultaneously concerned with action and research, and which simultaneously involves the individual and the group in the organization of a self-reflective community.

The self-reflective community established in action research is not only concerned with the transformation of its own situation. It is also forced to confront the non-educational constraints of education. This dialectic of the educational versus the non-educational draws the attention of the group towards education as a totality and its relationships with the social structure beyond education. It invites the group to consider not only its own domain of action, but the domain of educational action as part of a whole social domain. It invites the group to consider education as a whole, and thus the general need for educational reform in society. It is not only a process which reflects or responds to history; it envisages a profession made up of educational action researchers who see themselves as agents of history who must express their practical judgments about needed changes in education in their own considered action — in *praxis.*

This dialectical unity of the achievement of theory with achievements of practice is central to educational action research. The fifth requirement for an adequate and coherent educational science was that it must be based on an explicit recognition that it is practical, in the sense that the question of its truth will be determined by the way it relates to practice. Perhaps more than any other form of educational research, action research meets this requirement.

7 Conclusion

This chapter has considered educational action research in relation to the five requirements identified in Chapter 5 for an educational science.

It has shown how action research meets each requirement, and that educational action research can be justified in terms of the criteria established in the course of the earlier argument of the book.

In these earlier arguments it was shown that neither positivist nor interpretive educational research was adequate as educational science. This conclusion was derived from the central claim that both positivist and interpretive educational research lack a coherent view of the relationship between theory and practice in education. This is a claim of some significance: if it is true, much of the energy and the resources currently devoted to these dominant forms of educational research is misdirected.

This chapter has expounded some of the features of educational action research. It is clear that much contemporary action research falls short of the stringent requirements that have been set for it — both in principle and in practice. Some is merely flawed; some is sufficiently distant from meeting the requirements we have presented that it would be a mistake to call it 'action research' at all. Nevertheless, there are sufficient indications in the growing literature of action research that the requirements can be met, and that self-reflective communities of action researchers can have an impact on educational policy and practice. Despite its history of forty years or so, its potential is as yet barely tapped.

During those forty years, action research has risen on a wave of enthusiasm, has been through a decline, and has revived in popularity. Undoubtedly, it is plagued by enthusiasts; it is also resisted by entrenched interests. In the academy, it challenges the 'expert' authority of academic educational researchers, and in education systems, it challenges bureaucratic authority in its notion of participatory control. There is a growing awareness in the teaching profession of what is at stake here, however, and an increasing reluctance to accept that education should be controlled by non-practitioner groups. The increasing professionalization of teaching generates increasing demands for professional control. It is possible that some form of educational action research could be harnessed solely to the self-interests of the profession and lose its critical capacity. It is, therefore, increasingly important to see that educational acton research projects involve students, administrators, parents and others in all aspects of the research process in order to guard against the appropriation of action research as a prerogative of the profession. Nevertheless, the future of educational action research depends upon the profession demanding that its concerns be addressed by educational research; the control of educational research today is too much in the hands of bureaucratic and academic authorities.

By its nature, educational action research as critical educational science is concerned with the question of the control of education, and it comes out on the side of the control of education by self-critical communities of researchers, including teachers, students, parents, educational administrators and others. Creating the conditions under which these participants can take collaborative responsibility for the development and reform of education is the task of a critical educational science. Educational action research offers a means by which this can be achieved.

Further Reading

Tom Popkewitz's book, *Paradigms and Ideology in Educational Research* raises many of the issues discussed in this chapter. So too (though from a very different perspective) does Alasdair McIntyre in his *After Virtue: A Study of Moral Theory*. Some of our own recent writings attempt to discuss the prospects of relating educational research and critical theory. For example, Wilf Carr's 'Philosophy Values and Educational Science' and Stephen Kemmis's 'The Socially Critical School'.

Notes

1 MATTHEWS, M. (1980) *The Marxist Theory of Schooling: A Study of Epistemology and Education*, Brighton, Harvester, p. 80.
2 WITTGENSTEIN, L. (1974) *Philosophical Investigations*, trans. ANSCOMBE, G.E.M., Oxford, Basil Blackwell.
3 HABERMAS, J. (1971) *Toward a Rational Society*, trans. SHAPIRO, J.J., London, Heinemann.
4 FREIRE, P. (1970) *Cultural Action for Freedom*, Cambridge, Mass, Center for the Study of Development and Social Change.
5 STENHOUSE, L. (1979) 'The problem of standards in illuminative research', *Scottish Educational Review*, vol. 11, no. 1, p. 7 (reprinted in BARTLETT, L. *et al.* (Eds) *Perspectives on Case Study 2; The quasi-historical approach*, Geelong, Victoria, Deakin University Press).
6 SANFORD, N. (1970) 'Whatever happened to action research?' *Journal of Social Issues*, vol. 26, pp. 3–23. (reprinted in KEMMIS, S. *et al.*, (1982) *Action Research Reader*, Geelong, Victoria, Deakin University Press).
7 See STENHOUSE, L. (1975) *Introduction to Curriculum Research and Development*, London, Heinemann; (1978) 'Using research means doing research' University of East Anglia Centre for Applied Research in Education

(mimeo), (prepared for *Festschrift to Johannas Sandven*); (1980) 'Curriculum research and the art of the teacher', *Study of Society*, April, pp. 14–15.

8 POLANYI, M. (1962) *Personal Knowledge: Towards a Post-critical Philosophy*, London, Routledge and Kegan Paul, see p. 300.

9 GAUTHIER, D.P. (1963), *Practical Reasoning*, London, Oxford University Press, chapter 1.

10 ELLIOTT, J. and ADELMAN, C. (1973) 'Reflecting where the action is: The design of the Ford Teaching Project', *Education for Teaching*, vol. 92, pp. 8–20.

11 HENRY, J. (1985) *A Critical Analysis of Action Research-Based In-service Education: Four Case Studies*, unpublished Ph.D. thesis, Geelong, Victoria, Deakin University.

12 Habermas makes this point in this way: 'In actions, the factually raised claims to validity, which form the underlying consensus, are assumed naively. Discourse, on the other hand, serves the justification of problematic claims to validity of opinions and norms. Thus the system of action and experience refers us in a compelling manner to a form of communication in which the participants do not exchange information, do not direct or carry out action, nor do they have or communicate experiences; instead they search for arguments or offer justifications. Discourse therefore requires the virtualization of constraints on action. This is intended to render inoperative all motives except solely that of a cooperative readiness to arrive at an understanding, and further requires that questions of validity be separated from those of genesis. Discourse thereby renders possible the virtualization of claims to validity; this consists in our announcing with respect to the objects of communicative action (things and events, persons and utterances) a reservation concerning their existence and conceiving of facts as well as of norms from the viewpoint of possible existence. To speak as Husserl does, in discourse we bracket the general thesis. Thus facts are transformed into states of affairs which may or may not be the case, and norms are transformed into recommendations and warnings which may be correct or appropriate but also incorrect or inappropriate.' HABERMAS, J. (1974) *Theory and Practice*, trans. VIERTEL, J. Heinemann, London, pp. 18–19.

13 BERNSTEIN, B. (1975) 'Class and pedagogies: Visible and invisible', *Education Studies*, vol. 1, no. 1, pp. 23–41.

14 MCINTYRE, A. (1981) *After Virtue: A Study of Moral Theory*, London, Duckworth, p. 175.

15 *Ibid.*, p. 181.

16 HABERMAS, J. (1974), *op. cit.*, p. 29.

17 This point was stressed in chapter 5 where McCarthy (1975) was quoted: 'Thus, the conditions for ideal discourse are connected with an ideal form of life; they include linguistic conceptions of the traditional ideas of freedom and justice. "Truth", therefore, cannot be analysed independently of "freedom" and "justice".' ('Translator's introduction' to HABERMAS, J. *Legitimation Crisis*, Boston, Beacon Press, p. xvii.)

18 See LEWIN, K. (1946) 'Action research and minority problems', *Journal of Social Issues*, vol. 2, pp. 34–46. Early action research did not always live up

to these democratic aspirations, however; for a critique, see GRUNDY, S. and KEMMIS, S. (1981) 'Social theory, group dynamics and action research', paper presented at the 11th annual conference of the South Pacific Association for Education, Adelaide, July.

19 BEASLEY, B. (1981) 'The reflexive spectator in classroom research', paper presented to the annual meeting of the Australian Association for Research in Education, Adelaide, November.

20 HABERMAS, J. (1974), *op. cit.*, p. 29.

21 *Ibid.*, p. 40.

22 WERNER, B. and DREXLER, I. (1978), 'Structures of communication and interaction in courses for junior faculty members of the faculties of engineering', in BRANDT, D. *The HDZ Aacheu,* 4th International Conference on Improving University Teaching, Aachen, July.

Chapter 8

Educational Research, Educational Reform and the Role of the Profession

1 Introduction

The unifying theme of this book has been that the dominant views of educational research, the positivist and the interpretive, give inadequate accounts of the relationship between theory and practice in education. Chapter 4 argued that the notion of a 'gap' existing between theory and practice is actually endemic to these views of educational research and that there is no 'transition' from theory to practice or *vice versa*. Rather the key transition is from ignorance to knowledge and from habit to reflection about what one is doing when one is educating.

On the basis of this argument, it became clear that the strengths of positivist research were the weaknesses of interpretive research, and *vice versa*. The positivist approach, by ignoring how educational problems are always pre-interpreted, effectively eliminates their *educational* character; the interpretive approach, by insulating the self-understandings of practitioners from direct, concrete and practical criticism, effectively eliminates their *problematic* character. An adequate view of an educational science, therefore, must resist both the positivistic tendency to assimilate practical educational problems to theoretical scientific problems, and the interpretive tendency to assimilate theoretical understanding to a descriptive record of practitioners' own understandings. Instead, it must develop theories of educational practice that are rooted in the concrete educational experiences and situations of practitioners and which enables them to confront the educational problems to which these experiences and situations give rise.

The purpose of this conclusion is to consider some of the social implications of these epistemological arguments. The separation of theory and practice endemic to positivist and interpretive views of research is now institutionalized in a division of labour between 'theorists' and 'practitioners'. The task of eliminating any inadequacies in practitioners' conceptions of educational practice is not, therefore, merely a task of revealing any personal misconceptions that may have been accidentally picked up. It is also a task of freeing them from misconceptions systematically developed, promulgated and sustained in the dominant forms of educational research and educational policy. The epistemological separation of educational theory from educational practice has its social counterpart in the separation of educational researchers and policy-makers on the one hand from educational practitioners on the other.

For this reason, it is necessary to find a conception of the work of educational theorizing and the work of educational practice which overcomes the dichotomy between them — a dichotomy concretely realized in the separation between educational researchers and those whose work is education. To unify the work of educational theorizing and the practice of education, it will be useful to reconsider the conception of the profession introduced in Chapter 1, on the basis of the subsequent argument about what constitutes an educational science. Before doing so however, it is first necessary to return to the different approaches to educational science and show how each implies a different conception of educational reform. It will then be possible to show how the development of education is a critical task for a variety of groups concerned with education and to give an account of the role of the profession within this broader task.

2 Educational Research, Policy and Reform

For any educational research study, what might be called a 'political economy' of knowledge is created: certain persons initiate research work, certain persons do the work, certain products are produced, and certain interests are served by the doing of the work and the use of its products. The research initiators, research workers and users of the research may be different groups or they may overlap; the interests of these different groups are differently served by the conduct of the work and by what it produces.

Thus, the question 'for whom is educational research directed?' will be answered in different ways for different studies, just as the questions 'by whom is it conducted?' and 'about whom is it written?' will be answered in different ways for different studies. General answers of the kind 'for students' or 'for society' are all very well rhetorically; in reality, these generalized answers disguise the actual political economy of knowledge of the particular study in question. All students or society as a whole are not addressed by any research study; only a particular group of persons actually participates in the study, reads its reports, or acts on its findings, and this group is only a subset of the larger group of persons which actually has an opportunity to participate, read or act on the research and its findings. Particular studies are initiated by groups with certain interests, sponsored by groups with certain interests, conducted by groups with certain interests, and used by groups with certain interests. These interests vary and they may conflict. To give some obvious examples, certain policy-makers may want a programme legitimated or challenged, certain researchers may want publications or prestige, certain teachers may want their working conditions improved, certain students may want more control over the conditions of their learning, certain parents may want guarantees that their children can be successful, certain employers may want more efficient employees, and certain school heads or principals may want schools which operate smoothly and without interpersonal or intergroup tensions. It is therefore both legitimate and wise for anyone approached about the possibility of participating in an educational research study to ask whose interests are in fact likely to be served by the study.

Conventional educational research is an institutionalized activity. It is part of a structured system of roles and relationships in education departments and authorities, universities, schools and other institutions. Credentials may be a prerequisite for conducting it; it may require financial and administrative accountability structures to organize it; it may require the production of reports for government agencies or academic publications; permissions may be required for it to take place. Since it is usually an intervention, into the life and work of schools, it usually requires quite formal acts of recognition and legitimation. In terms of the distinction between education and schooling, it appeals to the rhetoric and values of education, but requires formal recognition within the institutional structures of schooling. Despite the rhetoric of disinterest, the actual political economy of educational research works within this institutionalized structure, often requires its blessing, and often serves its interests. Though characteristically structured by combativeness between interests and interest groups, educational research is part of the ideological apparatus by which education operates generally and flexibly to reproduce existing social relations in society at large. Its debates tend to focus on such issues as which curriculum package is to be preferred and should be prescribed rather than whether packages should be developed at all; the relative importance of particular aspects of the educational system rather than the contemporary relevance of the structures they create, the meaning of concepts rather than the interests of those who use them, or the self-understandings and perspectives of particular participants in education rather than the way their views have been formed by history. Being specialized by disciplines and focused on narrow problems, educational research often loses the broader perspective and sense of contradiction which makes educational criticism possible.

Although educational research is generally justified by reference to its contribution to educational reform, 'reforming education' almost invariably means reforming institutional structures. Educational researchers, therefore, have a 'natural' interest in educational policy as the administrative statement of guiding principles by which the educational system is organized and operated. On this view, educational theory is about general principles justifying educational arrangements, while educational policy is the administrative version of educational theory, binding participants to the system's principles. If this view is accepted, then almost all educational research is policy research, aiming to influence educational practice by changing the policies which regulate it.

This view simply incorporates the dichotomous view of educational theory as distinct from educational practice, and then makes this relationship concrete in the relationships between educational policy and practice. It projects an epistemological claim into the economic and political domain of power relationships existing in a division of labour between policy-makers, researchers and practitioners. What, in the argument of earlier chapters, was an epistemological mistake is now transformed into a cultural or political mistake.

Just as different approaches to educational research embody different views of the relationship between theory and practice, different approaches to educational research incorporate different perspectives on how research relates to reform. A choice between research approaches involves a choice about the presumed character of the 'object' of research (a 'phenomenon', as in the physical sciences; 'perspectives', as in interpretive science; or historically-formed *praxis* as in a critical educational science). If the choice between these approaches is made at the level of 'methodological' doctrines about 'science', then the presumptions about the nature of education as an 'object' of enquiry will tend to be confirmed, not because of the 'correctness' of these presumptions, but because each approach always produces results that satisfy its own criteria. In this way, research practice itself conventionalizes the research methodologies and traditions of the researchers who practise them.

If, however, approaches to educational research are considered from the standpoint of their claims about their own achievements, it becomes clear that the different views they take of what counts as an achievement relate to their particular views of how theory relates to practice and how research relates to reform. The positivist approach, for example, views educational events and practices as 'phenomena' susceptible of 'objective' treatment. It views schooling as a delivery-system whose effectiveness and efficiency can be improved by improvements in the technology of the system. Its form of reasoning is technical reasoning and its interest in technical control readily translates into an interest in the hierarchical or bureaucratic control of educational practitioners by systems administrators. Its views of policy is prescriptive; its view of reform is managerial. While in some extreme versions it envisages a technocracy in which researchers actually control education systems, it more frequently envisages an alliance between researchers and systems policy-makers in which researchers create theories which legitimate the administrative and social relationships which constitute institutionalized education.

Interpretive research sees education as a lived experience for those involved in educational processes and institutions. Its form of reasoning is practical; it aims to transform the consciousness of practitioners and, by so doing, aims to give them grounds upon which to decide how to change themselves. Its interest is in transforming education by educating practitioners; it assumes a relationship between researchers and practitioners in which rational persuasion is the only active force and in which practitioners are free to make up their own minds about how to change their practices in the light of their informed practical deliberation. Its view of policy is sceptical, since it trusts to the wisdom of practitioners rather than the regulatory power of institutionalized educational reform. It envisages a liberal and educative, rather than managerial and prescriptive, alliance between researchers, practitioners and policy-makers in which the wise policy is one which expresses general agreements and restricts professional judgment as little as possible.

Critical educational research, including collaborative action research, views education as an ideologically-formed historical process. Its form of reasoning is both practical and critical; it is shaped by an emancipatory interest in transforming education to achieve rationality, justice and access to an interesting and satisfying life for all. It counters the liberal faith in wise judgment with ideology-critique aimed at exposing the ideological restraints on the thinking of practitioners and policy-makers, and at exposing the interests which are preserved by the structure of institutionalized education. Its view of policy is critical, since its treats policy as the expression of ideology and the interests of dominant groups, and its view of reform is emancipatory. It envisages no alliance between researchers and practitioners or policy-makers, except as may be necessary to initiate a process of critical and self-critical reflection in democratic communities of researcher-practitioners.

Note that, while the first two approaches to educational research embody some notion of bringing practitioners' practices in line with theorists' theories or administrators' policies, critical educational science does not. It is as much concerned with practitioners' theories as it is with the way in which theorists' and administrators' practices create the conditions regulating practitioners' practices. In collaborative action research, the development of educational theories is carried out as an integral part of the development of education itself; the development of educational policies is carried out as an integral part of the democratic process of educational reform. Each is 'integral' in the sense that it is an indispensable aspect of the other. Just as there is no transition from theory to practice so there is no transition from policy to reform. The policy *is* emancipation; it is progressively realized in reform. 'In the power of self-reflection,' writes Habermas, 'knowledge and interest are one'.[1]

3 Educational Action Research and the Profession

In Chapter 1, it was suggested that 'professions' are usually characterized by reference to three distinctive features. The first was that 'professions' employ methods and procedures based on theoretical knowledge and research. The second was that the members of the profession have an overriding commitment to the well-being of their clients. The third was that, individually and collectively, the members of the profession reserve the right to make autonomous and independent judgments, free from external non-professional controls and constraints, about the particular courses of action to be adopted in any particular situation. Emancipatory action research suggests an image of the teaching profession which incorporates these features in a distinctive way.

In the first place, emancipatory action research provides a method for testing and improving educational practices, and basing the practices and procedures of teaching on theoretical knowledge and research organized by professional teachers. At the level of teaching and learning it provides a method by which teachers and students can explore and improve their own classroom practices. At the level of the curriculum, it provides a method for exploring and improving the practices which constitute the curriculum. At the level of school organization, it provides a method for exploring and improving the practices which constitute school organization, (for example, practices for the division of knowledge into 'subjects', for allocation of time and staff resources to these subjects, practices for assessing student learning, and practices of decision-making which regulate the operation of the school through school policy). At the level of school-community relations, action research provides a method for exploring and improving the practices which constitute the school as a specialized educational institution in the community (for example, practices of reporting to parents, of relating 'school knowledge' to contemporary environmental, social, political and economic concerns of the community, and of involving the community in curriculum decision-making and educational practice). In each case, action research offers a way of theorizing current practice and transforming practice in the light of critical reflection.

Throughout, emancipatory action research presents criteria for the evaluation of practice in relation to communication, decision-making and the work of education. It provides a means by which teachers can organize themselves as communities of enquirers, organizing their own enlightenment. This is a uniquely educational task — emancipatory action research is itself an educational process. It thus poses the challenge to teachers that they organize the educational process in their own classrooms on the same basis as their own professional development through critical self-reflection. This unity of method between the development of the profession and the education of students is a distinctive feature of the educational profession. Emancipatory action research provides an approach through which the development of a theoretical and research base for professional practice can be accomplished.

The second feature of a profession, its commitment to the well-being of its clients refers, in the case of the teaching profession, both to the education of students and to the educational role of the school in relation to parents and society at large. Perhaps it seems uncontroversial to argue that the central role of schools is educational. But if the role and function of schools is probed more critically it is obvious that schools are being continually limited in their educational work and are being increasingly compelled to adopt a passive, 'transmitter' role which leads them uncritically to reproduce the social, political and economic relations of the *status quo*. This is essentially a socialization role: the uncritical preparation of students for participation in the particular social and economic frameworks of society. Too often, schools take the structure of society for granted rather than treat it as problematic, even though it is a human and social construction, the product of many decisions and expectations. For schools to accept the assumption that our social structure is 'natural' or 'given' is to rob education of its critical function and to deprive schools of their critical role.

What this means is that if schools are to function as educational institutions then they must accept an obligation which reaches beyond its membership to consider, for example, government education policies, the terms and conditions of employment of teachers and community education. The profession, therefore, has a special responsibility to promote critical reflection in society at large as well as a responsibility for critical self-reflection on the rationality and justice of its own self-educational processes. Emancipatory action research is one way in which the profession's commitment to the well-being of its clients can be critically analyzed and extended.

If the educational profession is to have a right to make judgments about its practices, free from external non-professional constraints, its members must develop their professional practice on the basis of a distinctively educational science. Given the critical nature of education, however, the profession cannot seal itself off from the concerns and interests of its client groups. If it is to exercise its critical function, it must engage students, parents, employers and communities in curriculum decision-making, and, where possible, in the conduct of educational activities. The freedom of the profession exists within a community framework. To put it another way, since the practice of education is intrinsically political (serving some interests at the expense of others, distributing life-chances, and orienting students in particular ways to the life of society) teachers must take into account the values and interests of the various client groups served by schools.

The professional judgment of the teacher nevertheless remains a professional prerogative. All decisions of educational consequence cannot be taken by groups or committees representing the interests of all client groups for it is the nature of practical educational decision-making that decisions must be taken on the spot. It is for this reason that society requires professional teachers, not simply instructional technicians. In any case, the practical decisions of individual teachers should always be subject to two safeguards: first, they should be informed by critical educational theorizing and research; and second, they should be guided by a general commitment to the well-being of clients — a commitment concretely embodied in participatory processes of curriculum decision-making, which involve students, parents, employers and other community members.

Beyond the individual level, schools can organize for the critical development of staff groups to investigate school-level practices, and the profession as a whole can organize research networks which allow for the critical development of practice. To some extent, these activities already occur through school-based curriculum development and school-controlled in-service education. It is a matter of priority for the profession to stengthen these investigative networks.

4 Conclusion

Given the current state of the profession, current levels of teacher morale in a period of contraction, and the morale of students facing an uncertain future, a thorough-going critique of the organization of education systems is urgently needed. Of course, to assert that action research provides the means by which the education profession can single-handedly produce such a critique is Utopian. It requires freedom of discourse, a common commitment to assuring scope for unconstrained dialogue, proper precautions against self-interested domination and control of the process, and the freedom of decision-making for those involved. Utopian though this aspiration may appear, however, there seems to be no justifiable alternative. If the development of a critical theory, authentic insights, and wise and prudent decision-making can only be achieved under adverse circumstances, then there is no alternative but to implement them to the greatest possible extent and to articulate the impediments to their wider implementation wherever possible.

What can be achieved in this way is the establishment of communities of critical action-researchers committed to working with other individuals and groups outside the immediate learning communities. In practice, this requires teachers in schools forming critical communities of action researchers who progressively incorporate students and other members of school communities into their collaborative enterprise of self-reflection. At the system level, it means that advisers, organizers and curriculum developers must devolve the responsibility for learning about programmes and associated policies to teachers and others in the field, and commit resources to support this learning process within these action groups.

In these times of increasing bureaucratic management in education, the need for the profession to organize itself to support and protect its professional work is obvious. Moreover, if the central aim of education is the critical transmission, interpretation and development of the cultural traditions of our society, then the need for a form of research which focuses its energies and resources on the policies, processes and practices by which this aim is pursued is obvious as well. Emancipatory action research, as a form of critical educational science, provides a means by which the teaching profession and educational research can be reformulated so as to meet these ends.

Note

1 HABERMAS, J. (1972) *Knowledge and Human Interests*, trans. SHAPIRO, J.J., London, Heinemann, p. 314.

Bibliography

ADAMS, J. (1928), *Educational Theories*, London, Ernest Benn.
APPLE, M. (1979), *Ideology and Curriculum*, London, Routledge and Kegan Paul.
ARISTOTLE, (1973), *The Nicomachean Ethics*, tr. H.G. GREENWOOD, New York, Arno Press.
ARY, D. *et al.* (1972), *Introduction to Research in Education*, New York, Holt, Rinehart and Winston.
AYER, A.J. (1946), *Language, Truth and Logic*, 2nd edn., New York, Dover Publications.
AYER, A.J. (1964), *Man as a Subject for Science*, London, Athlone Press.
BAIN, A. (1879), *Education as Science*, London, Kegan Paul.
BANKS, O. (1976), *The Sociology of Education*, New York, Schocken Books.
BEARD, R., and VERMA, G.K. (1981), *What is Educational Research?* Gower Pub. Co.
BECKER, M.S. (1958), 'Problems of inference and proof in participant observation', *American Sociological Review*, vol. 23.
BENNETT, N. (1975), *Teaching Styles and Pupil Progress*, London, Open Books.
BERGER, P.L., and LUCKMAN, T. (1967), *The Social Construction of Reality*, London, The Penguin Press.
BERGER, P., BERGER, B., and KELLNER, H. (1973), *The Homeless Mind: Modernisation and Consciousness*, New York, Random House.
BERNSTEIN, B. (1975), 'Class and pedagogies: Visible and invisible', *Educational Studies*, vol. 1, no. 1, pp. 23–41.
BERNSTEIN, R.J. (1972), *Praxis and Action*, London, Duckworth.
BERNSTEIN, R.J. (1976), *The Restructuring of Social and Political Theory*, London, Methuen University Paperback.
BLEICHER, J. (1980), *Hermeneutics as Method, Philosophy and Critique*, London, Routledge and Kegan Paul.
BOHM, D. (1974), 'Science as perception-communication', in SUPPE, F. (Ed.), *The Structure of Scientific Theories*, Urbana, Ill., University of Illinois Press.
BOOMER, G. (Ed.) (1982), *Negotiating the Curriculum*, Sydney, Ashton Scholastic.
BOWLES, S., and GINTIS, H. (1976), *Schooling in Capitalist America*, London,

Routledge and Kegan Paul.

BREDD, E. and FEINBERG, W. (Eds) *Knowledge and Values in Social and Educational Research*, Philadelphia, Temple.

BROADFOOT, P. (1979) 'Educational research through the looking glass', *Scottish Educational Review*, vol. 11, no. 2, pp. 133–42.

BROCK-UTNE, B. (1980) 'What is educational action research?' *Classroom Action Research Network Bulletin*, no. 4, summer.

BROWN, L., HENRY, C., HENRY, J., and MCTAGGART, R. (1981), 'Action research: notes on the national seminar', School of Education, Geelong, Victoria, Deakin University (mimeo).

BROWN, L., HENRY, C., HENRY, J. and MCTAGGART, R. (1982), 'Action research: notes on the national seminar', *Classroom Action Research Network Bulletin*, no. 5, pp. 1–16.

CAMPBELL, D.T. (1974a), 'Evolutionary epistemology', in SCHILPP, P.A (Ed.), *The Philosophy of Karl Popper*, vol. 14, I and II, *The Library of Living Philosophers*, La Salle, Ill. Open Court.

CAMPBELL, D.T. (1974b), 'Qualitative knowing in action research', Northwestern University (mimeo), transcript of the Kurt Lewin Memorial Address to the American Psychological Association, 1 September.

CANE, B. and SCHRODER, C. (1970), *The Teacher and Research*, Slough, NFER.

CARNAP, R. (1967), *The Logical Structure of the World*, tr. R.A. GEORGE, Berkeley, Ca., University of California Press.

CARR, W. (1980), 'The gap between theory and practice', *Journal of Further and Higher Education*, vol. 4, no. 1, pp. 60–9.

CARR, W. (1985) 'Philosophy, values and educational science', *Journal of Curriculum Studies*, 17, 2, pp. 119–32.

CHALMER, A.F. (1978), *What is this Thing called Science?* Queensland, University of Queensland Press.

CHARLESWORTH, M. (1982), *Science, Non-Science and Pseudo-Science*, Geelong, Deakin University Press.

CICOUREL, A.V., and KITSUSE, J. (1963), *The Educational Decisionmakers*, Indianapolis, Ind., Bobbs-Merrill Co.

CODD, J. (1983) 'Educational research as political practice', paper presented to the Annual Meeting of the Australian Association for Research in Education, Canberra, November.

COMSTOCK, D. (1982) 'A method for critical research', in BREDO, E. and FEINBERG, W. (Eds) *Knowledge and Values in Social and Educational Research*, Philadelphia, Temple University Press.

CONNELL, W.F., DEBUS, R.L., and NIBLETT, W.R. (Eds) (1966), *Readings in the Foundations of Education*, Sydney, Novak.

CONNELL, W.F. *et al.* (1962), *The Foundations of Education*, Sydney, Novak.

CONNERTON, P. (Ed.), (1975), *Critical Sociology: Selected Readings*, Harmondsworth, Penguin.

COREY, S.M. (1953), *Action Research to Improve School Practices*, Columbia, New York Teachers' College.

CRONBACH, L.J., and SUPPES, P. (1969), *Research for Tomorrow's Schools*, London, Macmillan.

DEAKIN UNIVERSITY (1981), *The Action Research Reader*, Geelong, Deakin

University Press.

DEWEY, J. (1939), *Freedom and Culture*, New York, G.P. Putnam and Sons.

DOW, G. (Ed.) (1982), *Teacher Learning*, Melbourne, Routledge and Kegan Paul.

EISNER, E.W., and VALLANCE, E. (Eds), (1974), *Conflicting Concepts of Curriculum*, Berkeley, McCutchan.

ELLIOTT, J. (1976–77), 'Developing hypotheses about classrooms from teachers' practical constructs: An account of the Ford Teaching Project', *Interchange*, vol. 7, no. 2, pp. 2–20.

ELLIOTT, J. et. al., (1981), *School Accountability*, London, Grant McIntyre.

ELLIOTT, J. and ADELMAN, C. (1973) 'Reflecting where the action is: The design of the Ford Teaching Project', *Education for Teaching*, vol. 92, pp. 8–20.

ENTWISTLE, N.J., and NISBET, J.D. (1972), *Education Research in Action*, London, University of London Press.

FARGANIS, J. (1975), 'A preface to critical theory', *Theory and Society*, vol. 2, no. 4, pp. 483–508.

FAY, B. (1977), *Social Theory and Political Practice*, London, George Allen and Unwin.

FENTON, J. et al. (1984) *School-Controlled In-service Education*, a report of the Wimmera school-controlled in-service education project, Horsham, Education Department of Victoria (mimeo).

FEYERABEND, P.K. (1975), *Against Method: Outlines of an Anarchist Theory of Knowledge*, London, New Left Books.

FILMER, P. et al. (1972), *New Directions in Sociological Theory*, New York, Collier Macmillan.

FREIRE, P. (1970) *Cultural Action for Freedom*, Cambridge, Mass, Center for the Study of Change.

GADAMER, H.G. (1975), *Truth and Method*, London, Sheed and Ward.

GADAMER, H.G. (1977), 'Theory, science, technology: The task of a science of man', *Social Research*, vol. 44, pp. 529–61.

GAGE, N.L. (Ed.) (1973), *Handbook of Research on Teaching*, Chicago, Rand McNally.

GAUTHIER, D.P. (1963), *Practical Reasoning*, London, Oxford University Press.

GIDDENS, A. (1974), *Positivism and Sociology*, London, Heinemann.

GINTIS, H. (1972), 'Towards a political economy of education', *Harvard Educational Review*, vol. 42, pp. 70–96.

GLASER, B., and STRAUSS, A. (1967), *The Discovery of Grounded Theory*, Chicago, Aldine.

GOLDMAN, L. (1968), 'Criticism and dogmatism in literature', in COOPER, D. (Ed.) *The Dialectics of Liberation*, London, Pelican.

GOULDNER, A. (1976), *The Dialectic of Ideology and Technology*, London, Macmillan.

GRUNDY, S., and KEMMIS, S. (1981), 'Social theory, group dynamics and action research', paper presented at the 11th Annual Conference of the South Pacific Association for Teacher Education, Adelaide, July.

HABERMAS, J. (1970), 'Towards a theory of communicative competence', *Inquiry*, vol. 13.

HABERMAS, J. (1971), *Toward a Rational Society*, tr. J.J. SHAPIRO, London, Heinemann.

HABERMAS, J. (1972), *Knowledge and Human Interests*, tr. J.J. SHAPIRO, London, Heinemann.

HABERMAS, J. (1973a), 'A postscript to knowledge and human interest', *Philosophy of the Social Sciences*, vol. 3.

HABERMAS, J. (1973b), *Legitimation Crisis*, tr. T. MCCARTHY, Boston, Beacon Press.

HABERMAS, J. (1974), *Theory and Practice*, tr. J. VIERTEL, London, Heinemann.

HABERMAS, J. (1979), *Communication and the Evolution of Society*, tr. T. MCCARTHY, Boston, Beacon Press.

HAMILTON, D. *et al.* (Eds) (1977), *Beyond the Numbers Game*, London, Macmillan.

HAMILTON, D. (1980), 'Educational research and the shadow of John Stuart Mill', in SMITH, J.V. and HAMILTON, D. (Eds), *The Meritocratic Intellect: Studies in the History of Educational Research*, Aberdeen, Aberdeen University Press.

HANNAN, W. (1982) 'Assessment, reporting and evaluation in democratic education', *VISE News* (The information bulletin of the Victorian Institute of Secondary Education, 582 St. Kilda Road, Melbourne, Victoria, 3004, Australia), no. 31, July/August.

HANSON, N.R. (1958), *Patterns of Discovery*, Cambridge, Cambridge University Press.

HARGREAVES, D. (1967), *Social Relations in a Secondary School,* London, Routledge and Kegan Paul.

HARTNETT, A. and NAISH, M. (1976), *Theory and the Practice of Education*, London, Heinemann Education.

HELD, D. (1980), *Introduction to Critical Theory*, London, Hutchinson.

HEMPEL, C.G. (1966), *Philosophy of Natural Science*, Englewood Cliffs, N.J., Prentice Hall.

HEMPEL, C., and OPPENHEIM, P. (1948), 'The covering law analysis of scientific explanation', *Philosophy of Science*, vol. 15, no. 2, pp. 135–74.

HENRY, J. (1985) *A Critical Analysis of Action Research Based In-service Education: Four Case Studies*, unpublished Ph.D. thesis, Geelong, Victoria, Deakin University.

HIRST, P.H. (1966), 'Educational theory', in TIBBLE, J.W. (Ed.), *The Study of Education*, London, Routledge and Kegan Paul.

HIRST, P.H. (1974), *Knowledge and the Curriculum*, London, Routledge and Kegan Paul.

HIRST, P.H. (1983) 'Educational theory' in HIRST, P.H. (Ed.) *Educational Theory and Its Foundation Disciplines*, London, Routledge and Kegan Paul.

HORKHEIMER, M. (1972), 'Traditional and critical theory', in HORKHEIMER, M., *Critical Theory*, New York, The Seabury Press.

HOYLE, E. (1972), 'Education innovation and the role of the teacher', *New Forum*, vol. 14, pp. 42–4.

HOYLE, E. (1974), 'Professionality, professionalism and control in teaching', *London Educational Review*, vol. 3, no. 2, pp. 15–17.

JAY, M. (1973), *The Dialectical Imagination: The History of the Institute for Social Research and the Frankfurt School, 1923–50*, Boston, Little, Brown & Co.

JENCKS, C. *et al.* (1975), *Inequality: A Reassessment of the Effect of Family and Schooling in America*, Harmondsworth, Penguin.

JONICICH, G.M. (Ed.) (1962), *Psychology and the Science of Education: Selected Writings of Edward L. Thorndike*, New York, Teachers College Columbia University Press.

KALLOS, D., and LUNDGREN, U.P. (1979), 'Lessons from a comprehensive school system for curriculum theory and research', *Journal of Curriculum Studies*, reprinted in TAYLOR, P.H. (Ed.), *New Directions in Curriculum Studies*, Lewes, Falmer Press.

KARIER, C.J. (1974), 'Ideology and evaluation: In quest of meritocracy', in APPLE, M.W. *et al.*, (Eds), *Educational Evaluation: Analysis and Responsibility*, Berkeley, Ca., McCutchan.

KEDDIE, N. (1971), 'Classroom knowledge', in YOUNG, M.F.D. (Ed.), *Knowledge and Control*, London, Collier Macmillan.

KEMMIS, S. *et al.*, (Eds) (1982a), *The Action Research Reader*, Geelong, Victoria, Deakin University Press.

KEMMIS, S. (1982b) 'The remedial reading group: a case study in cluster-based action research' in KEMMIS, S. *et al.* (Eds) *The Action Research Reader*, Geelong, Victoria, Deakin University Press.

KEMMIS, S. (1982c) 'The Socially Critical School'. Paper presented at the annual conference of the Australian Association for Research in Education, Brisbane.

KOLAKOWSKI, L. (1972), *Positivist Philosophy*, Harmondsworth, Penguin.

KUHN, T.S. (1970), *The Structure of Scientific Revolutions*, 2nd edn, Chicago, University of Chicago Press.

LACEY, C. (1970), *Hightown Grammar*, Manchester, Manchester University Press.

LAKATOS, I. (1970), 'Falsification and the methodology of scientific research programmes', in LAKATOS, I. and MUSGRAVE, F. (Eds), *Criticism and the Growth of Knowledge*, Cambridge, Cambridge University Press.

LAKATOS, I., and MUSGRAVE, F. (Eds), (1970), *Criticism and the Growth of Knowledge*, Cambridge, Cambridge University Press.

LANGFORD, G. (1973), 'The concept of education', in LANGFORD, G. and O'CONNOR, D.J. (Eds), *New Essays in the Philosophy of Education*, London, Routledge and Kegan Paul.

LANGFORD, G. (1978), *Teaching as a Profession*, Manchester, Manchester University Press.

LANGFORD, G., and O'CONNOR, D.J. (Eds), (1973), *New Essays in the Philosophy of Education*, London, Routledge and Kegan Paul.

LEWIN, K. (1946), 'Action research and minority problems', *Journal of Social Issues*, vol. 2, pp. 34–6.

LEWIN, K. (1952), 'Group decision and social change', in SWANSON, G.E., NEWCOMB, T.M., and HARTLEY, F.E. (Eds), *Readings in Social Psychology*, New York, Holt.

LOBKNOWICZ, N. (1967), *Theory and Practice: History of a Concept from Aristotle to Marx*, Notre Dame, University of Notre Dame Press.

LOVELL, K., and LAWSON, K.S. (1970), *Understanding Research in Education*, London, University of London Press.

LUNDGREN, U.P. (1972), *Frame Factors and the Teaching Process*, Stockholm, Almqvist and Wiskell.

LUNDGREN, U.P. (1977), 'Model analysis of pedagogical processes', *Studies in Curriculum Theory and Cultural Reproduction*, vol. 2, Lund, Sweden, CWK Gleerup.

McCARTHY, T. (1975), 'Translator's Introduction' to HABERMAS J. *Legitimation Crisis*, Boston, Beacon Press.

McCARTHY, T. (1978), *The Critical Theory of Jurgen Habermas*, Cambridge, MIT Press.

McINTYRE, A. (1981) *After Virtue: A Study of Moral Theory*, London, Duckworth.

McTAGGART, R. *et al.* (1982), *The Action Research Planner*, Geelong, Victoria, Deakin University Press.

MAGER, R.F. (1962), *Preparing Instructional Objectives*, Palo Alto, Ca., Fearon.

MAO TSE TUNG (1971), 'On contradiction', in *Selected Readings from the Works of Mao Tse Tung*, Peking, Foreign Languages Press.

MARCUSE, H. (1964), *One-dimensional Man*, Boston, Beacon Press.

MARX, K. (1941) 'Theses on Feuerbach', in ENGELS, A. (Ed.) *Ludwig Feuerbach*, New York, International Publishers.

MARX, K. (1967), *Writings of the Young Marx on Philosophy and Society*, EASTON, L.D. and GUDDAT, K.H. (Eds), New York, Anchor Books.

MATTHEWS, M. (1980) *The Marxist Theory of Schooling: A Study of Epistemology and Education*, Brighton, Harvester.

MILL, J.S. (1963), *Collected Works*, Toronto, University of Toronto Press. (Originally written 1843.)

MUSGROVE, F. (1979), 'Curriculum, culture and ideology', *Journal of Curriculum Studies*, reprinted in TAYLOR, P.H. (Ed.), *New Directions in Curriculum Studies*, Lewes, Falmer Press.

NAGEL, E. (1969), 'Philosophy and educational theory', *Studies in Philosophy and Education*, vol. 7, pp. 5–27.

NAGEL, E. (1961), *The Structure of Science*, London, Harcourt Brace Jovanovich.

NIXON, J. (1981), *A Teachers' Guide to Action Research*, London, Grant McIntyre.

O'CONNOR, D.J. (1957), *An Introduction to the Philosophy of Education*, London, Routledge and Kegan Paul.

O'CONNOR, D.J. (1973), 'The nature and scope of educational theory', in LANGFORD, G. and O'CONNOR, D.J. (Eds), *New Essays in the Philosophy of Education*, London, Routledge and Kegan Paul.

OUTHWAITE, W. (1975), *Understanding Social Life: The Method Called Verstehen*, London, Routledge and Kegan Paul.

PARLETT, M., and HAMILTON, D. (1976), 'Evaluation as illumination: A new approach to the study of innovatory programs', in TAWNEY, D.A. (Ed.), *Curriculum Evaluation Today: Trends and Implications*, London, Macmillan Education.

PARLETT, M., and HAMILTON, D. (1977), 'Evaluation as illumination', in HAMILTON, D. *et al.*, (Eds), *Beyond the Numbers Game*, London, Macmillan.

PETERS, R.S. (1956), 'Education as initiation', in ARCHAMBAULT, R.D. (Ed.) *Philosophical Analysis and Education*, London, Routledge and Kegan Paul.

PETERS, R.S. (Ed.), (1973), *The Philosophy of Education*, London, Oxford University Press.

POLANYI, M. (1962), *Personal Knowledge: Towards a Post-critical Philosophy*, London, Routledge and Kegan Paul.

POPKEWITZ, T. (1984) *Paradigm and Ideology in Educational Research*, Lewes, Falmer Press.

POPPER, K.R. (1963), *Conjectures and Refutations*, London, Routledge and Kegan Paul.

POPPER, K.R. (1966), *The Open Society and its Enemies*, London, Routledge and Kegan Paul.

POPPER, K.R. (1972), 'Two faces of commonsense: An argument for commonsense realism and against the commonsense theory of knowledge', in *Objective Knowledge: An Evolutionary Approach*, Oxford, Clarendon Press.

REICH, C.A. (1970), *The Greening of America*, New York, Random House.

REID, L.A. (1962), *Philosophy and Education*, London, Heinemann.

REYNOLDS, J., and SKILBECK, M. (1976), *Culture and the Classroom*, London, Open Books.

RIORDAN, L. (1981), 'The formation of research communities amongst practising teachers: some problems and prospects', paper presented at the Annual Meeting of the Australian Association for Research in Education, Adelaide, November.

ROBOTTOM, I. (1983), *The Environmental Education Project: Evaluation Report*, Geelong, Victoria, School of Education, Deakin University.

RUSK, R.R., and SCOTLAND, J. (1979), *Doctrines of the Great Educators*, 5th edn, New York, St Martin's Press.

SANFORD, N. (1970) 'Whatever happened to action research?' *Journal of Social Issues*, vol. 26, pp. 3–13, Reprinted in KEMMIS, S. *et al.* (Eds) (1982) *The Action Research Reader*, Geelong, Victoria, Deakin University Press.

SCHOOL OF BARBIANA (1971) *Letter to a Teacher*, Harmondsworth, Penguin Education Special.

SCHUTZ, A. (1967), *The Phenomenology of the Social World*, Evanston, Northwestern University Press.

SCHWAB, J.J. (1969a) *College Curricula and Student Protest*, Chicago, University of Chicago Press.

SCHWAB, J.J. (1969b), 'The practical: A language for curriculum', *School Review*, vol. 78, pp. 1–24.

SHARP, R. and GREEN, A. (1976) *Education and Social Control: A Study in Progressive Primary Education*, London, Routledge and Kegan Paul.

SIMON, B. (1978) 'Educational research: Which way?', *Research Intelligence*, vol. 4, no. 1, pp. 2–7.

SKINNER, B.F. (1968), *The Technology of Teaching*, New York, Prentice Hall.

SMITH, B.O., STANLEY, W.O., and SHORES, J.H. (1950), *Fundamentals of Curriculum Development*, New York, World Book.

SMITH, J.V., and HAMILTON, D. (Eds.), (1980), *The Meritocratic Intellect: Studies in the History of Education Research*, Elmsford, Pergamon, Aberdeen University Press.

SOCKETT, H. (1963), 'Curriculum planning: taking a means to an end', in PETERS, R.S. (Ed.), *The Philosophy of Education*, London, Oxford University Press.

STAKE, R.E. (Ed.) (1975), *Evaluating the Arts in Education: A Responsive Approach*, Columbus, Ohio, Charles E. Merrill.

STANLEY, W.O., SMITH, B.O., BENNE, K.D. and ANDERSON, A.W. (1956), *Social Foundations of Education*, New York, Dryden.

STENHOUSE, L. (1968), 'The Humanities Curriculum Project', *Journal of Curriculum Studies*, vol. 1, no. 1, pp. 26–33.

STENHOUSE, L. (1975), *Introduction to Curriculum Research and Development*, London, Heinemann Education.

STENHOUSE, L. (1978) 'Using research means doing research', Norwich, Centre for Applied Research in Education, University of East Anglia (mimeo; prepared for Festschrift to Johannes Sandven).

STENHOUSE, L. (1979) 'The problem of standards in illuminative research', *Scottish Educational Review*, vol. 11, no. 1, p. 7 [reprinted in BARTLETT, L. et al. (Eds) *Perspectives on Case Study 2: The Quasi-historical Approach*, Geelong, Victoria, Deakin University Press.]

STENHOUSE, L. (1980) 'Curriculum research and the art of the teacher', *Study of Society*, April, pp. 14–15.

TAYLOR, P.H. (Ed.), (1979), *New Directions in Curriculum Studies*, Lewes, Falmer Press.

THOMPSON, J.B. (1981), *Critical Hermeneutics*, Cambridge, Cambridge University Press.

TIBBLE, J.W. (1966), *The Study of Education*, London, Routledge and Kegan Paul.

TOLSTOY, L. (1971), *War and Peace*, tr. C. GARNETT, London, Heinemann.

TOULMIN, S. (1972), *Human Understanding, Vol. 1: The Collective Use and Evolution of Concepts*, Princeton, N.J. Princeton University Press.

TRAVERS, R.M.W. (1969), *An Introduction to Educational Research*, London, Macmillan.

TYLER, R.W. (1949), *Basic Principles of Curriculum and Instruction*, Chicago, University of Chicago Press.

VON WRIGHT, G.H. (1971), *Explanation and Understanding*, London, Routledge and Kegan Paul.

WEBER, M. (1961), *The Theory of Social and Economic Organization*, New York, The Free Press.

WERNER, B., and DREXLER, I. (1978), 'Structures of communication and interaction in courses for junior staff members of the faculties of engineering', in BRANDT, D. (Ed.) *The HDZ Aachen*, 4th International Conference on Improving University Teaching, Aachen, July.

WESTBURY, I. (1979), 'Research into classroom processes: A review of ten years' work', *Journal of Curriculum Studies*, reprinted in TAYLOR, P.H. (Ed.), *New Directions in Curriculum Studies*, Lewes, Falmer Press.

WINCH, P. (1968), *The Idea of a Social Science*, London, Routledge and Kegan Paul.

WITTGENSTEIN, L. (1974) *Philosophical Investigations*, trans, G.E.M. ANSCOMBE, Oxford, Basil Blackwell.

WOLCOTT, M.F. (1977), *Teachers Versus Technocrats*, Eugene, Oregon, University of Oregon Press.

YOUNG, M.F.D. (Ed.) (1971), *Knowledge and Control: New Directions for the Sociology of Education*, London, Collier Macmillan.

Bibliography

Winch, P. (1958), *The Idea of a Social Science*, London: Routledge and Kegan Paul.

Wittgenstein, L. (1974), *Philosophical Investigations*, trans. G.E.M. Anscombe, Oxford: Basil Blackwell.

Wollheim, R.F. (1977), *F. H. Bradley*, Harmondsworth, England: Penguin Books.

Young, M.F.D. (ed.) (1971), *Knowledge and Control, New Directions for Sociology of Education*, London: Collier Macmillan.

Author Index

Subject Index